Recent Advances in Special Education and Rehabilitation

Recent Advances in Special Education and Rehabilitation

Ronald C. Eaves, Ph.D.
Department of Rehabilitation and Special Education
Auburn University
Auburn, Alabama

Phillip J. McLaughlin, Ed.D.
Division of Education for Exceptional Children
University of Georgia
Athens, Georgia

With 19 Contributing Authors

Andover Medical Publishers
Boston   London   Oxford   Singapore   Sydney   Toronto   Wellington

Andover Medical Publishers is an imprint of Butterworth–Heinemann.

Library of Congress Cataloging-in-Publication Data
Eaves, Ronald C., 1944–
Recent advances in special education and rehabilitation / Ronald C. Eaves, Phillip McLaughlin,
    with 19 contributing authors.
      p.   cm.
    Includes bibliographical references and index.
    ISBN 1-56372-064-7
    1. Handicapped children — Education — United States.   2. Handicapped
       children — Rehabilitation — United States.   3. Special Education —
       United States.   I. McLaughlin, Phillip J.   II. Title.
LC4031.E28 1993
371.9 — dc20
                                                                                      92-35946
                                                                                      CIP

British Library Cataloguing-in-Publication Data
A catalogue record for this book is available from the British Library.

Butterworth–Heinemann
80 Montvale Avenue
Stoneham, MA 02180

10 9 8 7 6 5 4 3 2 1

Printed in the United States of America

Contents

PART II

Instruction and Learning

Contributing Authors

M.L. Anderegg, Ph.D.
Assistant Professor of Education
Department of Early Childhood Education
Director, Regional Institute for School Enhancement
Cobb Educational Consortium
Kennesaw State College
Marietta, Georgia

William N. Bender, Ph.D.
Associate Professor
Division of Education for Exceptional Children
University of Georgia
Athens, Georgia

Clarence Brown, Ph.D.
Associate Professor
Department of Rehabilitation and Special Education
Auburn University
Auburn, Alabama

Philip Browning, Ph.D.
Professor and Chair
Department of Rehabilitation and Special Education
Auburn University
Auburn, Alabama

Craig Darch, Ph.D.
Professor of Special Education
Department of Rehabilitation and Special Education
Auburn University
Auburn, Alabama

Caroline Dunn, Ph.D.
Assistant Professor
Department of Rehabilitation and Special Education
Auburn University
Auburn, Alabama

Ronald C. Eaves, Ph.D.
Professor of Special Education
Department of Rehabilitation and Special Education
Auburn University
Auburn, Alabama

Raymond N. Elliott, D.Ed.
Area Head
Department of Special Education
University of Alabama
Tuscaloosa, Alabama

Richard A. Figueroa, Ph.D.
Professor
Division of Education
University of California
Davis, California

Susan L. Fister, M.Ed.
Educational Consultant
Education 1st
Educational Consultant
Special Educational Section
Utah State Office of Education
Salt Lake City, Utah

William D. Halloran, Ph.D.
Researcher
U.S. Department of Education
Office of Special Education and Rehabilitative Services
Washington, DC

Karen A. Kemp, M.A
Educational Consultant
Education 1st
Program Specialist
Professional Development
Utah Learning Resource Center
Salt Lake City, Utah

Cleborne D. Maddux, Ph.D.
Professor and Department Chairman
Department of Curriculum and Instruction
College of Education
University of Nevada
Reno, Nevada

Phillip J. McLaughlin, Ed.D.
Associate Professor
Division of Education for Exceptional Children
University of Georgia
Athens, Georgia

Nadeen T. Ruiz
Assistant Professor of Education
California State University at Sacramento
Sacramento, California

David A. Sabatino, Ph.D.
Professor and Chair
Department of Human Development and Learning
Adjunct Professor of Psychiatry and Pediatrics
School of Medicine
East Tennessee State University
Johnson City, Tennessee

Kris Scott
Special Education Doctoral Candidate
University of Georgia
Athens, Georgia

Hubert B. Vance
Director of Grants
Upper East Tennessee Educational Cooperative
East Tennessee State University
Johnson City, Tennessee

Glenn A. Vergason, Ed.D.
Professor Emeritus
Special Education Department
Georgia State University
Atlanta, Georgia

Paul H. Wehman, Ph.D.
Professor
Department of Physical Medicine and Rehabilitation
Virginia Commonwealth University
Richmond, Virginia

Lou Anne Worthington, M.S.
Program Associate
Department of Special Education
University of Alabama
Tuscaloosa, Alabama

Preface

We live in a period of unprecedented change. Gone are the days when human-service workers spent entire careers making "seat-of-the-pants" judgments, secure in the knowledge that helping exceptional people was an art, not a science. To be sure, many unanswered questions remain. Yet the number of recent court cases alone makes it clear that both lawyers and lay citizens can now question whether or not the best possible practices are being employed by working professionals.

As a multidisciplinary field, we have been heir to new advances from diverse sources: anthropology, computer science, education, neurology, and psychology, just to name a few. In past decades, we managed to pay mere lip service to our roots in these diverse fields, but the more recent advances have proven too potent to finesse in this way. For instance, who these days can hope to succeed in special education and rehabilitation without a knowledge of cultural pluralism, computer applications, assessment principles, pedagogy, cognitive psychology, and public policy?

In short, we have experienced an information explosion. As evidence, consider the mass government-funded projects, independent research, and new professional journals now being published. A decade ago, a professional could remain familiar with most of the relevant information in the area of special education and rehabilitation. That is no longer possible. Now, one can hardly stay abreast of one particular specialty within the field (e.g., assessment, behavior management). The problem stems not only from the information explosion, but also from the need to be well-versed in diverse areas.

It is the main purpose of this volume to provide the reader with a ready source of current information on the critical issues and trends in special education and rehabilitation. The format and content are designed to address the needs of practitioners, personnel trainers, and administrators who desire cutting-edge information about recent advances in the field. The chapters were written by nationally recognized scholars who graciously consented to contribute to the book. Without their unique knowledge and experience, this volume would surely have missed the mark.

Ronald C. Eaves
Phillip J. McLaughlin

PART I

Assessment

1

A Theory of Human Behavior

Ronald C. Eaves

This chapter integrates evidence from several disciplines to provide a framework to explain human behavior. Although some of its contents are speculative, most of its propositions are undergirded by research. I am unaware of any significant research that would invalidate the framework offered here.

THE IMPORTANCE OF EVOLUTION
Adaptive Advantage, Natural Selection, and Survival of the Fittest

According to evolutionary theory, the available resources of the planet are inadequate to supply the needs of all of the organisms that exist on it. Consequently, species are in constant competition with one another for survival. Successful species are those lucky enough to possess adaptive advantages over their competitors. For some species, the advantage lies in the large number of offspring they produce (e.g., many insects); although the vast majority will be eaten very soon after birth, the odds against *all* members of the species dying are greatly diminished. Other species (e.g., mammalian carnivores) possess the weapons of sharp teeth and claws, keen senses, and a propensity for violence. Thus, although their variations are dramatic, all successful species possess advantages for adapting to their environment that are sufficient to ensure their survival. Nature is said to select those species most fit for survival.

Environmental and Morphological Change

As its name implies, evolution is not a static phenomenon, but rather a dynamic one. An evolutionary "shuffling of the cards" occurs whenever the environment changes significantly. Thus, species unable to control their body temperatures may become extinct during periods of glacial cooling. Fish whose eggs are preserved in a dry state may flourish during significant periods of drought. In short, nature "favors" those species that can adapt to changing environments.

A second way that evolution may occur is through heritable morphological (i.e., structural) variations. In this case, a new individual is created that possesses

3

one or more genetically distinct attributes. This can occur in a number of ways: (a) by a mutation of the normal genetic structure, (b) by the cross-breeding of two varieties or species, or (c) by the repeating or crossing over of chromosomes during the reproductive process. To effect an evolutionary change, the morphological modification must be heritable and must represent an advantage over other species competing for the same resources. Morphological changes may be of two kinds: (a) the function of an existing structure may change (as apparently happened when reptilian "arms" transformed into avian wings), and (b) new structures may be added to old structures (as happened in the evolution of the human nervous system).

It is important to our discussion of a theory of human behavior to note that a change of the second type (known as structural accretion) does not commonly lead to the elimination of earlier structures and functions. Rather, it represents an advantage that is added to the advantages of earlier structures, which continue to perform their functions. Since the major components of the human brain (e.g., brain stem, cerebellum, limbic system, cerebrum) are accretions, these observations have a direct bearing on a theory of human behavior. Although the newer structures in the human nervous system perform regulating functions on older structures, the older structures retain a significant degree of independence in directing behavior (MacLean, 1970; Malmo, 1975).

In evolutionary terms, the only "goal" of a species, including *homo sapiens sapiens,* is successful adaptation. Some humans believe that our species exists to fulfill any number of higher-order goals (e.g., to dominate the earth, explore the universe, or discover the meaning of life). Yet I would argue that, although a few humans have some facility in addressing these goals, the overriding majority of humans see little point in these "higher purposes." This is especially true when such goals demand great effort and large amounts of time and have little immediate utility.

In summary, a useful theory of human behavior must take into account the phenomena discussed earlier. First, it must acknowledge the roles of natural selection and adaptation as instrumental in the origin and survival of *homo sapiens sapiens.* Second, it must recognize that each structure in the human nervous system had an original role that provided a survival advantage to our ancestral species. Third, a theory of human behavior must incorporate the fact that old structures did not cease to function in human beings after new neurological structures were added. Rather, the old structures continued to perform functions similar to those seen in the ancestral species from which human beings evolved. Finally, the study of human behavior would be more fruitful if we refrained from assigning high-minded goals to our species; greater insight can be gained by assuming that, like other species, we have but one goal: to adapt and survive. The implication is that the study of human behavior is best served by associating elements of human behavior with significant evolutionary morphology and by searching for their adaptive advantage.

ELEMENTS OF THE CENTRAL NERVOUS SYSTEM

Since the following discussion tends to isolate the elements of the human nervous system, it is important to note that, far from being separate entities that perform independent processes, these components operate as a coordinated system. Yet that is not to say that all components play an equal part in every human behavior. Instead, the performance we call human behavior may be likened to that of a polished symphony orchestra. Sometimes we are treated to a bravissimo solo; other times we experience a crescendo in which every musician contributes an indispensible element. To obtain a mental image of the components of the human brain, the reader may benefit from a perusal of Figure 1.1. Such an inspection should prepare the reader for the discussion that follows.

The Motor System

The central organ of the human motor system is the cerebellum. It exists in all land animals, first appearing in animals that initiated travel on legs. The cerebellum interacts extensively with other organs, including the tactile, visual, and auditory sensory receptors. It also receives information on equilibrium and the

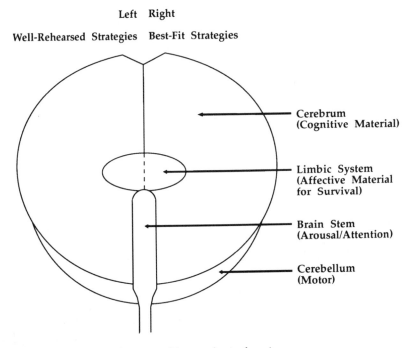

Figure 1.1 Major elements of human brain functions.

status of muscles and joints, and it communicates with the cerebral cortex, particularly the motor areas. It is generally accepted that the cerebellum serves a coordinating and integrating function because that are three times as many afferent fibers (i.e., input channels) as efferent fibers (i.e., output channels). This implies that the cerebellum reduces several bits of incoming information into a single signal to a muscle group.

The cerebellum in humans is highly complex and sophisticated. It makes possible the smooth coordination involved in pouring a cup of tea or writing a letter, as well as enabling the graceful movements of a prima ballerina and a professional athlete. Although its function is closely tied to posture and motion, a number of sources have linked the cerebellum to such wide-ranging behavior as complex emotions (Prescott et al., 1975) and motivation (Ito, 1984). However, before assigning a central role in the performance of such behavior to the cerebellum, we should bear in mind two points. First, the cerebellum apparently does not initiate behavior; rather, it integrates and coordinates signals from other brain locations. Second, all observable human behavior must involve the cerebellum. Yet the cerebellum is not the source of behavior, but the mechanism by which its display is possible.

The Sensory System and Bilaterality

Organisms capable of adapting to a complex and changing environment must have a means of monitoring that environment. Animal species accomplish this through the senses. For humans, the most important senses are vision, hearing, and touch; the least vital senses are smell and taste. The senses have complex neurological systems that send information to both deep brain structures and the cortex. One aspect of the visual, auditory, and tactile senses is of special interest. It relates to the fact that humans are bilateral; that is, most of the organs of the human body come in pairs that are juxtaposed in the body's left and right sides. Therefore, we have two arms, two lungs, two eyes, and so on. The environmental advantages provided by this fact abound. Clearly, the possession of two pairs of legs gives lizards a distinct locomotor advantage over their relatives, the snakes. For many paired organs, life can be sustained even though one of the pair is destroyed (e.g., a kidney).

As for the senses, bilaterality provides four advantages: (a) balance and equilibrium, (b) depth perception, (c) directional orientation, and (d) localization. The absence of these functions is life threatening, particularly among wild animals. The mechanism by which these advantages are possible lies in the chiasma, which is an anatomical intersection, or crossing over, of nerve fibers within the central nervous system. Chiasmata exist for four systems: vision, hearing, touch, and movement. The crossing over of most, but not all, of the neurons on one side of the body to the opposite side of the brain means that the right side of the brain largely deals with stimuli from the left field of the sensory system. Conversely, the left side of the brain deals largely with afferent stimuli from the right sensory field.

The Arousal and Attention System

Arousal has been strongly tied to the reticular formation, a netlike set of neurons in the brain stem that extends from the medulla to the reticular nuclei of the thalamus. The reticular formation, or reticular-activating system (RAS), receives sensory information from all of the major sensory pathways and projects this stimulation to the limbic system and diffusely to all areas of the cortex via the thalamus. The function of the RAS is one of general arousal; it alerts the rest of the brain that stimuli of interest are incoming. Separate sensory systems convey more specific information directly to their associated cortical sensory reception sites.

Research has shown that arousal requires the active participation of the RAS; a state of arousal cannot be achieved by stimulating the higher cortical regions if the RAS is anesthetized (Fuster & Uyeda, 1962; Moruzzi & Magoun, 1949). It is also apparent that novelty helps to distinguish which stimuli result in general arousal. The presentation of novel stimuli initiates arousal for several trials, but after repeated presentations, the organism becomes habituated to the previously novel stimuli and their arousal function ceases. Thus, the RAS prepares the brain for dealing with novel and potentially important sensory stimuli; it apparently does not serve to determine what responses might be appropriate to those stimuli.

The means by which the brain selectively attends to some stimuli while ignoring others are not known. Luria (1973) assumed that cortical units (the prefontal cortex in particular) communicate with the reticular formation to perform this function. To the extent that human beings can consciously choose to focus on some stimuli while inhibiting other stimuli from conscious awareness, it seems reasonable that selective attention is, at least in part, a frontal lobe function. Indeed, the work of Deutsch, Papanicolaou, Bourbon, and Eisenberg (1988) showed greater blood flow in the right, as contrasted with the left, frontal lobe during tasks requiring a high attention level. According to Springer and Deutsch (1989), the "finding suggests a very general role for the right hemisphere in attention and vigilance" (p. 121).

The Affective System

Based on both animal and human research, it has become clear that the limbic system (i.e., hippocampus, amygdala, septum, cingulate cortex, and mammillary bodies) and the nearby thalamus and hypothalamus (important parts of the diencephalon) are largely responsible for the selection and display of primitive survival behavior, much of which can be classified as emotional in nature. For instance, consider the "fight or flight" response so necessary for wild animals. Given an environmental stimulus that the brain interprets as a threat, a part of the brain (possibly the amygdala) selects fear or aggression as an appropriate response. This causes the hypothalamus, via a molecule called corticotropin-releasing factor (CRF), to signal the pituitary gland, which in turn sends adrenocorticotrophic hormone (ACTH) into the bloodstream. When ACTH reaches the adrenal glands, two more hormones are produced: epinephrine and norepinephrine, which are released into the sympathetic nervous system. Thus, an astounding array of physiological reactions is produced. The liver releases glucose into the bloodstream. The heart beats faster, transporting extra glucose and oxygen to the muscles for needed energy. Blood vessels in the skin contract so that cuts or bites bleed less and coagulate faster. Energy-draining digestive processes shut down temporarily. To increase the oxygen supply, the chest expands, bronchial tubes grow larger, and breathing is deeper and more rapid. Sweat glands open to regulate the anticipated increase in body temperature. Pupils dilate. Body hair may stand straight out, a defensive display, the purpose of which is hypothesized to make the organism appear larger and more formidable.

As can be seen from this example, the behaviors regulated by the hypothalamus and limbic system are many and varied. The hypothalamus alone is known to regulate (a) body temperature, (b) water balance (drinking, sweating, urination), (c) appetite, (d) blood pressure, (e) sexual behavior, (f) fear, (g) aggression, and (h) sleep. In addition, the hypothalamus stimulates feelings of pleasure and pain. According to Woodburne (1967), the hypothalamus functions as a *mediator* of emotions through its connections with the autonomic nervous system, but it does not "share in the experiencing of emotional or motivational states" (p. 227). Further, Woodburne states that "the limbic system is relatively separate from the strictly informational aspects of cortical function. It is, then, concerned with the affective aspects of experience" (p. 228). Recent research supports this assertion (Ebner, 1969; LeDoux et al., 1984; MacLean & Creswell, 1970; Norita & Kawamura, 1980; Pickard & Silverman, 1981; Swanson et al., 1974). These studies suggest that, under certain conditions, stimuli can be evaluated and affective responses can be initiated by the limbic system without input from cortical areas.

What is the adaptive advantage of the limbic system and diencephalon? Species that possess these structures are able to learn from their experiences. Thus, wild feline species are genetically aroused by rustling, squeaking, and scratching noises; they are innately attracted to animals that move away from them, or laterally in the visual field. Cats do not, however, recognize mice or birds as natural prey. The latter are identified as prey only after many environmental experiences that are associated with the satiation of hunger (Leyhausen, 1979). Cats and other predators must learn to recognize which species can be considered prey, which species may be life threatening and best avoided, how to effect the "killing bite" to different prey, and a variety of other survival skills. It is this ability of the individual to learn from and adapt to its environment that leads to the great evolutionary advantage of early mammals.

The Cognitive System

The limbic system and diencephalon provided mammals with the capacity to learn from environmental experiences; yet primates, with their grossly enlarged cerebrum, have a much greater capacity to learn, by virtue of their ability to deal symbolically with more complex and abstract relationships among variables. In humans, the development of language greatly expanded the formalization of the learning process. Thus, humans can learn adaptive behavior efficiently and without exposing themselves to the danger of actual experience.

The most important structure of the cerebrum is the cortex, which consists of the outer one-eighth–inch layer of the cerebrum. It is this thin outer layer of gray matter to which the capacity to think is attributed: to organize environmental stimuli, to communicate symbolically, to analyze elements of a whole, to synthesize diverse data, to evaluate and select among alternatives, and to initiate action. Below the gray matter is located a relatively thick layer of fibers that form axon pathways to other parts of the brain: the white matter. These fibers appear white because the neural axons and glial cells are coated with a fatty (lipid) substance known as *myelin*.

Although glial cells (or glia) outnumber neurons by a factor of 9 or 10 to 1, only three functions have so far been attributed to them: (a) they provide a guidance function for migrating neurons during early development, (b) they serve as physical support structures for axons, and (c) they provide nourishment to nerve cells. Galambos (1961) has postulated a more intriguing role for the glia; he suggested that they serve as the locations of engrams, the long sought-after repositories of memories. Although no compelling evidence exists to support or refute Galambos' hypothesis, the sheer mass of these structures invites speculation that glial cells could serve as the metaphorical "hard drive" of the brain, the place where memory is stored.

Like most other parts of the nervous system, the cerebrum is bilateral. Therefore, each of its four lobes (frontal, temporal, parietal, and occipital) exists in the left and right hemispheres of the cerebrum. The hemispheres are widely considered to be lateralized in their function; that is, there are fundamental differences in the cognitive processes of the left and right hemispheres. An early proposal by Semmes (1968) suggested that the left hemisphere functioned as a relatively independent set of localized areas; lesions or damage to an area resulted in specific deficits, the particular deficit depending on the location and extent of the damage. Similar (in size and location) damage to the right hemisphere often had no obvious effect on behavior. As a result, Semmes (1968) said that the right hemisphere functioned more diffusely and that its functions were not localized.

Ornstein (1991), Sperry (1974), Jaynes (1976), and many others have extended Semmes' (1968) proposal by asserting that the left and right hemispheres represent two separate and distinct cognitive processing styles. Sperry's (1974) description of his patients who had received a commissurotomy (i.e., the surgical cutting of the neural fibers of the corpus callosum) is an extreme representation of this view: "Each hemisphere . . . has its own private sensations, perceptions, thoughts, and ideas all of which are cut off from the corresponding experiences in the opposite hemisphere . . . . In many respects each disconnected hemisphere appears to have a separate 'mind of its own'" (p. 7). Of course, the experience of the commissurotomy patient may be quite different from that of the typical human being. As Table 1.1 shows, terms abound that have been used to

Table 1.1 Descriptive terms representing inferred symbolic abstractions of the left and right cerebral hemispheres

Left Hemisphere	Right Hemisphere
verbal	proverbial
logical, analytical, fragmentary	holistic, gestaltic, unitary, synthetic
rational	metaphorical
absolute	relative
intellectual	intuitive, insightful
convergent, focal	divergent, orientational
sequential, successive, digital	simultaneous, spatial, analogical
serial	parallel
discrete	continuous
realistic	fantastic
physical	metaphysical
differential	existential
explicit	implicit
crystallized intelligence	fluid intelligence
objective	subjective
appositional	propositional
scientific, technological	artful
functional	formal
classical	romantic
Western thought	Eastern thought

Note. Adapted from Springer, S.P., & Deutsch, G. (1989)

represent the inferred functional dichotomy of the hemispheres. In addition, a number of researchers have embraced the idea of dichotomous hemispheric functions (e.g., Bogen & Bogen, 1969; Galin, 1974; Ornstein, 1991). Yet many neuroscientists, such as Kolb and Whishaw (1990), recommend caution in accepting this notion. Although the number of research results is expanding rapidly, no one has developed a testable, comprehensive theory to explain these phenomena.

THE SIGNIFICANCE OF HUMAN NEUROLOGICAL STRUCTURES

As mentioned earlier, the neurology of *homo sapiens sapiens* represents an amalgam of successively more ancient structures that date back to our earliest ancestors. Our spinal cord is shared with all species of the vertebrate family. The brain stem, located at the top of the spinal cord, is almost all that is needed by fishes to survive. Early mammals evolved an added feature: a transitional cortex known as the limbic system. Later mammals and primates evolved the cerebral cortex, which reached its greatest elaboration in humankind.

Although the addition of new structures did not lead to the functional demise of older structures, one important change that occurred was the capacity of newer structures to adjust or modify, temporarily, the function of older structures. Thus, through the sympathetic nervous system, the diencephalon and limbic system increase both heart rate and respiration, while the function of the digestive system is shut down during periods of danger. This gives the organism an increased capacity to respond, depending on the nature of the species and the particular environmental circumstances. Further, the evolution of the cerebrum provided higher-order mammals additional control over the more ancient structures. Consequently, humans do not invariably attack weaker organisms that threaten them; the cerebral response to such a threat would more likely be the use of abstract reason, either to overcome the foe through tactical or strategic maneuvering or to avoid confrontation altogether.

It is postulated here that the superordinate control mentioned above (i.e., the idea that newer structures monitor and adjust the function of older structures) does not always operate. For instance, under ordinary circumstances, the limbic system does not usurp the regulatory functions of the brain stem. Likewise, in times of imminent danger (e.g., attack by a wild bear), the normal function of the limbic system cannot easily be overridden by the cortex of the brain. Under these circumstances, the limbic system will usually produce a better outcome than any behavioral strategy that the cortex can effect. Therefore, insofar as environmental events call for functions directly related to a particular brain structure, newer structures may be unable to supersede. If this proposition is confirmed by research, the semi-independent nature of the limbic system could explain a number of forms of emotional disturbance found in human beings (e.g., juvenile delinquency, sexual assault and other violent crimes).

THE ROLE OF MEMORY IN A THEORY OF HUMAN BEHAVIOR
The Significance of Memory

Some aspects of memory are discussed with a sense of mystery by lay people. Although we have little difficulty understanding the need to memorize mathematical algorithms, sight vocabulary, and traffic signals, the nature of other memories seems ill defined and strange. For instance, why should I still recall the smell of crayons and library paste from my first-grade classroom? While memories of the first sort have clear advantages, the only function of memories of the second sort would seem to be the nostalgic feelings they evoke. The key to understanding memories of the second type is the significance of first encounters. For instance, notice how readily we recall our first encounter with the death of a loved one, our first date, the first trophy won . . . or lost. The significance of these latter memories seems immediately apparent: they represent our understanding of the world, the events that can occur, our feelings about those events, and our behavioral responses to them. Thus, it seems reasonable to suggest that the purpose of memory is to provide the individual with environmental scenarios and response strategies that can be used when similar events recur.

Note that our first experiences of a particular environmental event are prominent in our memories (e.g., first bicycle, first job, first home). It will be recalled that the RAS and aspects of the frontal lobe are especially sensitive to such novel stimuli. After repeated exposures, previously novel stimuli become habituated and no longer arouse our concentrated attention. In terms of adaptation, the reason would seem to be that the first exposure to an environmental event has more potential importance than does the fiftieth or one-hundredth exposure. Thus, first exposures to important events are more vivid in our memories than later, similar events.

Types of Memory

Semantic Memory. There are many ways of classifying memory, but an especially useful dichotomy is the casting of what we recall into semantic and episodic memory (Springer & Deutsch, 1989). In this context the term *semantic* extends beyond its usual linguistic meaning to include the sum of our cognitive understanding of the world. Therefore, semantic memory not only involves specific rule-based skills used in speech, reading, and mathematics, but also sundry other skills like the manipulation of verbal intonation to convey meaning, playing a musical instrument, observing the rules of social etiquette, and appreciating beauty as well as the movement patterns in ballet. The importance of semantic memory in the storage of certain types of learning is universally recognized as crucial to an individual's successful adaptive behavior. Obviously, remembering one's phone number, the names of acquaintances, how to drive a car, and the process of long division enhances adaptation.

Episodic Memory. This type of memory is more ancient. It is called episodic memory because information is stored as specific events within the context of the individual's life. The transformation of life events into episodic memory involves the hippocampus and amygdala, two important elements of the limbic system. According to Winson (1985), memory processed by the hippocampus is represented as visual scenes because "language and abstract concepts . . . played no part in the lower mammalian brain" (pp. 217–218). Thus, the hippocampus has no mechanism for dealing with cognitive information, except by representing it in the context of life events.

Based on his own research and that of others, Winson has put forward a remarkable hypothesis: that dream sleep, a phenomenon that has puzzled scientists for generations, has the central function of allowing the brain to assimilate important information, integrate it with past experiences, and formulate strategies for future behavior. Whether or not dreams turn out to be integral to the process of long-term memory storage, the important point to understand about memory is that it provides the material used by humans to select judiciously from among alternative responses to environmental circumstances.

Limbic Memory and Cortical Memory

As mentioned above, strong evidence exists that the hippocampus is crucial in the long-term storage of episodic, or limbic, memory (Kesner, 1983; Winson, 1985). Whether it is involved in the storage of symbolic, or cortical, memory is in doubt. Although it appears certain that the bilateral removal of both the hippocampus and amygdala prevents the further consolidation of long-term episodic memory (Mishkin, 1978; Mishkin & Appenzeller, 1987), evidence exists that certain types of learning and retention remain possible: operant approach and avoidance behavior (Black et al., 1977; Means et al., 1970), classical conditioning (Schmaltz & Theios, 1972; Solomon & Moore, 1975), and discrimination learning (Isaacson & Kimble, 1972; Kimble & Kimble, 1970). Therefore, the existence of separate limbic and cortical memory consolidation mechanisms remains a viable hypothesis, although adequate explanations of the latter are not presently available.

NEUROLOGICAL BEHAVIOR CONTROL

By what mechanism does the brain monitor the environment and direct behavior? How does it know what to do in a given situation? Monitoring the environment is accomplished through the senses. As for responding to environmental situations, it is clear that external stimuli must be analyzed, judgments must be made as to appropriate responses, and, when needed, the necessary motor responses must be initiated and inhibited. Many researchers believe that it is in the frontal lobes that cognitive strategies stored in long-term memory are related to environmental stimuli. The eduction of such relations leads to the selection and implementation, by the frontal lobe, of the best available strategy for responding to particular environmental contingencies. What is the nature of the environmental stimuli and behavioral strategies? In what way does the system operate?

First, humans can face (a) wholly novel, (b) partially novel, or (c) highly familiar environmental stimulus sets. A wholly novel stimulus set refers to a first exposure to the stimuli causing arousal (e.g., a child's first day at school, one's first date, the first experience of being under fire in battle). It is well documented that individuals behave in unusual ways when confronted with such circumstances (Caldwell et al., 1951; Marshall, 1947; Tyhurst, 1951); yet one's choices are actually quite limited. Typically, organisms respond in only a few ways. They may (a) ignore the stimuli, (b) do nothing (be still), (c) emit trial-and-error responses, (d) flee, (e) become hysterical, or (f) aggress. Examples of some of these alternatives are well known. To illustrate, prey being stalked by a predator may become immobile, apparently to avoid being seen or to appear to be dead. In war, soldiers may fail to return fire from the enemy. In disasters, victims may fail to take obvious measures to save their own lives (e.g., hundreds of passengers on the *Titanic* failed to enter lifeboats that were readily available). Some accounts suggest that Thomas Edison employed trial-and-error methods extensively in discovering a viable filament for the electric lightbulb, including the use of a human hair drawn from a co-worker. Another common solution to novel stimuli is to run away from them (i.e., the organism may move to a new, more familiar environment). Finally, examples of apparently senseless aggression abound.

Responses to partially novel stimulus sets come into play when some stimuli in the set are familiar and other stimuli are novel. In this situation the brain relates the familiar stimuli with a similar past experience in an attempt to find a viable, plausible response strategy. At the limbic level, a predatory mammal (e.g., a cougar) may encounter a wolverine for the first time. Since the wolverine is small and has much in common with other, known prey, the cougar may attack, only to find that the wolverine is a vicious opponent. In this instance, the strategy failed, even though aspects of the stimulus set indicated that the strategy had a reasonable chance for success. At the cortical level, a human may recognize a painting by Picasso or a waltz by Chopin even though he or she has never been exposed to these particular works before. Likewise, children may delay making a request when they judge that a parent is in a cross mood. In these and many other instances, the individual identifies certain signature attributes of the stimulus set and generates a plausibly successful response on that basis.

A third type of strategy is used to respond to highly familiar environmental stimulus sets (e.g., the localization of known food sources or driving the family car). The stimuli are well known, as is the appropriate response to them. In every case, the organism has experienced the stimulus–response pair so many times that the association is overlearned. The process of making the association and engaging the response requires little concentrated mental effort and is more or less automatic. Examples include the acts of eating, dressing, using an elevator, adding single digits, and brushing one's teeth. The three means of directing behavior described above are very old phylogenetically; however, the behavioral focus is quite different, depending on whether the activity is conducted at the level of the limbic system or the cortex.

Limbic Behavioral Strategies

Consider some of the behavioral referents of activity within the limbic system: feeding, exploring (food getting), aggression (anger, rage), running away (fear), sex-related behavior (intercourse, masturbation), temperature regulation, respiration regulation, and feelings of pleasure and pain. All clearly concern very fundamental behavior that is important for survival. It is possible for humans to deal with these topics cognitively, with conscious awareness; that is, we can discuss good and bad food and the physical features of attractive men and women, and we can relish or disdain an upcoming boxing match. However, at the limbic level, there is a great deal of neurological activity that seems to be just outside of our normal conscious awareness. Yet, that is not entirely true. Rather, there are many levels of conscious awareness inside our brains.

Autonomic responses conducted by ancient structures in the brain *do* occur outside of the consciousness of the individual. Therefore, we need not remind ourselves to breathe, to digest our food, or to initiate heart beats. Such activities are actuated involuntarily, and ordinarily the organism is unaware of their occurrence. On the other hand, the organism is more conscious of activities conducted by the limbic system. For instance, every mammal initiates food-getting behavior when it feels the pangs of hunger, and, finding itself in the presence of a predatory enemy, the mammal initiates defensive behavior designed to escape or avoid the danger. To the extent that eating and escape afford a pleasurable feeling, the behavior is reinforced, and consequently the strategies used to obtain food and escape are more likely to recur. Although the animal's awareness of the relationships between the stimuli, its responses to those stimuli, and the consequences that follow must be considered rudimentary at best, it is certain that a limbic consciousness exists and that it is a step above whatever consciousness may be associated with the activities of the autonomic nervous system.

Recall that three means were postulated by which an organism may direct its behavior in response to particular environmental situations. For well-defined survival situations that have been experienced and successfully resolved repeatedly, I hypothesize that a learned behavioral strategy is retrieved from long-term episodic memory and implemented more or less automatically. Such is most likely the case for the highly repetitious function of food-getting among mammals. An alternative means of directing behavior is implemented when the environmental circumstance is ill defined or when some elements of the circumstance are relatively novel to the organism; that is, no well-rehearsed strategy for responding to the specific survival situation has been stored in long-term episodic memory. Under these conditions, assuming that some response is required, the organism searches its long-term memory for the stimulus set and strategy that most closely match the current situation. Should the strategy succeed, the organism adjusts the strategy to accomodate the novel elements of the environmental situation for future occasions. Should the strategy fail and the organism survive, the lack of success is noted, and the strategy is not repeated in the future. The four defining characteristics of limbic behavioral strategies are: (a) they deal with concrete observables; (b) language or other symbolic representations play no role; (c) they are affective and visceral in nature; and (d) they are fundamentally related to the survival of the organism and/or the species.

Cortical Behavioral Strategies

At the cortical level, the means for directing behavior are conceptually much the same, but the stimulus–response referents are quite different from those of the limbic system. While the limbic system is heavily invested in basic affective, visceral, survival responses to concrete, environmental situations, the life or death of the individual does not so commonly hinge on behavior directed by the cortex.

Also, cortical behavior is cognitive, symbolic, and abstract, rather than affective, emotional, and concrete in nature. Thus, the well-rehearsed behavioral strategies of the cortex include expressing verbal idioms, completing mathematical algorithms, displaying social conventions, discriminating different-sized wrenches, and other behavioral sequences that have been overlearned by the individual. Notice that all of the rules of language (e.g., phonology, morphology, syntax, semantics) and the majority of school-related objectives fall into this category. Strategies of this type have much in common with Jensen's (1980) Level I intelligence.

For the cortex, an alternative means for directing behavior can best be described by repeating a definition of intelligence once offered by Carl Bereiter: "What you do when you don't know what to do" (cited in Jensen, 1980, p. 232). Thus, like the limbic system, the cortex also faces circumstances for which no well-rehearsed behavorial strategies exist. When this occurs, as yet unknown elements of the cortex (although some would argue that the prefrontal lobe performs this function) attempt to identify the best match between the current stimulus set and some generalized stimulus–response scenario previously stored in long-term memory. Successes and failures are monitored by the cortex and, if the stimulus–response contingencies are important enough, may be stored in long-term semantic memory as new behavioral strategies or adjustments to old strategies. The defining characteristic of cortical behavioral strategies is that such strategies deal with abstract, symbolic representations, rather than with concrete, observable phenomena.

A Hypothesis to Explain Hemispheric Asymmetry. Table 1.1 shows researchers' attempts to characterize the differential functioning of the left and right cerebral hemispheres of the brain. I believe the description of cortical behavioral strategies presented above sheds light on these characterizations. I propose that the left cerebral hemisphere is specialized for mediating highly familiar, overlearned routines, or strategies, to adapt to abstract, symbolic stimuli. Left-hemisphere routines (as well as left-side limbic strategies) are well rehearsed and can be implemented relatively effortlessly. Unlike limbic strategies, left-hemisphere cortical strategies manipulate material symbolically. Within this view, representative left-hemisphere functions include such activities as the use of idiomatic speech (e.g., "Hi, how's it going?"), completion of a long-division problem, addressing an envelope, and so on. Seminal research by Goldberg, Vaughn, and Gerstman (1978) and Goldberg and Costa (1981) undergirds these assertions.

Of course, left-hemisphere functions can be much more complex than the examples given above. For instance, most 8-year-old children have practiced linguistic strategies involving complex rules to an extent that allows them to communicate relatively effortlessly with others of their culture. A competent auto mechanic should have little difficulty diagnosing a clogged fuel line in a car, although an average citizen would find the task overwhelmingly daunting. Finally, a computer programmer has vast experience in correcting program "bugs," whereas most humans are ignorant of such problems entirely. At bottom, whether or not more complicated strategies become left-hemisphere functions depends on the adaptive advantage they offer the individual. Thus, for most of us, clogged fuel lines and computer program "bugs" occur too infrequently to justify committing their solutions to memory. Instead, in our culture, the most common adaptive response to broken cars and computer programs that don't work is to select specialists who have practiced solutions to these problems to overlearning levels.

One interesting aspect of less complex left-hemisphere functions is that the individual need not know why a particular strategy works, only that it *does* work. Thus, both normal and mentally retarded children often learn a sequence of steps to compute multidigit multiplication problems successfully but fail to grasp how the steps take place value into account. At a more complex level, few individuals have a deep understanding of the syntactic rules of language, yet most of us use language to communicate with acceptable facility. Thus, humans, like other animals, typically develop and use strategies to adapt to specific situations; they are not developed to attain some normative model of perfection. On a day-to-day basis, this implies that, for many humans, effectively and efficiently adapting to the immediate environmental circumstance is the overriding goal of behavioral strategies. The adoption of long-term goals that would require a deeper cognitive understanding of the stimulus–response variables would appear to be an uncommon, and largely unnecessary, trait for most individuals.

If the left cerebral hemisphere handles explicit, highly organized, symbolic routines for responding to highly familiar, repetitive environmental circumstances, it seems plausible that the right hemisphere mediates responses to infrequently encountered symbolic stimuli that are poorly understood by the individual; that is, the right hemisphere handles symbolic material for which no well-practiced behavioral strategy exists. The notion that it deals with poorly understood phenomena would explain why the nature of the right hemisphere seems so alien to most humans and why it has been termed the "neglected hemisphere" by Springer and Deutsch (1989, p. 14). If the right hemisphere deals with poorly understood material, it follows that the material will appear to be more highly complex, abstract, and ambiguous than left-hemisphere material, which is better understood. This statement is consistent with the fact that terms used to infer the functions of the right hemisphere are invariably more complex, abstract, and ambiguous than those functions attributed to the left hemisphere (see Table 1.1). Also notice that this view explains why the right hemisphere is largely non-verbal. By definition, language is a tool used to codify *known* phenomena; the better understood the phenomena, the more facile we are in describing them linguistically. Because right-hemisphere material is, at best, only dimly grasped by the individual, it follows that verbal descriptions will be laborious and uncommunicative or even nonexistent.

Thus, because of its very nature, descriptions of how the right hemisphere might function in an actual situation are difficult to construct and will probably be flawed. Nevertheless, I offer the following as tentative examples. First, consider the possibly apocryphal story about how the theory of relativity first crystallized in the brain of Albert Einstein. As he rode in a vehicle traveling side-by-side with a second vehicle, he experienced the illusion of increasing speed that sometimes occurs when the other vehicle slows down. Apparently, his right hemisphere recognized that event as a metaphor for the notion that time, space, and velocity are interactive phenomena. Thus, this fairly commomplace experience provided the impetus for an incredible intuitive leap that had profound effects. In a very similar vein, cartoons depicting an apple dropping on Isaac Newton's head and ultimately leading to his defining of the laws of gravity no doubt imply a similar right-hemisphere phenomenon.

CONSCIOUSNESS
Mind and Body

Descartes developed the modern view of consciousness in the seventeenth century. For him, the mind (or soul) was noncorporeal; that is, it was distinct from the physical matter that makes up the human body. Indeed, the only connection between physical man and his mind was the pineal gland, which communicated the results of physical phenomena to the mind. The mind, or soul, then experienced passion (or feelings). Thus, Descartes' dichotomy of mind and body initiated a problem that has plagued psychology since its inception: How can human consciousness be explained in neurological terms? The question has been especially resistant to scientific investigation, largely because there has never been an accepted definition of the term consciousness, nor of its corollaries: phenomenal experience, feelings, mental awareness (or self-awareness), emotion, cognition, and the self.

The Problem of the Self

The concept of consciousness is inextricably bound to our notions of the self. Thus, we display consciousness only to the extent that we exhibit self-awareness. Self-awareness, in its turn, is largely a function of one's ability to describe verbally one's perceptions or beliefs about one's own personal attributes (e.g., ideas, motives, intelligence, attractiveness, strength) and experiences. Because our concepts of the self normally require an individual to reflect on his or her attributes and experiences linguistically, our tendency is to assign the label *conscious awareness* only to linguistic descriptions of the self. Yet there are a number of life experiences of which we are aware that are seldom submitted to linguistic analysis.

Linguistic Consciousness Versus Phylogenetic Consciousness

Much of the difficulty caused by the mind–body problem arises from the common human tendency to relate consciousness and the self to language. For instance, LeDoux (1986) offered three sets of evidence for accepting the view that consciousness (self-awareness) is tied to natural language systems: (a) species without well-developed language systems lack demonstrable self-awareness, whereas self-awareness is readibly exhibited by language-using humans; (b) commissurotomy patients, whose language functions are lateralized in the left hemisphere, exhibit right-hemisphere deficits in self-awareness; and (c) among commissurotomy patients whose language functions are bilateral, "each half-brain seems to possess an independent and well-developed sense of self" (LeDoux, 1986, p. 350). We probably relate consciousness to language systems because language is the tool we humans use to translate our experience into a readily understandable code. If we cannot express an experience through language, this is often taken as prima facie evidence that the experience does not qualify as a conscious experience. Rather, it may be seen as preconscious, subconscious, or unconscious.

Of course, if we tie consciousness to language, then only humans will exhibit consciousness, and, among humans, the left hemisphere will reign supreme. In contrast, I would argue that there exists no overarching reason why consciousness demands linguistic explication for its existence. Further, if we are willing to relate consciousness to important evolutionary structures in the brain, then several levels of consciousness result. For instance, the visceral (limbic) thrill, such as that felt by sky divers as they wait for their parachutes to open, qualifies as a conscious experience, whether or not the sensations are given linguistic tags. Likewise, the feeling of rage that may result from a physical attack requires no verbal description to justify its existence as a conscious experience. Viewed in this way, it a fair, although speculative, hypothesis that mammalian species experience a similar conscious awareness when placed in similar environmental circumstances. Of course, this hypothesis would hold only to the extent that the species in question each possess comparable brain structures.

The Problem of the Self, Consciousness, and Behavioral Control

Another problem presented by traditional conceptualizations of consciousness is the implicit requirement that an organism be in control of its behavior if the response is to be considered a conscious response. The concept of the *self,* which is intimately tied to our language system, is paramount in this tradition. Three examples of this situation may help to crystallize the problem: (a) when a human being emits behavior "involuntarily" and "without a 'conscious' decision to act," as in an emergency, the behavior may be viewed as an unconscious act; (b) the consequences for unpremeditated crimes of passion are less severe in our society than preplanned crimes of a similar nature, presumably because the "conscious self" played no active part in deciding to commit the crime; and (c) numerous scientific discoveries have been attributed to "unconscious" mental activity (e.g., Loewi's discovery of acetylcholine, the inhibitor of heart rate). In each of these examples, it is as if the "conscious self" were an entirely different entity than the "unconscious self" that emitted the behavior. However, I would argue that such behavior is unconscious only insofar as the cortical-linguistic system (i.e., ordinarily the left hemisphere) was omitted from neurological activity that directed the behavior. That is, the neurological mechanisms for engaging in the behavior did not include the traditional *self,* that part of our neurology that manipulates variables linguistically. Was the behavior conscious? To the extent that the person was aware of his behavior, even though linguistic awareness might have come after the fact, the behavior was conscious. From this point of view, humans may be seen to have many selves, which, under certain circumstances, function independently from the traditional, linguistic self. Therefore, well-practiced activities (e.g., identifying the key to start the ignition of your car) generally require no prior, conscious approval from the linguistic self; it is as if the self need not be bothered with such trivial pursuits. In emergency situations and acts of passion, there is no time to make prudent, informed decisions. In these instances, it seems likely that linguistic, cortical control was overridden by limbic functions. As LeDoux (1986) remarked, "Emotional expression can thus proceed without the intervention of conscious feelings" (p.353). Finally, "unconscious" scientific discoveries are probably a function of the nonlinguistic, right hemisphere of the cortex; that is, the crucial patterns may be identified by the right hemisphere, particularly when no tested, rehearsed strategy exists in the left hemisphere.

When the requirement of language is dropped and consciousness is defined as the *totality of an organism's mental experiences, that is, its awareness of its sensations, behavior, and surroundings,* then much of the mind-body problem disappears. This definition requires the acknowledgment of several selves, each corresponding to important phylogenetic systems in the brain. Further, the question, "How can human consciousness be explained in neurological terms?" then becomes a straightforward scientific question, subject to experimentation.

CRITICAL PERIODS

During the normal course of brain development, eight distinctive events take place: (a) neuronal induction, (b) neuroblast proliferation, (c) cell migration, (d) neuron aggregation, (e) neuron differentiation, (f) neuron death, (g) synapse elimination, and (h) myelination. Although the timing and sequence of these processes are regulated genetically, the environment can and does have its own moderating effects on their progression (Kellaway, 1989). Such environmental effects seem to be maximized when they occur during critical periods. A critical period is an interval of time during which specific processes must occur without significant interference. Should the process not take place at the appointed time, the subsequent integrity of the neurological system in question is jeopardized. For instance, when maternal rubella occurs during the first trimester of pregnancy, it often leads to mental retardation and visual and hearing impairments in the infant; should rubella be contracted later in the pregnancy, the dangers are much less threatening. All of the known critical periods occur either prior to birth or during the developmental period.

Evidence for Critical Periods

As might be expected, the existence of critical periods is better represented in animal research than in human research. Thus, Hubel and Wiesel (1970) were able to effect functional blindness in kittens simply by depriving them of visual stimuli for as little as 3 or 4 days during critical periods. Likewise, Woolsey (cited in Mishkin & Appenzeller, 1987) found that removal of a mouse's whiskers (critical in the search for food) soon after birth prevented corresponding neurons in the sensory cortex from developing. In a series of studies, Harlow (e.g., 1960, 1962) showed that infant monkeys deprived of close, physical contact with their mothers became much more fearful adults than did monkeys that were raised normally. Further, isolation-reared monkeys became self-injurious and aggressive toward other members of their own species.

Some research exists to support the existence of similar critical periods among humans. For instance, Skeels and Dye's (1939) comparison of experimental- and control-group orphans demonstrated dramatically higher IQs among the former group as a result of enriched environmental arrangements. Likewise, Lazar and Darlington's (1982) review of eleven preschool intervention projects for low-income families concluded that the projects had produced significant positive effects on a number of dimensions: cognition, achievement, attitudes, and values. Such results have generated increased interest in early childhood education, since remedial and compensatory programs for older individuals have less impressive outcomes.

At least one human critical period is well documented in neurological research: that of language learning. It has been known for a century that when left-hemisphere injury occurs very early in life, the effects are largely overcome (cf., Alajouanine & Lhermitte, 1965; Hécaen, 1976). However, should language development be impeded during the critical period, language deficits may be difficult or impossible to overcome. There is some debate about the length of the critical period for language learning. Lenneberg (1967) argued that the interval ranged from 2 years of age to early puberty, whereas Krashen (1973) restricted the period from 2 years to 5 years of age. Nevertheless, several lines of investigation support the notion that the acquisition of a new language becomes increasingly difficult with age (Kolb & Whishaw, 1990).

Myelination, a process by which support structures envelop, insulate, and protect axons, is considered by most neurologists to be a sign of the functional maturity of a differentiated group of neurons. The fact that myelination of the cortex, the last brain structure to attain maturity, reaches a plateau sometime during late adolescence (Kolb & Whishaw, 1990) is another source of evidence that the developmental years broadly represent a critical period among humans. It is therefore interesting that studies have repeatedly shown that general cognitive ability, as measured by most intelligence tests, also approaches an asymptote during this age span (Jensen, 1980).

Implications of Critical Periods for Human Behavior

After the publication of Jensen's (1969) article, "How Much Can We Boost IQ and Scholastic Achievement?" a series of arguments, replies, and rejoinders by various scholars appeared in *American Psychologist.* One much-discussed hypothetical situation was raised by Hebb (1970): What would happen if a child were raised from infancy to adulthood in a wine barrel and fed through the bung hole? Environmentalists argued that such a child, deprived almost entirely of stimulation from the environment, would be grossly abnormal in its cognitive abilities, whatever its genetic endowment might be. Their point was that Jensen's attribution of an 80%–20% split between hereditary and environmental contributions to one's intellectual attainment was meaningless. Not surprisingly, the point was not settled in the debate. However, approximations to the child-raised-in-a-wine-barrel scenario are occasionally well documented in the literature. The best-known example is the case of Genie (Curtiss, 1978; Fromkin et al., 1974). Genie was discovered at age 13, the victim of extreme environmental deprivation. Apparently she had been isolated by her father in a small room from the age of about 20 months to the age of 13 years, 9 months. Two indices of the neglect Genie suffered were the harness she wore (her only "clothing") to prevent her from handling her own feces and a potty chair to which she was strapped, at times for 24 hours a day.

At the time she was found, "Genie . . . was an unsocialized, primitive human being, emotionally disturbed, unlearned, and without language" (Fromkin et al., 1974, p. 84). By age 17 years, Genie's mental age was determined to be 5 years, 8 months, a value that far exceeded her language skills. By that time it was quite clear that Genie had begun to develop language, although her speech was considerably different from that of normal children. For instance, she used no interrogatives, demonstratives, or rejoinders. Negatives were merely added to the beginnings of sentences. Thus, there appears to be a practical answer to the question, "How much does the environment influence cognitive outcomes?" The answer is that the environment is profoundly influential, particularly during the early years.

Although environments as extreme as those reflected by Harlow's research and Genie's experience are exceedingly rare, recent statistics on the extent of such social ills as child abuse, drug abuse, neighborhood violence, and "latchkey" children imply that a sizable number of children grow up in grossly impoverished environments. There can be no doubt that the range from the most impoverished homes to the most enriched homes is vast. Based on what is known about critical periods, it is a plausible assumption that the existence of such deprivation during childhood exacts a tremendous cost on the general welfare of our society.

CULTURE, NEUROLOGY, AND HUMAN BEHAVIOR
The Socialization of a Species

Animals that live in groups necessarily develop rules for behavior. Among lower mammals, rules govern which individual gets the best food, the most comfortable resting place, the opportunity for sexual fulfillment, and so on. Since these animals lack elaborate, formal language systems, the primary teacher is rude experience. Consequently, dominance, based on strength and agility, plays a major role in determining an individual's position in the group pecking order.

Among humans, the social rules, or cultural norms, are more refined, but the system serves a similar purpose. That is, rules are designed to reduce conflict and promote harmony and order within the group. One means by which humans impart cultural norms to their offspring is through the creation of myths that serve as models for behavior (Hirsch, 1987). Thus, children are taught virtuous behavior through stories about the legendary honesty of George Washington and Abe Lincoln, the bravery of American fighting men during war, and the perseverance-through-hardship exhibited by such individuals as Helen Keller and George Washington Carver. These myths describe how a culturally defined "good" person behaves. Although they are often presented as universal truths, they are much more closely tied to the kinds of behavior required of the members of any gregarious, cooperative society.

The formal means by which society instills its members with its cultural mores are many and varied. Much of the early training is conducted by a child's parents and immediate family. Although schools have recently specialized more in skill training, one of the important original purposes of schooling was the inculcation of good citizenship. Religious institutions have also played a major role in the socialization process, as have youth groups, such as Boy Scouts and Little League teams. Another mechanism for ensuring approbatory behavior is the legal system, including our laws, courts, police forces, and other elements of the criminal-justice system.

To the extent that individuals learn and conform to the socially expected behavior described above, I propose that the neural mechanisms responsible for their storage and expression are no different from other well-rehearsed routines handled by the left cerebral hemisphere. Once again, the distinguishing characteristic of left-hemishpere functioning is its virtually automatic expression of repetitiously practiced responses to highly familiar environmental stimuli.

One important implication of this hypothesis is the assertion that the left hemisphere does not specialize only in language-oriented behavior, as it has often been argued; rather, it handles any systematized responses that can be described as dealing with abstract, symbolic (i.e., cognitive) material. A related implication concerns the fact that social behavior like that described above has traditionally been described as emotional or affective behavior. However, if my hypothesis is correct, a person's assimilation of cultural and social norms is a cognitive function. Thus, it should be orthogonal to status in the affective domain, which is regulated largely by the limbic system. In keeping with the notion of positive manifold (Jensen, 1980), it also follows that the development of social skills should be positively correlated with standing on other cognitive achievements (e.g., speech, reading, arithmetic).

Culture and the Right Hemisphere

At this point, it is appropriate to ask whether or not culture influences the function of the right cerebral hemisphere. I would postulate that it does, although the influences are difficult to explicate because the right hemisphere deals with relationships between complex, abstract variables that humans find difficult to describe linguistically. A few examples may help to reveal how such a process might work.

There has recently been a good deal of interest in the possible meaning of body language among humans. Thus, folding one's arms across one's chest is believed to connote skepticism, defensiveness, or contemplation, depending on other aspects of the environmental context. Moving in close to a communicant, particularly face to face, may be an attempt to intimidate or an expression of anger, depending on the use of other elements of the body (e.g., narrowed eyes, set jaw). Further, such behavior as clasping the hands behind one's back and crossing one's legs are thought to convey certain inner states by some researchers. At present, none of the postulated meanings of these gestures is well established in the research literature. Yet a number of gestures have widely accepted meanings. For instance, most humans draw similar meaning from frowns, smiles, and the forceful pounding of fists. I would argue that the latter illustrations represent such well-understood patterns that they have become left-hemisphere functions for most humans. Because they are so familiar and consistent, they seem not at all strange to us. On the other hand, the meanings of the first illustrations (e.g., crossed arms and legs) remain obscure and not a little strange, causing our left hemisphere to be skeptical of their postulated nature.

Our culture's use of proverbs would seem to be another example of right-hemisphere function. Consider the proverb, "Beware of Greeks bearing gifts." Simply committing the story of the Trojan horse to memory falls far short of the intended purpose of this saying. I suggest that the real intention is for the individual to notice events in his own life that are similar to those in the story of Troy and to respond cogently. Thus, the salesman who promises an abundance of free merchandise simply for trying his product may be viewed with suspicion by some buyers, but others, who fail to recognize the similarity of patterns, may welcome the salesman into their homes. All proverbs would seem to serve the same purpose. Therefore, "A bird in the hand is worth two in the bush" relates to all risk-taking ventures, and "Never count your chickens before they hatch," refers to all situations in which it is dangerous to behave as if a promising event, which may never reach fruition, has already taken place.

The use of figurative language would also seem to be a good prospect for right-hemisphere functioning. For instance, consider the metaphorical language in "Jane was a tiger on the tennis court." A literal translation of the sentence, a left-hemisphere function, would produce a very distorted and inaccurate interpretation of the intended message. Only by interpreting the word "tiger" as a metaphor for aggressiveness, energy, and tenacity can a proper understanding of the sentence be attained. Similes serve essentially the same purpose. Thus, to use another metaphor, "a word (or a look) may speak volumes."

Although space limitations prevent a lengthy discussion of them, still other widely recognized aspects of adaptive living fit nicely into the notion that culture has vast influence on both linguistic and nonlinguistic right-hemisphere functioning. Several are supported by research, whereas others await empirical study. To name but a few: (a) the use of verbal and figural analogies; (b) the production and interpretation of poetry, visual art, music, and dance; (c) the use of exaggeration and humor; (d) visual scanning (as in reading); (e) the formation of generalizations; (f) finding the main idea of an event or story; (g) the characterization of people and places; (h) decoding maps; (i) the use of synonyms and antonyms; (j) the prediction of outcomes; (k) evaluating a speaker's purpose; (l) the classification of objects, events, and ideas; (m) drawing implications; (n) distinguishing fact from opinion; (o) problem solving; (p) the use of connotative language; (q) solving jigsaw puzzles and conundrums; (r) making comparisons; (s) determining causes and effects; (t) the use of syllogisms in logical reasoning; and (u) gestalt completion.

To be sure, not all of these examples will prove to represent right-hemisphere functions for all individuals. To the extent that the specific environmental stimuli are no longer novel, but rather are highly familiar and well practiced, the individual will process responses via the left cerebral hemisphere. For instance, individuals who have developed a routine for the application of Venn diagrams when faced with syllogistic reasoning problems would be expected to use the left hemisphere to process solutions, whereas those without a working knowledge of Venn diagrams would be hypothesized to employ the right hemisphere.

SUMMARY

This chapter draws from several disciplines in an attempt to develop a cohesive theory of human behavior. It focused on eleven propositions. Although some of these propositions have not appeared in the literature before, most are consistent with existing research. In summary form, here are the propositions.

First, theorizing about human behavior benefits from an acceptance of a basic tenet of evolutionary theory. That is, species are selected by nature because of their ability to adapt and survive. We needlessly complicate our theory if we insist on attributing higher purposes to humans. Because our neurological system evolved through accretion, there is good reason to believe that phylogenetically earlier structures retain a significant degree of independent functioning. Consequently, it is reasonable to relate important human behavior to such neurological structures as the limbic system and the left and right cerebral hemispheres.

Humans have at least two means by which behavioral strategies are stored in long-term memory and related to environmental stimuli. Episodic memory is related to the limbic system, and semantic memory is coupled with the cerebral cortex. Episodic memory is concrete and represents actual events in adaptive living. Semantic memory is abstract and symbolic in nature.

Aside from hit-or-miss attempts to respond to absolutely novel stimuli, two types of behavorial strategies are available for use. First, when stimuli are relatively unfamiliar, an organism can analyze the stimulus situation for elements that approximate some known, generalized pattern or gestalt. The response ultimately chosen is the one associated with the identified pattern or gestalt. The use of this type of behavioral strategy is handled by the right side of the brain. When stimuli are highly familiar and important for adaptation, the left side of the brain rehearses and overlearns successful strategies to these stimuli. Such strategies are identified and implemented relatively effortlessly by the organism.

The essential distinction between the limbic system and the cerebral cortex concerns the nature of the material they deal with. The limbic system deals with survival behavior that is affective, concrete, and visceral. The cortex is concerned with cognitive behavior that is abstract, highly complex, and symbolic. Yet both employ the behavioral strategies described earlier.

The concept of consciousness, which has traditionally been linked with the linguistic, left hemisphere, has proved to be an obstacle to the understanding of human behavior. Evidence supports the assertion that, in addition to linguistic consciousness, both limbic and right-hemipshere functions constitute their own forms of consciousness.

Critical periods may be much more influential in the development of human behavior than is widely assumed. Although few human critical periods have been confirmed, there are strong hints from both animal and human research that the provision (or omission) of certain experiences can have profound effects on adult behavior. Likewise, culture has profound effects on the behavior of individual members of our species. To the extent that culture fails to instill consistent, reasonable rules of behavior in its offspring, the culture will suffer because gregarious, cooperative societies depend on order, harmony, and a reduction of conflict to survive and flourish.

REFERENCES

Alajouanine, T., & Lhermitte, F. (1965). Acquired aphasia in children *Brain, 88,* 653–662.

Black, A.H., Nadel, L., & O'Keefe, J. (1977). Hippocampal function in avoidance learning and punishment. *Psychological Bulletin, 84,* 1107–1129.

Bogen, J.E., & Bogen, G.M. (1969). The other side of the brain: III. The corpus collosum and creativity. *Bulletin of the Los Angeles Neurological Society, 34,* 191–220.

Caldwell, J.M., Ransom, S.W., & Sacks, J.G. (1951). Group panic and other mass disruptive reactions. *United States Armed Forces Medical Journal, 2,* 541–567.

Curtiss, S. (1978). *Genie: A psycholinguistic study of a modern-day "wild child."* New York: Academic Press.

Deutsch, G., Papanicolaou, W.T., Bourbon, A.C., & Eisenberg, H.M. (1988). Visuospatial tasks compared via activation of regional cerebral blood flow. *Neuropsychologia, 26,* 445–452.

Ebner, F. (1969). A comparison of primitive forebrain organization on metatherian and eutherian mammals. *Annals of the New York Academy of Science, 167,* 241–257.

Fromkin, V.A., Krashen, S., Curtiss, S., Rigler, D., & Rigler, M. (1974). The development of language in Genie: A case of language acquisition beyond the "critical period." *Brain and Language, 1,* 81–107.

Fuster, J.M., & Uyeda, A.A. (1962). Facilitation of tachistoscopic performance by stimulation of midbrain tegmental points in the monkey. *Experimental Neurology, 6,* 384–406.

Galambos, R. (1961). A glia-neural theory of brain function. *Procedures of the National Academy of Science, 47,* 129–136.

Galin, D. (1974). Implications for psychiatry of left and right cerebral specialization. *Archives of General Psychiatry, 31,* 572–583.

Goldberg, E., & Costa L.D. (1981). Hemispheric differences in the acquisition and use of descriptive systems. *Brain and Language, 14,* 144–173.

Goldberg, E., Vaughan, H.G., Jr., & Gerstman, L.J. (1978). Nonverbal descriptive systems and hemisphere asymmetry: Shape versus texture discrimination. *Brain and Language, 5,* 249–257.

Harlow, H.F. (1960). Primary affectional patterns in primates. *American Journal of Orthopsychiatry, 30,* 676.

Harlow, H.F. (1962). The heterosexual affectional system in monkeys. *American Psychologist, 17,* 1–9.

Hebb, D.O. (1970). A return to Jensen and his social science critics. *American Psychologist, 25,* 568.

Hécaen, H. (1976). Acquired aphasia in children and the ontogenesis of hemispheric functional specialization. *Brain and Language, 3,* 114–134.

Hirsch, E.D. (1987). *Cultural literacy: What every American needs to know.* Boston: Houghton Mifflin.

Hubel, D.H., & Wiesel, T.N. (1970). The period of susceptibility to the physiological effects of unilateral eye closure in kittens. *Journal of Physiology, 206,* 419–436.

Isaacson, R.L., & Kimble, D.P. (1972). Lesions of the limbic system: Their effects upon hypotheses and frustration. *Behavioral Biology, 7,* 767–793.

Ito, M. (1984). *The cerebellum and neural control.* New York: Raven Press.

Jaynes, J. (1976). *The origin of consciousness in the breakdown of the bicameral mind.* Boston: Houghton Mifflin.

Jensen, A.R. (1969). How much can we boost IQ and scholastic achievement? *Harvard Educational Review, 39,* 1–123.

Jensen, A.R. (1980). *Bias in mental testing.* New York: Free Press.

Kellaway, P. (1989). Introduction to plasticity and sensitive periods. In P. Kellaway & J.L. Neobels (Eds.), *Problems and concepts in developmental neurophysiology* (pp. 3–28). Baltimore: Johns Hopkins University Press.

Kesner, R.P. (1983). Mnemonic functions of the hippocampus: Correspondence between animals and humans. In C.D. Woody (Ed.), *Conditioning representation of neural function.* New York: Plenum Press.

Kimble, D.P., & Kimble, R.J. (1970). The effect of hippocampal lesions on extinction and "hypothesis" behavior in rats. *Physiology and Behavior, 5,* 735–738.

Kolb, B., & Whishaw, I.Q. (1990). *Fundamentals of human neuropsychology* (3rd ed.). New York: W.H. Freeman.

Krashen, S.D. (1973). Lateralization, language learning and the critical period: Some new evidence. *Language Learning, 23,* 63–74.

Lazar, I., & Darlington, R. (1982). Lasting effects of early education: A report from the consortium for longitudinal studies. *Monographs of the Society for Research in Child Development, 47* (Serial No. 195).

LeDoux, J.E. (1986). The neurobiology of emotion. In J.E. LeDoux & W. Hirst (Eds.), *Mind and brain: Dialogues in cognitive neuroscience* (pp. 301–354). Cambridge: Cambridge University Press.

LeDoux, J.E., Sakaguchi, A., & Reis, D.J. (1984). Subcortical efferent projections of the medulla geniculate nucleus mediate emotional responses conditioned to acoustic stimuli. *Jounal of Neuroscience, 4,* 683–698.

Lenneberg, E. (1967). *Biological foundations of language.* New York: Wiley.

Leyhausen, P. (1979). *Cat behavior.* New York: Garland Press.

Luria, A.R. (1973). *The working brain.* Harmondsworth, England: Penguin.

MacLean, P.D. (1970). The triune brain, emotion, and scientific bias. In F.O. Schmitt (Ed.), *The neurosciences: Second study program* (pp. 336–349). New York: Rockefeller University Press.

MacLean, P.D., & Creswell, G. (1970). Anatomical connections of the visual system with limbic cortex of monkey. *Journal of Comparative Neurology, 138,* 265–278.

Malmo, R.B. (1975). *On emotions, needs, and our archaic brain.* New York: Holt, Rinehart, and Winston.

Marshall, S.L.A. (1947). *Men against fire.* New York: William Morrow.

Means, L.W., Walker, D.W., & Isaacson, R.L. (1970). Facilitated single alternation go, no-go acquisition following hippocampectomy in the rat. *Journal of Comparative and Physiological Psychology, 72,* 278–285.

Mishkin, M. (1978). Memory in monkeys severely impaired by combined but not by separate removal of amygdala and hippocampus. *Nature, 273,* 297–298.

Mishkin, M., & Appenzeller, T. (1987). The anatomy of memory. In R.R. Llinis (Ed.), *The workings of the brain: Development, memory, and perception* (pp. 88–102). New York: W.H. Freeman.

Moruzzi, G., & Magoun, H.W. (1949). Brain stem reticular formation and activation of the EEG. *Electroencephalography and Clinical Neurophysiology, 1,* 455–473.

Norita, M., & Kawamura, K. (1980). Subcortical afferents to the monkey amygdala. *Brain Research, 190,* 225- ⋅ ⋅.

Ornstein, R. (1991). *The evolution of consciousness.* New York: Prentice-Hall.

Pickard, G.E., & Silverman, A.J. (1981). Direct retinal projections to the hypothalamus piriform cortex, and accessory optic nuclei in the golden hamster as demonstrated by a sensitive anterograde horseradish peroxidase technique. *Journal of Comparative Neurology, 196,* 155–172.

Prescott, J.W., Read, M.S., & Coursin, D.B. (Eds). (1975). *Brain function and malnutrition: Neuropsychological methods of assessment.* New York: John Wiley & Sons.

Schmaltz, L.W., & Theios, J. (1972). Acquisition and extinction of a classically conditioned response in hippocampectomized rabbits *(Oryctolagus cuniculus).* *Journal of Comparative and Physiological Psychology, 79,* 328–333.

Semmes, J. (1968). Hemispheric specialization: A possible clue to mechanism. *Neuropsychologia, 6,* 11–26.

Skeels, H.M., & Dye. H.B. (1939). A study of the effects of differential stimulation on mentally retarded children. *Proceedings of the American Association on Mental Deficiency, 44,* 114–136.

Solomon, P.R., & Moore, J.W. (1975). Latent inhibition and stimulus generalization of the classically conditioned nictitating membrane response in rabbits *(Oryctolagus cuniculus)* following dorsal hippocampal ablations. *Journal of Comparative and Physiological Psychology, 89,* 1192–1203.

Sperry, R.W. (1974). Lateral specialization in the surgically separated hemispheres. In F.O. Schmitt & F.G. Worden (Eds.), *The neurosciences: Third study program* (pp. 5–19). Cambridge, MA: MIT press.

Springer, S.P., & Deutsch, G. (1989). *Left brain, right brain.* New York: W.H. Freeman.

Swanson, L.W., Cowan, W.M., & Jones, E.G. (1974). An autoradiographic study of the efferent connections of the ventral lateral geniculate nucleus of the albino rat and cat. *Journal of Comparative Neurology, 156,* 143–163.

Tyhurst, J.S. (1951). Individual reactions to community disaster. The natural history of psychiatric phenomena. *American Journal of Psychiatry, 107,* 764–769.

Winson, J. (1985). *Brain and psyche.* New York: Vintage Books.

Woodburne, L.S. (1967). *The neural basis of behavior.* Columbus: Merrill.

2

Describing the Cognitive Aspects
of Intelligence

David A. Sabatino
Hubert B. Vance

The history and evolution of psychology are reflected in the quest to quantify intelligent behavior. This includes understanding how both higher- and lower-order nervous systems learn; what role external factors such as enrichment, stimulation, conditioning, and other manipulations may play; and, of course, the all-important inter- and intrasubject variation in human adaptability.

The word *adaptability* was chosen for its broad utility in describing intelligence. Theoretically, the greater the intelligence, the greater is the ability to adapt to environments and to learn specific tasks required in that process. This logic has been argued throughout history and culminated in the Spearman (1923), Thorndike (1927), and Thurstone (1938) debates in the second quarter of the twentieth century. The urgency to define intelligence as either specific traits or as a general factor, or as some combination of specific traits and general factor, continues to be more than a theoretical debate. It was, and is, the very basis for designing intelligence tests. It is a continuing study of the process by which humans solve problems.

Problem solving is adaptability. The application of thought through language in the search to bring solutions to problems as an adaptation is also intelligence. Thus, we frequently hear people described as intelligent when they display behaviors that otherwise might be regarded as shrewd, cunning, and perceptive. Often, intelligence is associated with the ability to demonstrate outstanding performance in a disciplinary body that requires informational mastery. Intelligence is used as a summary descriptor of intelligent behavior.

Cognition by definition means the ability to control one's environment (Halstead, 1947). Herein lies a very important difference between humans and most other living beings. Most species have some biological ability to adapt to their natural environment, wherein humans lack the ability to adapt directly to nature. The act of generating purposeful intelligent behaviors is paramount to our survival. We possess the power to communicate our internal thoughts (using abstract symbol and conceptual systems) through language. People must express cognitive traits as conscious intelligent behaviors to offset for physical and biological inferiority.

The behavioral sciences' interest in cognition continues for several reasons (Glasser, 1981). Certainly, the future of humankind depends on our ability to adapt to a radically changing environment, one that changes within the generational period. The bank of information to be maintained doubles every five years. Therefore, the behavioral sciences will be under additional stress to identify the amounts, speed, and retention necessary to demonstrate human adaptability (Glover & Corkill, 1990). We are the first generation to create artificial intelligence, and as world survival issues become even more pressing, reliance on the interaction of human cognitive capability and computer applications will greatly extend our problem-solving capacity.

That is a sharp contrast to special education's current interest in the formative cognitive processing of information (Hynd et al, 1988). Special education appears driven to determine who can and cannot achieve a certain type and amount of information (learning task) in a rigid learning environment. It is not terribly interested in the uniqueness we witness in the human mind as a problem-solving information processor. Instead, special educators focus on the intellectual product and not on the processes of cognitive capacities (Hartlage & Telzrow, 1983).

If the behavioral sciences and special education are to take cognitive re-education seriously, the capacities that contribute to the structure of the intellect must be differentiated. Why? There is evidence that stimulating cognitive capabilities produces increased learning (Gouvier & Adams, 1986). If a child's environment is not enriched during the preschool years, then cognitive re-education may be needed later in that person's life (Melamed & Rugle, 1989). Education for the masses is necessary to ensure democracy. Education for the disabled is important to improve the quality of life for that group of citizens. However, enriching the learner's capability to develop the mental resources necessary to solve problems related to independent living and competitive employment may become very important in the immediate future (Lyon et al., 1988). Longer-term cognitive education may play a substantial role in reducing welfare dependency. More importantly, however, the identification of specific cognitive genius that resides in those with advanced development may enhance the collective good and ensure a stable and prosperous social order.

This chapter argues that special education is dependent on summary statements such as IQ and must take seriously the exploration of cognitive dysfunction in students. It is our premise that, ultimately, regular education can provide its own tutorial and remedial services. In contrast, special education should be about the task of cognitive re-education of students with cognitive dysfunction. This argument is predicated on the capacity of psychology to define diagnostically useful cognitive structures and on the capacity of the schools to apply information about those structures. This means that outmoded twentieth-century categories of handicapped will be removed and disability will be defined as cognitive dysfunction and undergo cognitive re-education.

THE PAST AND THE FUTURE

Hundreds of years before Binet, various cultures attempted to find ways in which specific learning styles, learning speed, accuracy, memory, and specific job traits could be studied in controlled environments on tasks that provided economy of measurement. For centuries, tests of human cognitive performance have been required, for example, for advancement in the Roman army, for civil-service positions in second-century China, and for graduation to the lyceum following British or European schools (Bowman, 1989).

Forerunners in the history of mental measurement were interested in developing instruments that could define the development of specific cognitive traits (Lichtheim, 1885). In the United States, the search emphasized reliability and validity. Individual trait measures were eliminated in favor of highly stable summary scores. Cognitive traits were summarized as intelligence, which become synonymous with IQ, a global summation, that became an American twentieth-century trade mark.

INTELLIGENCE AND COGNITION

Considerable confusion exists regarding the definitions of intelligence and cognition, as evidenced by the inconsistent use of the terms. There is a common belief that if intelligence is ascertained, cognitive development can be described from those results. Intelligence, when viewed as a general factor, is a summation of various, often undifferentiated, cognitive traits (Thurstone, 1938). Intelligence can be viewed as Intelligence*s*, or specific cognitive traits, if a theoretical structure exists to explain how these traits process information for the learner (Guilford, 1967). It is often difficult to know if cognitive composition is implied when intelligence is referenced and especially when it is summed as a score. Operationally, intelligence and cognition are used quite differently in special education. Intelligence is used to suggest a score, frequently for a classification or a placement decision. Consequently, predictive validity is often viewed as the *sine qua non* of an intelligence test.

Cognition, or the measurement of cognitive traits, demands construct and concurrent validity. Most cognitive traits are given names based on observed functions (e.g., visual or auditory perception, memory). Generally, that function is observed in some motoric product or output. It is difficult to obtain standardized measures that do not also measure a manual-motor or vocal-motor response mode. In ascertaining specific cognitive traits, the amount of specificity is always an issue. Intelligence is a safe construct, and it is usable because it permits generalizations to be made about a student's ability to interact successfully with the general curriculum. Intelligence is operationally defined as what an intelligence test measures. The majority of intelligence tests for children are designed to measure school success.

Intelligence, to most people, is the ability to function intellectually. With school children, that implies an index to determine their rates of academic achievement. There is a very high positive correlation between verbal intelligence test performance and reading comprehension (Vance, 1981). There is only a moderate relationship between verbal intelligence and success as measured by salary, job satisfaction, and long-term employability (Jensen, 1980). A key factor is that intelligence is viewed as a summation of many types of performance on many types of tasks. It is a performance average and therefore highly stable, and stability means that it does not change much without an explanation (e.g., environmental impoverishment, neural damage).

Cognition is the economic use of symbol and conceptual systems to convey information that abstractly represents that which occurs in nature. Cognition is the immediate adaptability to environmental circumstances and represents our understanding of what may happen under the skull cap to generate intelligence (Sternberg, 1984). Just as humans provide names to all those things observed in nature, we also devise names to describe those cognitive aspects of how information must be processed by the nervous system. Cognition occurs in both concrete learning (nonsymbolic) and abstract learning (symbol systems such as reading, math, and even speaking). *Cognitive trait* is the name given to a characteristic that we believe occurs in the processing of information (e.g., memory, reasoning, conceptualization).

Cognitive traits are generally thought to respond to directive teaching that may not have anything to do with academic learning or grade-level instruction (Shurtleff et al., 1986). Therefore, most of us would scoff at the notion that the IQ can be raised through a miracle diet. On the other hand, most educators believe that specific cognitive traits can be modified. Yet few educators teach children to think, increase their memory, enhance abstract reasoning, or develop spatial-relations skills. The consequence is that the value of education in developing adaptability or problem solving has been lost to increasing academic achievement rates.

INTELLIGENCE TESTS AND EDUCATION

Today, education in general and special education in particular have a love-hate relationship with intelligence tests. Research on special education administrators shows that they view the importance of intellectual assessment and testing as a necessary evil. This view exists for several reasons.

Each year, public schools are faced with a number of children who fail to master the school curriculum. The public schools have sought to explain these failures as an absence of suitable student intelligence to achieve academically. In fact, intelligence test scores provide a primary index for the placement of children into special education programs. Much of the justification for special education, as an alternative to regular education, resides in the fact that people differ intellectually. Yet the reality is that knowledge of intelligence does not answer questions related to what to teach and how to teach. The truth is that the combination of achievement and intelligence scores does little to explain how children learn, what is apparently wrong, and what may need to be fixed. No wonder that modern educators are confused and ambivalent over the "help" they receive from concepts such as intelligence.

OLD PITFALLS FOR NEW APPLICATIONS

In response to that confusion, special educators have continued to cheapen the process of diagnosing how learning occurs in various children who evidence academic and social problems. Currently, there is an assumption that specific cognitive development is ascertained within the administration of intelligence tests. Some states require that cognitive strengths and weaknesses be described for children who receive special education services. The incomprehensible aspect of this requirement is that these cognitive descriptions are to be obtained from intelligence tests. What is said to be a cognitive trait is but a subtest on a Wechsler Intelligence Scale for Children (WISC-III) or a Kaufman Assessment Battery for Children (KABC).

When a group of special education teachers were recently asked if cognitive development was ascertained in children placed into special education, nearly 90% replied in the affirmative. When asked where and how these cognitive data were generated, nearly 90% noted that they were drawn from the subtests of intelligence tests. Less than 10% reported that data on cognitive development were obtained through observation, school records, or other aspects of the prereferral and diagnostic process. They believed that the administration of an intelligence test, a perceptual-motor test, and an academic achievement test constitutes a comprehensive test battery.

In summary, there appears to be a strong belief among educators that a person's level of cognitive development is ascertained during the individual administration of intelligence tests. There appears to be considerable confusion between ascertaining intelligence and describing cognitive abilities related to learning. Cognitive traits can be observed and measured in response to specific learning tasks, if the task is not too complex. Children who interact successfully with the curriculum do self-sort on their cognitive strengths. Cognition in the apt learner defines the nature of the learner's interests and attitudes. Not so with disabled learners, however; cognitive dysfunction must be determined and a re-education plan developed for them.

With normal learners, intelligence is a functional construct that may be useful in guiding and directing them somewhat in their school programs. They will generally be self-directive on the basis of their cognitive strengths. Intelligence is a very limited construct with disabled learners inasmuch as it fails to define the nature of the learner. Intelligence tests are summary measures or products from many specific trait (motor, spatial, percepto-cognitive) measures. There is no such thing as an all-purpose intelligence test capable of describing a predetermined set of cognitive dysfunctions.

LEARNING DISABILITIES: A COGNITIVE DYSFUNCTION

Learning disability is now diagnosed by psychometric discrepancy — a regression between intelligence and academic achievement standard scores. It has become an academic underachievement deficit, not a cognitive disability. In the early years, learning disabilities were defined as informational processing deficits. The reason for the change in eligibility requirements was to control (reduce) the number of children found eligible for special educational services. Two of the major contributors to the change in eligibility requirements were school psychologists and special education directors. All school psychologists can obtain intelligence and academic achievement test scores. Not all school psychologists can describe cognitive dysfunction. Special education directors can readily understand summary intelligence test scores, but they cannot all understand cognitive dysfunctions.

Most school psychologists are ill prepared to ascertain cognitive dysfunction, and particularly neuropsychological aspects of disability. For those who can, the schools will not provide them the time to do so. School psychologists no longer write reports; they fill in blanks on a form that requests WISC-III scale scores and IQs. There are blanks for Bender Visual-Motor Gestalt Test raw errors and developmental age equivalents. And there is another blank for adaptive behavior if mental retardation is suspected. Academic achievement is measured by an educational diagnostician, and a multidisciplinary team examines these scores and rules on eligibility. There is no room for determining cognitive dysfunction in this simplistic placement scheme.

The reduction in the description of the unique behaviors associated with a student's learning and behavioral characteristics becomes lost in the effort to define people's traits objectively. In the words of Matarazzo (1990), ". . . objective testing and clinical sanctioned and licensed psychological assessment are vastly different, even though assessment usually includes testing" (p. 1000). Objective diagnosis derived from psychological assessment is impossible. Diagnosis requires a large measure of subjectivity. Tests do not derive diagnostic values; people do. The value of any test is no greater than the person using it. The inability to see beyond the standardized observation and to be able to create other behavioral sampling conditions has become a major issue that is well addressed in one example. We defy any diagnostician or multidisciplinary diagnostic group to write meaningful short- or long-term goals, including enabling instructional activities, on the basis of IQ and achievement test data. These scores do not provide the basis for making instructional and behavioral management decisions about highly complex learner characteristics in disabled persons.

"As a consequence, an increasing number of attorneys recognize that even in our nation's most advanced centers for psychological assessment, the measurement of intelligence (or personality, memory, or other psychological functions) is not, even today a totally objective, completely science-based activity. Rather, in common with much of medical diagnosis, experience in our nation's courtrooms is forcefully making clear to psychologists that the assessment of intelligence, personality, or type and level of impairment is a highly complex operation that involves extracting diagnostic meaning from an individual's personal history and objectively recorded test scores. Rather than being totally objective, assessment involves a subjective component" (Matarazzo, 1990, p. 1000).

A learning disability, as a cognitive dysfunction, cannot be found by IQ testing. Subtest scatter may be helpful in beginning the process if it is evaluated in light of how information is processed through the cognitive structures of the nervous system. People who administer tests are technicians, generating data for psychologists and the diagnosticians to use. Individuals who synthesize data from structured and unstructured observations into an integrated whole to derive diagnostic impressions and develop management schemes are diagnosticians. In uncovering cognitive dysfunction, diagnosticians develop and test hypotheses using a wide range of instruments and observational procedures.

The aftermath of current testing practices is horrendous. For instructional and behavior-management purposes, a group of children are classified as learning disabled on the basis of the statistical relationship between two scores. We treat special education eligibility and placement as if they were an intervention. The diagnostic value of any assessment procedure begins with declaring eligibility and the concomitant placement of children into various forms of special educational programs. If the only decision to be made is to determine if a special educational program is needed, then children should be placed on teacher recommendation, and diagnosis leading to intervention should be eliminated (Reynolds, 1981).

The value of diagnostic decisions in developing intervention strategies has been layered over with so-called procedural safeguards, such as multidisciplinary assessment. The principal requirement of writing the most effective intervention programs for the disabled student is being met in name only. The heart of defining an instructional and behavioral intervention is in the description of the learner's information processing. Then, the task to be learned and the learning environment can be altered to accommodate the learner; hence, the process of cognitive re-education begins.

COGNITIVE DYSFUNCTION

To understand the importance of cognitive functionality in selected populations of disabled learners, it may be helpful to examine how specific professions serving the disabled reference cognitive dysfunction. We can accomplish this by contrasting special education and vocational rehabilitation. These companion professions often serve the same client at different times in the disabled person's life. However, both medical and vocational rehabilitation also provide services to a number of clients who have achieved productive and successful lives only to have an accident or illness render them with a cognitive dysfunction.

One of the differences between special education and rehabilitation resides in how rehabilitation uses diagnostic information to obtain a prognosis (Ben-

Yishay et al., 1987). The philosophy that drives special education is often one that does not require a prognosis based on the learner's cognitive structures. In an examination of several hundred individualized education programs (IEPs), Janssen, Isles, O'Keefe, and Sabatino (1988) found that short-term objectives are generally academic or behaviorally oriented to some grade level or age-appropriate social skill, whereas the long-term goals are very global and rarely address any culmination of the collective interventions utilized. That may be one reason that IEPs fail to change across grades from year to year. When a rehabilitation team receives a 56-year-old successful sitting judge who has had a massive cerebrovascular accident (stroke), the amount of recovery expected is guided by prognostic estimates of cognitive function based on thorough neuropsychological diagnoses. Hence, what is ascertained are degrees of cognitive dysfunction, and a service plan is developed on these data accordingly (Orsini et al., 1988). In contrast, it is difficult to find disabled children receiving special education services where there are prognostic statements (goals). The absence of prognostic statements in special education means that clarification of the type and amount of services required is also lacking. Such oversights include the range of support services and adjustment to task and environment, which must be supported by family members.

Contrast the special education scenario with the following rehabilitation case. A highly successful 36-year-old businessman suffered a closed-head injury in an automobile accident, which left him with a severe motor-speech apraxia, right hemiplegia (weakness), and limited usable vision (legal blindness). Because of his powerful political and family connections within the community and state and the amount of insurance coverage available, it would not have been difficult to spend hundreds of thousands of dollars on travel training, speech therapy, braille instruction, and other re-educational therapies. That course of action was not taken. The amount of cognitive dysfunction to the language-learning centers, including recent and short-term retention, was so massive as to render this adult a highly inconsistent learner with only remote memory. It was considered more important to focus on quality-of-life aspects, such as activities of daily living, instead of submitting him to an academic relearning program. He received cognitive re-education in adaptive skills for independent living and a number of new leisure activities that he could enjoy.

To providers of adult rehabilitation services, cognitive function is the specific appraisal of brain function in areas of motor speech; manual motor speed and accuracy; strength and coordination of upper and lower extremities; laterality; expressive, receptive, and central language conceptual capacity to use vocabulary meaningfully; short- and long-term specific memory function; other abilities to learn and maintain information; and personality factors (Sohlberg & Mateer, 1989).

Establishing the presence of cognitive dysfunction in children is nearly ignored, yet it is an essential clinical practice that could revitalize special education in providing cognitive (re-)education. When asked recently to observe a 7-year-old boy repeating the first grade for the second time, we were told an interesting and highly indicative case history. The major behaviors observed were that the child preferred to work and play in isolation and was a highly inconsistent learner. He would have periods of seemingly excellent adjustment to peers, teachers, tasks, and the classroom environment. These periods might last an entire morning or afternoon, but rarely did they last all day. For no apparent reason this physically well-developed and attractive child, with a verbal IQ in excess of 120 and measured academic achievement above the third-grade level, would display an emotional storm. He displayed anger to the point of rage, disregarding verbal directions during these 10- to 15-minute periods, followed by an apathetic, almost semicomatose state that would last for 15 to 30 minutes.

He had been described by a pediatrician as displaying an attention-deficit disorder with hyperactivity and was administered Ritalin (CIBA Pharmaceutical Co.) and Cylert (Abbott Laboratories, Pharmaceutical Products Div.) at maximum dosages with no change in behavior. A child psychiatrist described him as having poor ego strength and lacking the personality integrity necessary for maintaining self-control owing to thoughts of anger that he could not deal with at a conscious level. Nearly a year of play therapy did not help. The multidisciplinary team considered him seriously emotionally disturbed and placed him in a self-contained classroom for disruptive children. A rigorous classroom engineering system was used with all the children in that room. Predictably, he would display perfect behavior for a period of time, then display an emotional episode and fail to respond to physical restraint, wrecking the behavior-management system.

This child had a history of spinal meningitis at the age of 4 years. He did not display severe explosive episodes prior to the illness. During the illness he had a high fever (in excess of 105°F) for several days, requiring alcohol baths and medication. Not all inappropriate or unwanted behavior is learned or can be brought under voluntary control. Children with histories of neurological insult or who exhibit behavior known to be associated with neurological impairment may require a different form of management. In the 1930s clinicians were reporting detailed observations of patients with large unilateral lesions, noting an apparent asymmetry in the effects of left and right hemisphere lesions. The best-known descriptions are those of Goldstein (1942), who suggested that left hemisphere lesions produce "catastrophic" reactions characterized by fearfulness and depression, whereas right hemisphere lesions produce "indifference." Systematic study of these contrasting behavioral effects showed that catastrophic reactions occurred in 62 percent of the left hemisphere sample, compared with only 10 percent for right hemisphere cases. In contrast, indifference was more common in the right hemisphere patients, occurring in 38 percent, as compared with only 11 percent of the left hemisphere cases.

It is obvious that a simple left/right distinction of catastrophic/indifference reactions is far too simple; both the site and the side of the lesion are important in understanding the changes in emotional behavior. This ought not to surprise us, however, because the same is true of cognitive behaviors. To understand the organization of emotional processes, we must therefore attempt to fractionate the components of the behaviors as we have done in the study of cognitive processes.

This child was not seriously emotionally disturbed; he was displaying sequelae to postneurological impairment.

Neuropsychological assessment and a pediatric neurologist confirmed the diagnosis. With antidepressant medication and the use of self-control measures involving self-isolation in a time-out room at the onset of the auras that preceded these events, the child was easily returned to the regular class. His only instructional problem was that he did not retain material during the aura and was informationally confused following the catastrophic reactions. By timing individual resource-room teaching with the reactions, he became an "A" student. Many so-called social–personal patterns are not emotional disturbances in a social-learning or behavioral sense; they are cognitive dysfunctions.

Thousands of children display inconsistent patterns in either learning or retaining information. Others have difficulty retaining perceptual information. Some have difficulty retaining language units or understanding language concepts. Still others have difficulty expressing them. An important aspect of differential diagnosis is determining when conceptual language learning (mental retardation) and receptive or expressive language learning problems are present. We are reminded of a child with a very high IQ who failed to learn to read. On observation, this child was having transient (petit mal) seizures that lasted a few seconds approximately every 3 minutes. He could not maintain arousal long enough to master word-recognition skills. When the teaching activities were timed with observations of his arousal/attention sets, his word-recognition skills soon exceeded grade level.

COGNITIVE DIAGNOSIS?

Diagnosis is decision making. The value of diagnosis must be seen in the interventions offered. A test score is not a diagnosis; comparisons of test scores are not diagnoses. Diagnosis with handicapped populations is defining disability in type and amount in order that appropriate levels and intensity of intervention can be offered. Reschley (1978) discussed the level of inference used in the predictions made about individuals based on diagnoses of minimal brain damage and/or learning disabilities: ". . . assessment which results in a high level of inference is usually not related to intervention, and is therefore of questionable benefit to individuals" (p.38). In this case and in others, a prediction orientation can no longer be supported. These types of decisions based on prediction are often helpful to the school but are often damaging to the individual and misleading to others. Reynolds (1975) wrote that ". . . consequently, schools require a decision orientation rather than simple prediction [orientation]; they need one that is oriented to individuals rather than institutional payoff. In today's context, the measurement technologies ought to become integral parts of instruction, designed to make a *difference in* the *lives* of *children* and not just a prediction about their lives" (p. 15).

The extant assessment process may serve only to further discriminate among children, using bureaucratic criteria that may act as a rejection process against the very student who needs or can profit the most from assistance. Do we continue to be weather forecasters, sometimes after the storm, instead of problem solvers?

The diagnostic process should cover the specific subskills that comprise each academic skill area of those cognitive traits that are used (theoretically at least) to process information. This information must be acquired through both formal and informal observational procedures. Specific cognitive traits can be obtained from any observation if the observer (or test administrator) uses the assessment task as a diagnostic process and is in search of something other than a product measure — IQ. Careful observation of the student's test performance and individual responses to test items can be analyzed closely for specific information processing errors.

In attempting to supplement the results of formal tests with more education-ally oriented information, many professionals have included different types of informal assessment procedures in the evaluation process. Teacher-made tests and various observational techniques have been widely used to combat the problems associated with formal assessment. However, these procedures have problems associated with precision. Informal assessment techniques must meet the same criteria for use as do formal procedures or they are worthless. Identifying cognitive dysfunctions provides the diagnostician the opportunity to recommend specific skill retraining (cognitive re-education) and specific educational interventions (Telzrow, 1989).

A CASE STUDY IN COGNITIVE RE-EDUCATION

Kevin was a 17-year-old high school junior when he sustained a head injury while driving home from his job as a grocery stock boy. He was comatose for 14 days and spent the next 2 months in a medical center. Kevin suffered diffuse injury to his brain as the result of the head-on collision. Major damage was particularly noted in the occipital lobes due to the contrecoup force causing the brain to bounce inside the skull. When he returned home he had problems with immediate memory and directionality. His speech and both written and spoken language returned and appeared normal.

While Kevin was in the hospital, the speech and language pathologist developed some cognitive strategies that Kevin could use to organize his thought processes. The occupational and physical therapists worked with him to develop manual-motor speed and accuracy. Although the function on his left side returned to normal, his right side remained weak. He regained full use of his legs, but the manual-motor speed and accuracy in his right hand were now 50% slower than in his left hand.

Following Kevin's return home, a home-bound teacher was employed. That instructional activity was not productive and was very frustrating to Kevin. On the recommendation of the home-bound teacher, Kevin was evaluated for special educational services and was returned to school in an expanded resource room for learning-disabled high school children.

The medical rehabilitation team outlined a tutorial support for academic subject areas that Kevin would take in the regular classroom. Kevin found the regular classroom a sea of confusion and floundered miserably. A vocational-rehabilitation counselor was asked to help. The counselor arranged a neuropsychological assessment and obtained the hospital therapy records, contacting the speech and language pathologist. The following educational plan was developed for Kevin.

Kevin would attend social science, English, and biology classes in the morning, using a tape recorder and writing key-word notes. He would receive how-to-study and tutorial assistance in the resource room during his third period (replacing study hall). In the afternoon he would attend a functional math course and English in the special education self-contained classes. He would complete the day with computer programming classes, which he liked and which did not require recent memory.

The first thing each morning Kevin would have a daily orientation session with the special education resource teacher to make sure he had the right materials, books, and so forth. All examinations were orally administered in the resource room by an aide. At the close of the day Kevin would "check out" with the special education resource teacher and outline his homework assignments.

One of Kevin's major out-of-school assignments was to begin a community reorientation training program since he would literally get lost in the high school building. Every day, immediately after school, an occupational therapist would provide him one-half hour of directional training that included using compensatory strategies. Kevin's goal was to take driver's education and requalify for his driver's license. The problem was, of course, that he could not find his way home from the school or to the store. A system of locations and landmarks was devised and a map "cookbook" was developed that greatly aided the directionality problems. Kevin took driver's training in the summer of his senior year and now drives and finds his way around the community using his maps. He has since expanded these maps to include a growing regional set of direction-finding guides.

Kevin's homework was networked with paid peers, and the benefit of travel training and tutoring with the peers soon became obviously successful, especially when Kevin converted homework to the computer in his home. Kevin kept a computer diary, which he reviewed each evening; the purpose of this diary was to become aware of feelings associated with all other activities and relationships. The diary was the basis for his counseling sessions with the rehabilitation and community agency counselors that he saw weekly. Kevin's friends developed, in cooperation with his family, a social activity weekend schedule.

Kevin's senior year was patterned on his junior year with expanded computer technology and programming courses. In the spring semester, his vocational-rehabilitation counselor helped him take one course in computer technology at the area vocational-technical school, which was only about 20 minutes from his house. He re-entered his old job the summer after his senior year but could not keep the list of work activities organized well enough, and it was his decision to find different employment. He spent the summer in partnership with a friend running a highly successful yard mowing and trimming business. Summer evenings were spent in the gym on a weight-training program.

Kevin graduated from high school and is having a successful year at the vocational-technical school, where he has obtained a part-time job in a computer store. As with all disabled persons, the learner with cognitive dysfunctions must have short-term goals that address immediate problems. Since students with cognitive dysfunctions must make pervasive and complicated adjustments in all areas of living, longer-term goals require the careful integration of all domains: cognitive, social, affective, and psychomotor. Classifying students with cognitive dysfunctions using traditional disability categories and placing them into time-worn special education programs may complicate already existing problems. Schools must recognize that students with cognitive dysfunctions have several common and overlapping problems, such as concentrating and focusing attention; retaining information; new learning; organizing their time, feelings, and thoughts; and general reasoning, problem solving, and decision making. They frequently display poor self-control and high levels of impulsivity, lack insight into feelings, and fail to understand some of the behaviors they produce. In response to feelings associated with limited control over their lives, they suffer from low levels of personal esteem and high levels of self-doubt.

The school will need to use teaching methods that concentrate on cognitive processing as academic skills are taught (Howell et al., 1979). Focus should be on the interaction between teacher and student, not necessarily on the material itself. The schools must project long-term goals (integrated into a continuous service plan) for the student and family, not just year-to-year objectives. All through the school years, two major goals, independent living and competitive employment, must be viewed as capstones and include transitional services as the student moves from school to community. All goals should include the family and draw freely on the services of other agencies.

NEUROPSYCHOLOGICAL TEST BATTERY

Today the psychologist has the ability to detail cognitive traits in two ways. The first is to develop a systematic scheme that explains how information is processed and then to develop hypotheses in response to observations and test data as to where percepto-cognitive failure occurs (Sabatino & Miller, 1979). In this manner the psychologist raises questions related to how information is processed and, using standard clinical procedures, attempts to answer those questions. The second is to obtain additional comprehensive assessment data using neuropsychological procedures (Filskov & Boll, 1981). These two procedures work well in combination. By raising speculation about which cognitive traits may be dysfunctional, a wider instrument band simply has the robustness of permitting greater hypothesis testing. It is also reassuring to find agreement among tests with high convergent validity, and equally so when divergent measures indicate other (possibly cognitive) strengths.

Neuropsychological tests do have the capability of providing voluminous amounts of specific cognitive information (Reynolds, 1989) and indeed more information than is sometimes necessary, at a labor-intensive cost of a full day's assessment time. For this reason, it may be practical to avoid test batteries and use a system of theoretical constructs. The search then is for answers to specific questions phrased as hypotheses from pointed observations, developmental and medical histories, and data obtained from other observers and earlier assessments. It is also important to consider the use of computer-aided scoring and interpretation when using neuropsychological procedures (Adams & Brown, 1986).

The Wechsler Scales (Wechsler, 1974,1991), Binet-type instruments (Terman & Merrill 1960; Thorndike et al., 1986), and Kaufman Assessment Battery for Children (Kaufman & Kaufman, 1981) do not constitute comprehensive cognitive assessment instruments (Kaplan, 1989). In general, they produce highly stable IQ scores and permit some hypothesis testing through subtest contrasts. Principally, however, they promote the development of hypotheses, many of which relate to the development and function of how and which various cognitive traits process what information. Neuropsychological procedures are time consuming and require in-service education for the special education audience, who currently have only minimal exposure to their use (Samuels, 1975). These procedures do provide systematically ordered data, some of which are more medically oriented (e.g., localization of possible lesion sites), but they also provide highly structured information on motor, manual-motor, vocal-motor, visual-perceptual, visual-spatial, auditory-perceptual, perceptual integration, perceptual organization, and various aspects of language functionality, laterality, directionality, and specific academic achievement functions (McCarthy & Warrington, 1990).

The answer to Senf's (1979) question, "Can neuropsychology really change the face of education?" (p. 51), should be a positive one. There are several reasons for this, including the fact that many educators and psychologists do not view psychological and neurological conditions as relevant to the treatment process and, accordingly, ". . . biological causes for disability have increasingly become of less concern to the practicing special educator" (Reed, 1979, p.52). Although the neuropsychology evaluation was designed to demonstrate sensitivity to the effects of brain injury (Reitan, 1964), it also provides a comprehensive profile of specific cognitive abilities (Prigatano, 1986).

NEUROPSYCHOLOGICAL ASSESSMENT BATTERIES

There are three major neuropsychological evaluation batteries. Some neuropsychologists define their practice according to a particular method, whereas others are eclectic and borrow selectively from several approaches. Three major neuropsychological evaluation batteries will be reviewed briefly. These methods are described in more detail by Grant and Adams (1986) and Filskov and Boll (1981).

Halstead-Reitan Approach

The Halstead-Reitan Battery (Halstead, 1947; Reitan & Davidson, 1974; Reitan & Wolfson, 1985) is characterized by the use of rather long and extensive subtests of specific traits in various cognitive categories (often requiring 6 to 8 hours to administer). This procedure thoroughly assesses a number of areas of cognitive function but has been criticized for not thoroughly assessing new learning and memory abilities, as opposed to previous (remote) memory and pre-accident/illness learning. Most practitioners in the Halstead-Reitan tradition include additional measures of learning and memory in their evaluation of individuals with traumatic brain injury. Of all the approaches to the neuropsychological evaluation, the Halstead-Reitan method has generated the largest amount of scientific documentation on its validity in identifying brain damage and localizing brain lesions. It has an adult orientation and requires rigorous interpretation. It is generally used in medical settings to support neurological diagnosis.

Luria-Nebraska Approach

The Luria-Nebraska Battery (Christiansen, 1979) is a collection of short tests based on Luria's work and the elucidation of his methods by Anna-Lise Christiansen. The Luria-Nebraska Battery requires 3 to 4 hours to administer. It does not provide as much detailed information usable on brain lesion localization as does the Halstead-Reitan, but it does provide highly usable intervention data for cognitive traits having greater application to special education. When augmented by Wechsler or Binet-type tests and, where indicated, tests of aphasia, it becomes an excellent procedure for determining cognitive dysfunction. Although generally cited as not ascertaining cognitive complexities in reasoning and planning, it has a children's version that addresses pre-learning cognitive tasks fairly well. Reliability and validity data on the Luria-Nebraska Battery indicate the test is stable and well developed (Spier, 1982).

Boston Battery

The Boston Battery (Kaplan, 1989) emphasizes observation of the patient's behavior in determining the presence of brain impairment and specific brain lesions. Its strength is that it promotes systematic structuring of neuropsychological information on specific cognitive traits using standard psychometric procedures. The major value of this approach is that it places most emphasis on the psychologist's observations of the client's test performance than on the scores produced. For this reason it is highly recommended as a beginning point for school psychologists who may not yet have much detailed information on neuropsychological cognitive trait assessment.

SUMMARY

No evaluation can assess all the abilities or traits that learners use in processing information. An evaluation conducted a year ago will not accurately represent the subject's cognitive growth and development or changes in cognitive abilities needed to plan interventions a year later. Cognitive diagnosis should be completed on an as-needed basis, not on a 3-year cycle as is required today in special education. Furthermore, no report can be exhaustive. Communication and open exchange among the members of the intervention team are essential. More and more often the psychologist is not in attendance at multidisciplinary team meetings. In communicating placement decisions based on an IQ score there may be no need for the presence of the psychologist. However, in communicating the nature of cognitive disabilities in face-to-face exchanges among the intervention team members, the psychologist's role is critical.

Space limitations prevent a thorough review of the major cognitive structures and how they can be assessed through both informal and standardized observation. Such structures include perceptual and motor traits, as well as those generally referred to as cognitive traits. In fact, it is probably more accurate to refer to those information-processing behaviors related to learning as percepto-cognitive traits rather than as purely cognitive. In lieu of a complete discussion, we offer, in outline form, a breakdown of the traits in Table 2.1. The importance

Table 2.1 Some Important Percepto-cognitive Traits Related to Human Adaptive Behavior and Academic Achievement

Arousal
  Attention and concentration
Learning and Memory
  Remote and delayed memory
  Immediate (perceptual) memory
  Memory interference
  Sequential memory
Visual–Spatial Abilities
Visual–Motor Perception
Manual Motor and Proprioception
  Tactile perception
Auditory Perception
Perceptual Integration and Perceptual Organization
Language Learning and General Reasoning
  Language structure and function
    Tangentiality
    Garrulousness
    Prosody
    Inflection
    Sequencing
  Motor speech
Emotional Adjustment and Depression

of understanding how information flows into the nervous system — from the sensory end organs, through the perceptual discrimination and memory interpretation of sensory data, into lower (perceptual-to-language conceptual-symbol conversions) and then the higher cognitive (language mediation and association capabilities) — becomes clear in attempting to hypothesize how academic learning (information processing) occurs. The structure presented in Table 2.1 is not complete, but as the reader will witness, it provides a far greater range of descriptive information on cognitive development than normally appears in most school psychological reports.

REFERENCES

Adams, K.M., & Brown, G.G. (1986). The role of the computer in neuropsychological assessment. In I. Grant & K.M. Adams (Eds.), *Neuropsychological assessment of neuropsychiatric disorders.* New York: Oxford University Press.

Ben-Yishay, Y., Silver, S.M., Piasetsky, E., & Rattock, J. (1987). Relationships between employability and vocational outcome after intensive holistic cognitive rehabilitation. *Journal of Head Trauma Rehabilitation, 2,* 35–48.

Bowman, M.L. (1989). Testing individual differences in ancient China. *American Psychologist, 44,* 857–993.

Christiansen, A.L. (1979). *Luria's neuropsychological investigation text* (2nd ed.). Copenhagen: Munsksgaard.

Filskov, S.J., & Boll, T.J. (Eds.) (1981). *Handbook of clinical neuropsychology.* New York: John Wiley & Sons.

Glasser, R. (1981). The future of testing: A research agenda for cognitive psychology and psychometrics. *American Psychologist, 36,* 923–936.

Glover, J.A., & Corkill, A.J. (1990). The implications of cognitive psychology for school psychology. In T.B. Gutkin & C.R. Reynolds, *The Handbook of School Psychology* (2nd ed.). New York: John Wiley & Sons.

Goldstein, K. (1942). *After effects of brain-injuries in war.* New York: Grune & Stratton.

Gouvier, I., & Adams, K.M. (1986). Cognitive retraining with brain-damaged patients. In D. Wedding, A.M. Horton, & J. Webster (Eds.). *The neuropsychology handbook: Behavioral and clinical perspectives.* New York: Springer.

Grant, I., & Adams, K.M. (1986). *Neuropsychological assessment of neuropsychiatric disorders.* New York: Oxford University Press.

Guilford, J.P. (1967). *The Nature of human intelligence.* New York: McGraw-Hill.

Halstead, W.C. (1947). *Brain and intelligence.* Chicago: University of Chicago Press.

Hartlage, L.C., & Telzrow, C.F. (1983). The neuropsychological bases of educational intervention. *Journal of Learning Disabilities, 16,* 521–528.

Howell, K.W., Kaplan, J.S., & O'Connell, G.Y. (1979). *Evaluating exceptional children: A task analysis approach.* Columbus: Charles E. Merrill.

Hynd, G.W., Connor, R.T., & Nieves, N. (1988). Learning disability subtypes: Perspectives and methodological issues in clinical assessment. In M.G. Tramontana & S.R. Hooper (Eds.), *Assessment issues in child neuropsychology.* New York: Plenum Press.

Janssen, D., Isles, T., O'Keefe, S., & Sabatino, D. (1988). The intent of secondary special education. *Illinois Vocational Educational Journal, 67,* 17–26.

Jensen, A.R. (1980). *Bias in mental testing.* New York: Free Press.

Kaplan, E. (1989). A process approach to neuropsychological assessment. In T. Boll & B.K. Bryant (Eds.), *Clinical neuropsychology and brain function: Research measurement and practice*. Washington, DC: American Psychological Association.

Kaufman, A.S., & Kaufman, N.L. (1981). *Kaufman Assessment Battery for Children — Manual*. Circle Pines, MN: American Guidance Services.

Lichtheim, L. (1885). On aphasia. *Brain, 7*, 433–484.

Lyon, G.R., Moats, L, & Flynn, J.M. (1988). From assessment to treatment: Linkage to interventions with children. In M.G. Tramontana & S.R. Hooper (Eds.), *Assessment issues in child neuropsychology*. New York: Plenum Press.

Matarazzo, J.D. (1990). Psychological assessment versus psychological testing: Validation from Binet to the school, clinic, and courtroom. *American Psychologist, 46*, 999–1017.

McCarthy, R.A., & Warrington, E.K. (1990). *Cognitive neuropsychology: A clinical introduction*. New York: Academic Press.

Melamed, L.E., & Rugle, L. (1989). Neuropsychological correlates of school achievement in young children: Longitudinal findings with a construct valid perceptual processing instrument. *Journal of Clinical and Experimental Neuropsychology, 11*, 745–762.

Orsini, D.L., Van Gorp, W.G., & Boone, K.B. (1988). *The neuropsychology casebook*. New York: Springer-Verlag.

Prigatano, G.P. (1986). *Neuropsychological rehabilitation after brain injury*. Baltimore: Johns Hopkins University Press.

Reed, H.B.C. (1979). Biological defects and special education: An issue in personnel preparation. *Journal of Special Education, 13*, 9–35.

Reitan, R.M. (1964). *Manual for administration and scoring the Reitan-Indiana Neuropsychological Battery for Children (ages 5 through 8)*. Indianapolis: University of Indiana Medical Center.

Reitan, R.M., & Davidson, L.A. (1974). *Clinical neuropsychology: Current status and application*. New York: Hemisphere.

Reitan, R.M., & Wolfson, D. (1985). *The Halstead-Reitan Neuropsychological Test Battery: Theory and clinical interpretation*. Tucson: Neuropsychology Press.

Reschley, D.F. (1978). *Non biased assessment and school psychology*. Des Moines: Department of Public Instruction, State of Iowa.

Reynolds, C.R. (1989). Measurement and statistical problems in neuropsychological assessment of children. In C.R. Reynolds & E. Fletcher-Janzen (Eds.), *Handbook of clinical child neuropsychology*. New York: Plenum Press.

Reynolds, C.R. (1981). Neuropsychological assessment and the habilitation of learning: Consideration in the search for the aptitude X treatment interaction. *School Psychology Review, 10*, 342–349.

Reynolds, M.C. (1975). Trends in special education: Implications for measurement. In M.D. Reynolds & W. Hivehy (Eds.), *Domain-referenced testing in special education*. Minneapolis: University of Minnesota.

Sabatino, D.A., & Miller, T.L. (1979). *Describing learner characteristics of handicapped children and youth*. New York: Grune & Stratton.

Samuels, S.J. (1975). An outside view of neuropsychological testing. *Journal of Special Education, 9*, 57–61.

Senf, G.M. (1979). Can neuropsychology really change the face of special education. *Journal of Special Education, 13*, 51–52.

Shurtleff, H.A., Fay, G.E., Abbott, R.D., & Berninger, V.W. (1986). Cognitive neuropsychological correlates of academic achievement: A levels of analysis assessment model. *Journal of Psychoeducational Assessment, 6*, 298–308.

Sohlberg, M.M., & Mateer, C.A. (1989). *Introduction to cognitive rehabilitation*. New York: Guilford Press.

Spearman, C.E. (1923). *The nature of intelligence and the principle of cognition.* London: MacMillan.

Spier, P.A. (1982). The Luria-Nebraska Neuropsychology Battery revisited: A theory in practice or just practicing? *Journal of Consulting and Clinical Psychology, 50,* 301–306.

Sternberg, R.J. (1984). Mechanisms of cognitive development: A componential approach. In R.J. Sternberg (Ed.), *Mechanisms of cognitive development.* New York: W.H. Freeman.

Telzrow, C.R. (1989). Neuropsychological applications of common educational and psychological tests. In C.R. Reynolds & E. Fletcher-Janzen (Eds.), *Handbook of clinical child neuropsychology.* New York: Plenum Press.

Terman, L.M., & Merrill, M.A. (1960). *Stanford Binet Intelligence Scale Form L-M.* Boston: Houghton Mifflin.

Thorndike, E.L. (1927). *The measurement of intelligence.* New York: Bureau of Publications, Teachers' College, Columbia University.

Thorndike, R.L., Hagen, E.L., & Sattler, J.M. (1986). *Stanford-Binet Intelligence Scale* (4th ed.). Chicago: Riverside.

Thurstone, L.L. (1938). Primary mental abilities. *Psychometric Monographs,* (1).

Vance, H.B. (1981). Intellectual factors of reading disabled children. *Journal of Research and Development in Education, 4,* 11–24.

Wechsler, D. (1974). *Wechsler Intelligence Scale for Children — Revised Manual.* New York: The Psychological Corporation.

Wechsler, D. (1991). *Wechsler Intelligence Scale for Children — III.* San Antonio: The Psychological Corporation.

3

Critical Issues in the Diagnostic Assessment of Children with Autistic Disorders

Lou Anne Worthington
Raymond N. Elliott

The assessment of children with autism poses formidable challenges for diagnosticians. The distinguishing features of autism, along with the heterogeneity of this population, make assessment particularly difficult (Factor et al., 1989). Autism is perhaps best conceptualized as a "spectrum disorder" with expressed symptoms ranging along a severity continuum (Lord, 1991). Diagnosticians should be well versed in assessing the diversity of behaviors of individuals with autism and should be equipped with the knowledge and skill needed to differentiate autism from closely associated disorders. Further complicating the diagnostic assessment process is the admixture of both developmental delay and deviance that many individuals with autism display across language, cognitive, and social domains (Freeman & Ritvo, 1986; Roberts, 1989; Rutter & Schopler, 1987). Consequently, the adoption of both a deviance *and* delay orientation to assessment is critical in making the autism diagnosis (Baron-Cohen, 1991; Siegel, 1991; Wolff, 1991).

Many have questioned the adequacy of currently available diagnostic instruments in the area of autism (Eaves & Hooper, 1987–1988; Hinerman, 1983; Rescorla, 1988; Sloan, 1987). In fact, Gilberg (1989) maintained that such instruments were not necessary for the "experienced" psychiatrist or psychologist. Although clinical experience certainly is essential for those involved in the diagnostic process, the poor interrater agreement of clinical diagnoses has been well documented (Gresham, 1985; Kauffman, 1989; Martin, 1988; Spitzer & Siegel, 1990; Steinhausen & Erdin, 1991a, 1991b).

The authors submit that many of the diagnostic instruments in this area have serious technical limitations and consequently fail to meet many of the primary standards set forth in the *Standards for Educational and Psychological Testing* (American Educational Research Association [AERA], American Psychological Association [APA], & National Council on Measurement in Education

[NCME], 1985). Although several rather limited test reviews have been undertaken (Harris, 1987; Morgan, 1988; Parks, 1986, 1988), we shall attempt to extend upon these reviews by addressing four critical issues pertinent to diagnostic instruments in this area. We have chosen to review these instruments within a critical issues framework because we believe that four problematic issues characterize most of these instruments. Embedded in the discussion will be recommendations for future instrument development. The four critical issues to be addressed are the need for (a) a clear delineation of the purposes of diagnostic assessment, (b) assessment instruments to be based on current diagnostic criteria, (c) integration of both clinical and psychometrical approaches in the assessment process, and (d) the need for the diagnosis of autism to be holistic, multidisciplinary, and multimethod in orientation. The chapter will conclude with a brief presentation of a suggested diagnostic model.

ISSUE 1: NEED FOR CLEAR DELINEATION OF THE PURPOSES OF DIAGNOSTIC ASSESSMENT

The comprehensive assessment of children and youth with autism requires that professionals from a variety of disciplines be involved in the diagnostic process (Harris, 1987; Lord, 1991; Parks, 1988). Consequently, professionals may encounter nomenclatural problems that impede the assessment process. Hinerman (1983) recognized the potential confusion and questioned the use of the "diagnostic instrument" terminology when applied to autism. McLoughlin and Lewis (1986) defined diagnosis as ". . . the effort to establish the cause of an illness and to describe the appropriate treatment" (p. 3). Since etiological aspects of autism cannot be identified in the majority of cases, and therefore autism is not generally recognized as an illness with known biological precursors (Bagley & McGeein, 1989; Freeman & Ritvo, 1986; Goodman, 1989; Smalley, 1991; Steffenberg, 1991; Szatmari & Jones, 1991), the meaning of the term *diagnosis* in reference to autism is not always clear. Consequently, autism may be best conceptualized as a theoretical "construct" or group of behaviors/symptoms that explain a rare group of behaviors and are thought to be due to an underlying disease process.

Assessment instruments designed for identification or diagnostic purposes should answer the fundamental question, "Does this child have autism?" To answer this question, identification/diagnostic instruments should be developed by defining and assessing those unique aspects of autism by careful normative study of (a) children in the normal population, (b) children with closely associated disorders, and most importantly, (c) children with autism. These instruments must be well standardized and include relevant populations in their studies of reliability and validity. Because the autism diagnosis has important long-term implications for those so diagnosed, developers should provide in-depth information regarding their instruments' technical merits and should adhere to psychological testing standards. As Buros (in Sattler, 1990) once said, "Tests not accompanied by detailed data on their construction, validation, uses, and limitations should be suspect" (p. 1).

Eight instruments, depicted in Table 3.1, that are generally considered diagnostic or are used for identification purposes are reviewed. These eight instruments are (a) *Diagnostic Checklist for Behavior Disturbed Children* (E-2; Rimland, 1971); (b) *Behavior Rating Instrument for Autistic and Atypical Children* (BRIACC; Ruttenberg et al., 1977); (c) *Autistic Behavior Checklist* (ABC; Krug et al., 1980a); (d) *Childhood Autism Rating Scale* (CARS; Schopler et al., 1988); (e) *Behavior Observation System* (BOS; Freeman et al; 1978); (f) *Autism Diagnostic Observation Schedule* (ADOS; Lord et al., 1989); (g) *Autism Descriptors Checklist* (ADC; Friedman et al., 1983); and (h) *Autism Diagnostic Interview* (ADI; Le Couteur et al., 1989). Generally, available diagnostic instruments include questionnaires, observation systems, rating scales and checklists, and parental interviews.

Table 3.2 provides a summary of the intended purposes of the instruments. All have been used to discriminate autism from closely associated disorders, which is the criterion used for inclusion in this chapter review. Close inspection of the purposes of several of these instruments, however, suggests that they do not reflect the most current diagnostic psychiatric criteria for autism. For example, the E-2 was designed to identify only those children who meet Kanner's (1943) criteria for classical autism, criteria now considered to be too exclusive (Parks, 1988; Rutter & Schopler, 1987; Short & Marcus, 1986). Additionally, the closely associated disorders among which the instruments have been designed to distinguish are, in some instances, not reflective of current criteria.

According to the *Standards for Educational and Psychological Testing* (AERA, APA, NCME, 1985), test developers have the responsibility to revise their instruments when new research or significant changes in the construct being measured make the test inappropriate for its intended uses. Given that the two major psychiatric classification systems have undergone significant changes in the past decade, those instruments developed in the 1970s and early 1980s have potential problems with both content and construct validity.

Table 3.3 presents an overview of the standardization samples reported for the selected instruments. Information regarding some of the samples either was not offered or was not described in the fashion commonly employed in the assessment literature. With the exception of the ABC, the samples for standardization, reliability, and validity were not always carefully distinguished. Additionally, some of these instruments are characterized by both a lack of detailed standardization information and inadequate sample sizes. As the symptoms of autism are known to vary considerably across age and intellectual ability, the glaring omission of data of this nature is of particular concern. Separate norms for normal children, children with autism, and children with closely associated disorders, along with detailed demographic information, are noticeably absent for most of these instruments.

In summary, those involved in the assessment of children with autism should clearly delineate the purpose of assessment: that is, identification. By

Table 3.1 Overview of Autism Diagnostic Assessment Instruments

Instrument	Nature of Instrument	Instrument Highlights
Rimland E-2	Multiple-choice Parental questionnaire	Focus on child functioning and early development Retrospective questionnaire
BRIACC	Eight scales are completed from direct observation	Requires trained raters Behaviors are operationally defined Post hoc recording system
ABC	Behavioral checklist	Part of a larger assessment battery Provides sample profiles Designed for public school use
CARS	Rating system	Well-defined behavioral criteria Requires minimal training Adapted for adolescents and adults
BOS	Direct observation	Requires rater training Observed behaviors are objectively defined Computer analysis of raw scores
ADOS	Standardized observation system	Is an interactive schedule Examiner is a participant/observer Assessment is naturalistic
ADC	Retrospective parental checklist and direct observation system	Large number of items Observed behaviors are well defined
ADI	Standardized Investigator-based Interview with child's principal caregiver	Age range from 5 years to early adulthood Retrospective interview within a detailed standardized coding system

Table 3.2 Purposes of Autistic Disorder Diagnostic Assessment Instruments

Instrument	Purpose(s) of Instrument and Information Sources
Rimland E-2	The E-2 was designed to differentiate subgroups of children with autism (i.e., classical autism Kanner's [1943] syndrome) from children who are "autistic," "autisticlike," "childhood schizophrenic" (Krall, 1989; Morgan, 1988; Rimland, 1984).
BRIACC	The BRIACC was developed to assess the functioning and progress of autistic children in psychoanalytically oriented daycare and has been found to discriminate among subgroups of autistic children, children with developmental aphasia, and children with mental retardation (Morgan, 1988; Parks, 1986; Powers, 1988; Schreibman, 1988; Short & Marcus, 1986).
ABC	The ABC was designed to differentiate individuals with autism from those diagnosed as severely mentally retarded, deaf-blind, severely emotionally disturbed, or normal (Krug et al., 1980b).
CARS	The CARS was designed to identify children with autism and to differentiate children with other developmental disabilities who are not autistic (Schopler et al., 1988).
BOS	The BOS was developed to differentiate autistic children from mentally disabled children and to identify subgroups of autistic children (Freeman et al., 1984).
ADOS	The purpose of the ADOS is to discriminate persons with autism from individuals with other disabilities and from individuals with normal functioning (Lord et al., 1989).
ADC	The ADC was designed to differentiate among subgroups of autistic individuals (Fisch et al., 1988).
ADI	The ADI was designed for use in the differential diagnosis of pervasive developmental disorders (Le Couteur et al., 1989).

Table 3.3 Standardization Samples of the Diagnostic Instruments*

Instrument	Source(s)	Type Sample	Sample Size
Rimland E-2	Rimland, 1971	E-2 forms were collected from parents and professionals; some description of professional diagnoses of sample subjects was provided.	2,218
ABC	Krug et al., 1980a, 1980b	Checklists were completed by professionals from all disabilities; sample subjects ranged in age from 18 months to 35 years; 2.5-to-1 male-to-female ratio; 172 individuals had a previous diagnosis of autism; 423 diagnosed as severely mentally retarded; 254 as severely emotionally disturbed; 100 diagnosed as deaf-blind, and 100 were normal. Manual provides detailed demographic data by age, gender, geographic location, language, age, etc.	1,049
CARS	Schopler et al., 1988	Demographic data were reported by sex, race, social class, age, and IQ, although separate norms were not provided; tabular sample data were not clearly referred to in the manual.	1,606
BOS	Freeman et al., 1979	Sample included 59 children who met National Society for Autistic Children (1978) definition; 40 children were diagnosed as mentally retarded, and 41 as normal, ages ≥23 months to <65 months.	140

*Information was either not available or was not clearly described for some of the instruments.

conceptualizing autism as a construct rather than as a disease entity, instrument selection for the diagnostic assessment should be designed to answer the question, "Does this child have autism?" Consequently, future instrument development should include specific group norms with appropriate demographic data for individuals and youths with autism or with closely associated disorders, and for individuals in the normal population. Caution is advised because many instruments do not reflect current diagnostic criteria and do not report essential normative data. Instrument selection should reflect these limitations.

ISSUE 2: NEED FOR INSTRUMENTS TO CORRESPOND TO CURRENT DIAGNOSTIC CRITERIA

The relationship between definition and assessment is reciprocal (Eaves, 1982). Perhaps the single greatest weakness in the diagnostic assessment of children with autism is the lack of instruments designed to reflect the current diagnostic criteria for autism (Lord, 1991; Rutter & Schopler, 1988). Diagnostic instruments have been criticized for their diversity in theoretical approaches since Kanner first identified this group of children in 1943 (Eaves & Hooper, 1987–88; Lord, 1991; Parks, 1988; Short & Marcus, 1986). Although not without criticism, psychiatric classification systems have reached considerable consensus within the past decade (Cox, 1991; Rutter & Schopler, 1987). Two widely used diagnostic schemes, the *Diagnostic and Statistical Manual of Mental Disorders– Revised* (DSM-III-R; APA, 1987) and the *International Classification of Disorders* (World Health Organization, 1990) have both identified four criteria for autism: (a) onset in infancy and childhood, (b) deviance in social relationships, (c) communication abnormalities, and (d) restricted repertoire of activities and stereotypical patterns of behavior. Diagnostic instruments generally have not been updated to reflect these core criteria. Table 3.4 presents the dimensions measured and the criteria used in the development of current instruments. Close inspection indicates that although several of these instruments measure important aspects of autism, they generally do not, as Lord (1991) noted, correspond conceptually to the four diagnostic criteria identified by these two major psychiatric classification schemes. A diversity of criteria and definitions were used during instrument development, some of which do not reflect the most current knowledge base and/or current classification systems.

The DSM-III-R criteria are the most widely used in the United States (Green, 1990), and this classification scheme has been praised by many for its attempts to reflect the current autism knowledge base and for its increased objectivity in delineating the specific behaviors believed to distinguish autism from other disorders (Factor et al., 1989; Wolff, 1991). The DSM-III-R provides a framework that can be used to guide the diagnostic process. Using this framework, both strengths and weaknesses of currently available instruments can be evaluated.

First, because the majority of children with autism (termed *autistic disorder* in the DSM-III-R) are also mentally disabled, the DSM-III-R and several

Table 3.4 Dimensions Measured and Criteria Used for Development of the Diagnostic Instruments

Instrument	Dimensions Measured	Criteria Used for Instrument Development and Data Sources
Rimland E-2	Developmental and medical history	Instrument is based on Kanner's (1943) syndrome criteria.
BRIACC	Eight scales designed to measure relationship to adult; communication; drive for mastery; vocalization and expressive speech; sound and speech reception; social responsiveness; body movement; and psychobiological development	Instrument was developed using children identified as autistic by Kanner's (1943) classic criteria.
ABC	Five subtests: sensory; relating; body and object; language; social and self-help	Instrument was developed using Creak's (1961) points; Rutter's (1978) definition; National Society for Autistic Children (1978) definition; DSM-III-R (APA, 1987); Kanner's (1943) definition.
CARS	Fifteen scale items: relating to people; imitation; emotional response; body use; object use; adaptation to change; visual response; listening response; taste, smell, and touch response and use; fear or nervousness; verbal communication; nonverbal communication; activity level; level and consistency of intellectual response; general impressions	Items incorporate Kanner's (1943) primary autism features; Creak's (1961) characteristics; National Society for Autistic Children (1978) definition; Rutter's (1978) definition; DSM-III-R criteria.
BOS	Four groups of behaviors rated: solitary; relation to objects; relation to people; and language	Instrument is based on the inclusion of items of the National Society of Autistic Children (1978) definition.

ADOS	Items designed to measure asking for help; symbolic play; reciprocal play; giving help to interviewer; taking turns in a structured task; descriptive gesture and mime; description of agents and actions; telling a sequential story; reciprocal communication; ability to use language to discuss socioemotional topics	Items were analyzed using a draft version of the ICD-10 (World Health Organization, 1990).
ADC	Items divided into ten categories: interpersonal relationships; communication and affect; sound and speech reception; vocalization and expressive speech; visual behavior; learning and memory; maintenance of sameness; self-care; stereotypy; and body movement	Items were based on developmental symptomatology (Fisch et al., 1985).
ADI	Items focus on three areas: quality of reciprocal social interaction; communication and language; and repetitive, restricted, and stereotyped behaviors	Items are reflective of ICD-10 criteria (Le Couteur et al., 1989)

professionals (Siegel, 1991; Rutter & Schopler, 1987) have recognized the need to assess the individual's behavior within the context of the child's mental rather than chronological age. The criterion used to determine mental age should be clearly specified by instrument developers, since Rutter and Schopler (1987) appropriately noted that mental age can be defined in many ways (i.e., verbally, nonverbally, by global intellectual ability, or by adaptive functioning). As noted earlier, many current diagnostic instruments do not provide this essential information. We suggest that the child's developmental level across the domains of cognition, language, and socialization be considered in the selection of all assessment tools used in the diagnostic process. A frequent criticism of current diagnostic instruments is that many are unable to diagnose or identify the higher-functioning child with autism (Rutter & Schopler, 1988; Sloan, 1987; Teal & Wiebe, 1986). Improved normative procedures, along with more sophisticated instrument development methodology, would greatly enhance the potential for identifying these individuals.

Each of the diagnostic instruments has provided at least some evidence to support its ability to discriminate between populations identified as autistic and mentally retarded. Reviews of research in this area have been provided by Morgan (1988) and Parks (1986, 1988). However, most of the instruments have not been investigated to determine their ability to discriminate children with autism from those suffering from other disorders mentioned in the DSM-III-R (e.g., schizophrenia, hearing impairments, visual impairments, schizoid and schizotypal personality disorders, tic disorders, and stereotypical habit disorders). Research in this area should become a focus in the future development of diagnostic instruments.

The DSM-III-R recognizes the lifelong debilitating impact of autism on the lives of those so diagnosed and expressly recognizes that the disorder varies greatly. Its impact is highly dependent on the degree of severity. Table 3.5 presents an overview of the extent to which current diagnostic assessment instruments have incorporated developmental and severity features into their test designs. Most of the current diagnostic instruments appear to have integrated, to some degree, both developmental and severity features into their instrument designs. Several approaches have been used, ranging from developmental history-taking to the use of test items based on specific developmental time periods. Although several developers have incorporated specific considerations into their instruments, it appears that more research is needed regarding the differentiation of high- and low-functioning individuals.

The DSM-III-R acknowledges that neurological dysfunctions are believed to predispose the individual to autism, and it specifically identifies autism's association with ". . . maternal rubella, untreated phenylketonuria, tuberous sclerosis, anoxia during birth, encephalitis, infantile spasms, and fragile X syndrome" (p. 37). The collection of pertinent developmental history and medically relevant information would provide support for the autism diagnosis. The E-2 and the ADI are two instruments that include medical and developmental history in their instrument designs. The E-2, a retrospective parental questionnaire, and the ADI,

Table 3.5 Developmental and Severity Considerations

Instrument	Developmental and Severity Features
Rimland E-2	Many items on the Rimland E-2 emphasize early development; a cut-off score differentiates children with Kanner's classical autism from other autistic subgroups.
BRIACC	Items are sequenced along progressive levels, although these levels have not been studied longitudinally (Parks, 1986). BRIACC ratings are made on a 10-point severity range (Ruttenberg et al., 1977).
ABC	Comparative profiles based on chronological age are provided by the authors (Krug et al., 1980a). In a study by Volkmar, Cicchetti, Dykens, Sparrow, Leckman, and Cohen (1988), a factor analysis revealed that chronological age and developmental level emerged as factors.
CARS	Ratings from 1 to 4 based on a continuum of normality are required and the total score yields a non-autistic to mild-to-moderate autism to severe-autism determination (Schopler et al., 1988).
BOS	A study by Freeman et al. (1984) using small samples provided support that the BOS can differentiate high-functioning vs. low-functioning children with autism. Some of the BOS behaviors appear to vary as a function of chronological and mental age (Freeman et al., 1978; Freeman et al., 1980).
ADOS	Ratings of abnormality on a scale of 0 to 2 are required. Studies undertaken by the authors were limited to verbal children and adolescents with verbal abilities of 3 years or higher (Le Couteur et al., 1989).
ADC	Items are scored based on significant developmental time periods, and severity ratings along a 6-point scale are used (Friedman et al., 1983).
ADI	As this instrument is designed for children with a chronological age of 5 years or more, a mental age of at least 2 years or more, a standardized history-taking approach is used. This instrument focuses on obtaining information regarding key developmental milestones (Le Couteur et al., 1989).

a standardized primary-caregiver interview, were designed to address medical concerns and to ascertain the age of autism onset. Although these concerns are critical to the diagnostic process, a truly comprehensive diagnostic assessment should go well beyond questionnaires and interviews and would include, as recommended by Freeman and Ritvo (1986), (a) the collection of developmental history data, (b) inspection of maternal records, (c) inspection of the child's medical records, (d) medical and neurological evaluations, (e) sleep electroencephalograms (EEGs), (f) metabolic screening, (g) chromosomal evaluations, and (h) audiometric screening.

In summary, the DSM-III-R implies a diagnostic assessment framework for the diagnosis of autism. Because several diagnostic instruments are characterized by a diversity of theoretical approaches, they may be limited in their applicability to current DSM-III-R criteria. Although the publication of the DSM-IV is imminent (Siegel, 1991), future instrument development should attempt to more closely match the most current diagnostic criteria and to employ, to the maximum extent possible, the assessment framework provided by the classification scheme.

ISSUE 3: NEED FOR AN INTEGRATION OF CLINICAL AND PSYCHOMETRIC APPROACHES TO THE DIAGNOSTIC ASSESSMENT OF AUTISM

Lord (1991) succinctly addressed this need in her statement: "Instruments should correspond conceptually, as well as statistically, to current diagnostic criteria for autism. . . ." (p. 70). Certainly not unique to the diagnostic assessment of autism, psychiatric classification systems historically have not employed multivariate statistical procedures to support diagnostic criteria, and their failure to do so has been criticized (Gresham, 1985; Lord, 1991; Martin, 1988). As Martin (1988) maintained, current diagnostic classification schemes reflect an admixture of both psychiatric tradition and empirical research, and they reflect, at least to some degree, the bias of the psychiatrists and mental health professionals responsible for criteria development.

The virtues and deficiencies of both clinically and psychometrically driven classification approaches have been described (Achenbach & Edelbrock, 1983a; Council for Children with Behavioral Disorders, 1987; Gresham, 1985; Kauffman, 1989; Martin, 1988; Walker & Fabre, 1987). The authors contend that the assessment needs of individuals with autism require the integration of both, as each yields unique and valuable diagnostic information. As explained by Parks (1988), the final diagnosis necessitates at least some clinical judgment. Kaufman and Kaufman (1977) also addressed this issue: "The clinical information that may be derived by observing the child's behavior during a test-taking session, and by interpreting *qualitative* aspects of his test performance, is at least as important as the scores themselves" (p. 153).

Throughout the research on autism is the consistent finding that these individuals display behavior that follows peculiar developmental patterns (Freeman

& Ritvo, 1986; Hobson, 1991). Siegel's (1991) atypical ontogenetic approach (i.e., children with autism progress through predictable stages of atypical behavior) to understanding both delay and deviance provides valuable insight for the diagnostic assessment of individuals with autism. An adoption of her approach would require that both quantitative and qualitative aspects of the individual's behavior be assessed in the diagnostic process. Siegel (1991) has maintained that developmental models, such as those frequently incorporated into diagnostic instruments, are limited, as they have focused exclusively on the *form* rather than the *function* of behavior. Developmental models, she argued, tend to rely on a fixated normal developmental progression of autistic behavior in order to explain autistic symptomatology. Siegel has argued that autistic behaviors, such as hand-flapping, follow an atypical developmental progression. By extending Siegel's approach to developmental assessment, it appears that while diagnostic instruments may provide information regarding the normality or developmental appropriateness of behaviors, they cannot always provide insight into the function that the behavior serves for the child. Determining the function of behavior may sometimes require a qualitative, rather than a quantitative, approach to assessment. Diagnosticians can greatly enhance the diagnostic process by providing qualitative interpretations of the observed behavior of these individuals and thereby select instruments that can either confirm or discount their judgments. No instrument, no matter how technically sophisticated, can supplant qualitative judgments of this nature.

While psychiatric classification schemes have relied heavily on clinical experience, the failure to incorporate psychometrically supported techniques into diagnostic criteria is quite striking among autism-diagnostic instruments. Typically, most of these instruments have been based on diagnostic criteria, with little attempt to support the validity of the dimensions psychometrically. In previous reviews of diagnostic instruments in the area of autism (Parks, 1986, 1988; Morgan, 1988), not one reviewer criticized the general lack of factor-analytic support for these diagnostic instruments. Rather, it appears sufficient to test developers and reviewers alike that ample evidence of both content and construct validity is provided when the instruments are developed on the basis of diagnostic criteria. Although psychiatric classification schemes are based at least in part on empirical research, this does not logically exempt test developers from employing more sophisticated techniques, such as factor analysis, to support the construct of their instruments. Nunnally (1978) has stated, "In the better factor analysis investigations, the conceptual models and the mathematical models are carefully thought out and interwoven" (p. 328). For example, if the four DSM-III-R diagnostic criteria for autistic disorder are used as the model for instrument development, factor-analytic support for these criteria (or dimensions) should be provided. Additionally, factor analysis would provide support for both the common and unique variances of these four criteria (Crocker & Algina, 1986). Ideally, the diagnosis of autism should include both clinical and psychometrical approaches as each has merit, and both can and should serve as complements to the other.

Although their samples were quite limited, the BOS and the BRIACC are notable exceptions to the general failure to include factor-analytic support in their instruments (Cohen et al., 1978; Freeman et al., 1980; Wenar & Ruttenberg, 1976). Two studies have highlighted the utility and benefits of such procedures. In the Eaves and Hooper (1987–88) study, the factor structure of the *Pervasive Developmental Disorder Rating Scale* (Eaves, 1981, 1990) was used to compare dimensions measured by the ABC, BOS, BRIACC, and CARS. The results provided some support for the dimensions of these instruments, although it was noted that many items may be placed inappropriately within their respective scales/dimensions. The authors concluded that data-reduction techniques, such as factor analysis, have many benefits, including (a) a more efficient approach to identifying pertinent variables, (b) optimizing the variance explained, and (c) aiding in the differential diagnostic process. Rescorla's (1988) cluster analytic study of the *Child Behavior Checklist* (Achenbach & Edelbrock, 1983b) provided support that not only can such a procedure differentiate among various groups but it can also partition individuals with autism into subgroups.

Through the provision of psychometric support for the dimensions measured by diagnostic instruments, more meaningful interpretation of reliability and validity studies can be realized. Previous instruments reviews (Morgan, 1988; Parks, 1986, 1988; Powers, 1988; Schreibman, 1988; Short & Marcus, 1986) have suggested that several of these instruments have failed to report the full gamut of reliability and validity data supportive of their intended purposes. The authors extend these reviews by addressing the general lack of factorial support provided by the developers of these instruments.

ISSUE 4: THE DIAGNOSIS OF AUTISM WARRANTS A HOLISTIC, MULTIDISCIPLINARY, MULTIFACETED APPROACH TO ASSESSMENT

Despite the numerous criticisms of diagnostic instruments previously cited, the authors recognize that no one assessment instrument can yield the information needed to make a diagnosis of autism. Consequently, the diagnosis of autism may be most accurate when assessment is approached as a *process* using a case formulation approach, with extensive efforts made to confirm the diagnosis through the careful selection of instruments (Krall, 1989; Martin, 1988). Although more broad-based, this approach is roughly analogous to Kaufman's (1979) profile approach to intelligence testing. The collection of various data across multiple domains by a variety of professionals can yield answers to critical diagnostic questions.

Similar to the "best estimate" diagnosis described by Young, O'Brien, Gutterman, and Cohen (1987), this approach to diagnostic assessment requires a multidisciplinary team. Empirical research within the past 10 years has yielded a wealth of information regarding the unique profiles of individuals with autism across domains (i.e., medical, neurological, cognitive, social, communicative).

Each professional involved in the diagnostic process should be knowledgeable regarding the unique characteristics these individuals display in their respective areas of expertise (Goodman, 1989; Lincoln et al., 1988; Shah & Frith, 1986; Shapiro & Hertzig, 1991).

Numerous professionals (Freeman & Ritvo, 1986; Harris, 1987; Kauffman, 1989; Lord, 1991; Olley & Rosenthal, 1985; Sattler, 1982; Schreibman, 1988) have recommended that assessment of a child's developmental history; adaptive behavior; and cognitive, social, communicative, neurological, and medical status, along with an assessment of familial factors, be undertaken. When aggregated, these data can provide substantial support for the diagnosis of autism. Once the diagnosis is made, they can provide guidance for additional assessment designed for intervention or program-planning purposes.

Several researchers have recommended that multiple sources and methods of data collection be incorporated into the diagnostic process (Kauffman, 1989; Young et al., 1987). A frequently voiced criticism in the diagnostic assessment of individuals with autism is the overreliance on one source or method of data collection (Lord, 1991; Parks, 1988; Rutter & Schopler, 1987, 1988; Young et al., 1987). As Parks (1988) noted, data from various sources and methods of diagnostic assessment should converge on, and provide support for, the autism diagnosis. Although the frequent failure of multiple sources/methods of data collection to converge has been cited as an assessment problem not unique to the diagnosis of autism, the adoption of a multisource, multimethod orientation to the assessment process has received considerable support, and the problematic issues have been resolved primarily through the increased reliability that occurs through data aggregation (Campbell & Fiske, 1959; Epstein, 1983; Howard, 1990; Martin, 1988). In reality, a diagnostic team cannot expect all assessment data to converge in a singular diagnosis of autism. Rather, the diagnostic team should interpret all data in concert and make a collective decision regarding the diagnosis through an analysis of the strengths and weaknesses of data-collection sources. For example, parental retrospective reports have often been criticized for poor reliability (Lord, 1991; Robbins, 1963), as have one-time observations (Lord, 1991). Interpretation of data from multiple sources and methods requires a coordinated team effort. Diagnostic team members each bring to the diagnostic effort an area of expertise germane to their discipline, and the unique contribution of each member is vital to the diagnosis of autism.

As can be ascertained from Table 3.1, autism-diagnostic instruments are characterized by a diversity of methodological approaches (e.g., rating scales, interviews, observation systems) and diverse data sources (e.g., parents, teachers, physicians). As Parks (1988) noted in her review of autism-diagnostic instruments, each method and source has merit, yet none can stand alone to make the autism diagnosis. Sloan (1987) and Parks (1988) have suggested that the use of one method or one source of data collection is limited, as they each sample important, yet different, aspects of autism.

In addition to applying a multimethod, multisource approach to assessment, the diagnostic process might best begin with the incorporation of omnibus pathology measures (Martin, 1988). This approach suggests that it is necessary to start with broad-based assessment measures that tap a wide range of behaviors and then move to more specific types of measurement in order to arrive at an accurate diagnosis. A cluster analytic study by Rescorla (1988) using the *Child Behavior Checklist* (Achenbach & Edelbrock, 1983b), an instrument generally considered to be omnibus, has received support for its utility in identifying children with autism. Although additional validation of this and similar instruments is needed, such omnibus measures hold promise for enhancing the diagnostic assessment process during the initial phase of assessment. If an omnibus measure is used during the initial phase of diagnostic assessment, and results from this assessment converge on, or provide tentative support for, an autism diagnosis, then the selection of instruments designed to make more subtle distinctions (e.g., distinguishing autism from schizophrenia) may be appropriate in the later phases of diagnostic assessment.

As an extension of this argument for the use of omnibus pathology measures, more traditional instruments across the domains of social, communication, and cognition have been empirically validated for use with the autistic population during the past decade (Lincoln et al., 1988; Olley & Rosenthal, 1985; Rescorla, 1988; Shah & Frith, 1986; Volkmar et al., 1987). Commensurate with the profile attack approach cited previously, the use of these instruments with the autistic population has yielded valuable information that can provide support for the autism diagnosis. Rather consistent profiles for children with autism have been observed across socialization, communicative, and cognitive domains (Lincoln et al., 1988; Rescorla, 1988; Rodrique et al., 1991; Shah & Frith, 1986; Volkmar et al., 1987). As noted by Parks (1988), the administration of these broad-domain assessment procedures with adequate normative bases may prove beneficial in the decision-making process.

A COMPREHENSIVE MODEL FOR THE DIAGNOSTIC ASSESSMENT OF CHILDREN WITH AUTISM

By integrating the recommendations from each of the issues previously discussed, a model for the diagnostic assessment can be readily designed. This model, depicted in Figure 3.1, superimposes a multigating model similar to that proposed by Walker and Fabre (1987) with a systems approach model for assessment by Eaves and McLaughlin (1977). Neither of these two models appeared entirely adequate for the diagnostic assessment process for children with autism, and consequently significant adaptations were made to meet the unique diagnostic assessment needs of these children.

The diagnostic assessment process is perhaps best undertaken in three distinct phases, with an emphasis on team decision-making points at the conclusion of each phase. Using a multigating approach (Walker & Fabre, 1987), the decision to continue assessment at the conclusion of each phase should be contingent on the extent to which assessment data collected are suggestive of an autism diagnosis. These decision-making points are critical, as they assist the diagnostic team in (a) collectively assimilating the data collected during the respective phase, (b) providing information regarding the selection of instruments most appropriate for use with the child in the next phase, (c) preventing unnecessary continuation of assessment when the assessment data are not supportive of an autism diagnosis, and (d) yielding assessment data that are more substantive as the phases progress.

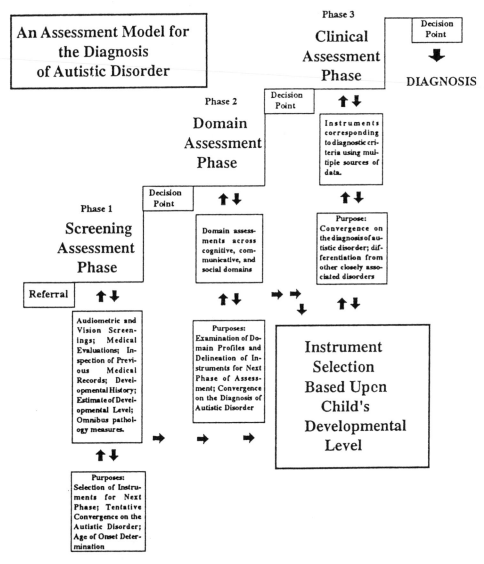

Figure 3.1   A multi-gating model

REFERENCES

Achenbach, T.M., & Edelbrock, C.S. (1983a). Taxonomic issues in child psycho-pathology. In T.H. Ollendick & M. Hersen (Eds.), *Handbook of child psychopathology* (pp. 65–93). New York: Plenum Press.

Achenbach, T.M., & Edelbrock, C.S. (1983b). *Manual for the Child Behavior Checklist*. Burlington: Department of Psychiatry, University of Vermont.

American Educational Research Association, American Psychological Association, & National Council on Measurement in Education. (1985). *Standards for educational and psychological testing*. Washington, DC: American Psychological Association.

American Psychiatric Association. (1987). *Diagnostic and statistical manual of mental disorders*. (3rd ed., rev.). Washington, DC: American Psychiatric Association.

Bagley, C., & McGeein, V. (1989). The taxonomy and course of childhood autism. *Perceptual and Motor Skills, 69,* 1264–1266.

Baron-Cohen, S. (1991). The development of a theory of mind in autism: Deviance and delay? *Psychiatric Clinics of North America, 14*(1), 33–51.

Campbell, D.D., & Fiske, D.W. (1959). Convergent and discriminant validity by the multi-trait–multimethod matrix. *Psychological Bulletin, 56,* 81–105.

Cohen, D.J., Caparulo, B.K., Gold, J.R., Waldo, M.C., Shaywitz, B.A., Ruttenberg, B.A., & Rimland, B. (1978). Agreement in diagnosis: Clinical assessment and behavior rating scales for pervasively disturbed children. *Journal of the American Academy of Child Psychiatry, 17,* 589–603.

Council for Children with Behavioral Disorders. (1987). *Position paper on the definition and identification of students with behavioral disorders*. Reston, VA: Council for Children with Behavioral Disorders.

Cox, A.D. (1991). Is Asperger's syndrome a useful diagnosis? *Archives of Disease in Childhood, 66*(2), 876–891.

Creak, M. (1961). Schizophrenia syndrome in childhood. Progress report of a working party. *Cerebral Palsy Bulletin, 3,* 501–504.

Crocker, L., & Algina, J. (1986). *Introduction to classical and modern test theory*. Fort Worth, TX: Holt, Rhinehart, & Winston.

Eaves, R.C., (1981). The psychotic behavior rating scale. Unpublished manuscript.

Eaves, R.C. (1982). A proposal for the diagnosis of emotional disturbance. *Journal of Special Education, 16,* 463–476.

Eaves, R.C. (1990). *The Pervasive Developmental Disorder Rating Scale*. Opelika, AL: Small World.

Eaves, R.C., & Hooper, J. (1987–88). A factor analysis of psychotic behavior. *Journal of Special Education, 21,* 122–132.

Eaves, R.C, & McLaughlin, P. (1977). A systems approach for the assessment of the child and his environment: Getting back to the basics. *Journal of Special Education, 11,* 99–111.

Epstein, S. (1983). The stability of confusion: A reply to Mischel and Peake. *Psychological Review, 90,* 179–184.

Factor, D.C., Freeman, N.L., & Kardash, A. (1989). Brief report: A comparison of DSM-III and DSM-III-R criteria for autism. *Journal of Autism and Developmental Disorders, 19,* 637–640.

Fisch, G.S., Cohen, I.L., Wolf, E.G., & Friedman, E. (1985). The Autistic Descriptors Checklist (ADC): A preliminary report. *Journal of Autism and Developmental Disorders, 15,* 233–235.

Freeman, B.J., & Ritvo, E.R. (1986). The syndrome of autism: Establishing the diagnosis and principles of management. In E.W. Bell (Ed.), *Autism: A reference book* (pp. 37–44). White Plains, NY: Longman.

Freeman, B.J., Ritvo, E.R., Guthrie, D., Schroth, P., & Ball, J. (1978). The Behavior Observation Scale for Autism: Initial methodology, data analysis and preliminary findings on 89 children. *Journal of the American Academy of Child Psychiatry, 17,* 576–588.

Freeman, B.J., Ritvo, E.R., & Schroth, P.C. (1984). Behavior assessment of the syndrome of autism: Behavior Observation System. *Journal of the American Academy of Child Psychiatry, 23,* 588–594.

Freeman, B.J., Schroth, P., Ritvo, E., Guthrie, D., & Wake, J. (1980). The Behavior Observation Scale for Autism (BOS): Initial results of factor analyses. *Journal of Autism and Developmental Disorders, 10,* 343–346.

Freeman, B.J., Tonick, E.R., Ritvo, E.R., Guthrie, D., & Schroth, P. (1979). *The Behavior Observation Scale for Autism (BOS): Frequency analysis.* Paper presented at the Psychological Association Meetings, New York, NY, September, 1979.

Friedman, E., Wolf, E.G., & Cohen, L.L. (1983). *Autistic Descriptors Checklist (ADC).* Staten Island: New York State Institute for Basic Research in Developmental Disabilities.

Gilberg, C. (1989). Habilitation for children with autism: A Swedish example. In C. Gilberg (Ed.), *Diagnosis and treatment of autism* (pp. 329–345). New York: Plenum Press.

Goodman, R. (1989). Infantile autism: A syndrome of multiple primary deficits. *Journal of Autism and Developmental Disorders, 19,* 409–423.

Green, J. (1990). Is Asperger's a syndrome? *Developmental Medicine and Child Neurology, 32,* 743–746.

Gresham, F.M. (1985). Behavior disorder assessment: Conceptual, definitional, and practical considerations. *School Psychology Review, 14,* 495–509.

Harris, S.L. (1987). Infantile disorders and childhood schizophrenia. In C.L. Frame & J.L. Matson (Eds), *Handbook of assessment in childhood psychopathology* (pp. 323–340). New York: Plenum Press.

Hinerman, P.S. (1983). *Teaching autistic children to communicate.* Rockville, MD: Aspen Systems Co.

Hobson, R.P. (1991). What is autism? *Psychiatric Clinics of North America, 14*(1), 1–17.

Howard, G.S. (1990). On the construct validity of self-reports: What do the data say? *American Psychologist 45,* 292–294.

Kanner, L. (1943). Autistic disturbances of affective contact. *Nervous Child, 2,* 217–250.

Kauffman, J.M. (1989). *Characteristics of behavior disorders of children and youth* (4th ed.). Columbus, OH: Merrill Publishing Co.

Kaufman, A.S. (1979). *Intelligent testing with the WISC-R.* New York: John Wiley & Sons.

Kaufman, A.S., & Kaufman, N.L. (1977). *Clinical evaluation of young children with the McCarthy Scales.* Orlando, FL: Grune & Stratton.

Koegel, R.L., Rincover, A., & Egel, A.L. (1982). *Educating and understanding autistic children.* San Diego: College Hill.

Krall, V. (1989). *Developmental psychodiagnostic assessment of children and adolescents.* New York: Human Sciences Press.

Krug, D.A., Arick, J., & Almond, P.J. (1980a). *Autism screening instrument for educational planning.* Portland: ASIEP Educational Co.

Krug, D.A., Arick, J., & Almond, P.J. (1980b). Behavior checklist for identifying severely handicapped individuals with high levels of autistic behavior. *Journal of Child Psychology and Psychiatry, 21,* 221–229.

Le Couteur, A., Rutter, M., Lord, C., Rios, P., Robertson, S., Holdgrafer, A., & McLennan, J. (1989). Autism Diagnostic Interview: A standardized investigator-based instrument. *Journal of Autism and Developmental Disorders, 19,* 363–387.

Lincoln, A.J., Courchesne, E., Kilman, B.A., Elmasian, R., & Allen, M. (1988). A study of intellectual abilities of high-functioning people with autism. *Journal of Autism and Developmental Disorders, 18,* 505–524.

Lord, C. (1991). Methods and measures of behavior in the diagnosis of autism and related disorders. *Psychiatric Clinics of North America, 14*(1), 69–80.

Lord, C., Rutter, M., Goode, S., Heemsbergen, J., Jordan, H., Mawhood, L., & Schopler, E. (1989). Autism Diagnostic Observation Schedule: A standardized observation of communicative and social behavior. *Journal of Autism and Developmental Disorders, 19,* 185–212.

Martin, R.P. (1988). Assessment of personality and behavior problems. New York: Guilford Press.

McLoughlin, J.A., & Lewis, R.B. (1986). *Assessing special students* (2nd ed.). Columbus, OH: Merrill Publishing Co.

Morgan, S. (1988). Diagnostic assessment of autism. *Journal of Psychoeducational Assessment, 6,* 139–151.

National Society for Autistic Children, (1978). National Society for Autistic Children definition of the syndrome of autism. *Journal of Autism and Developmental Disorders, 8,* 162–167.

Nunnally, J.C. (1978). *Psychometric theory.* (2nd ed.). New York: McGraw-Hill.

Olley, J.G., & Rosenthal, S.L. (1985). Current issues in school services for students with autism. *School Psychology Review, 14,* 166–170.

Parks, S.L. (1986). The assessment of autistic children: A selective review of available instruments. In E.W. Bell (Ed.), *Autism: A reference book* (pp. 244–251). White Plains, NY: Longman.

Parks, S.L. (1988). Psychometric instruments available for the assessment of autistic children. In E. Schopler & G.B. Mesibov (Eds.), *Diagnosis and assessment in autism* (pp. 123–136). New York: Plenum Press.

Powers, M.D. (1988). Behavioral assessment of children and adults with autism. In E. Schopler & G.B. Mesibov (Eds.), *Diagnosis and assessment in autism* (pp. 139–165). New York: Plenum Press.

Rescorla, L. (1988). Cluster analytic identification of autistic preschoolers. *Journal of Autism and Developmental Disorders, 18,* 475–492.

Rimland, B. (1971). The differentiation of childhood psychoses: An analysis of checklists for 2,218 psychotic children. *Journal of Autism and Childhood Schizophrenia, 1,* 161–174.

Rimland, B. (1984). Diagnostic checklist from E-2: A reply to Parks. *Journal of Autism and Developmental Disorders, 14,* 343–345.

Robbins, L.C. (1963). The accuracy of parental recall of aspects of child development and of child rearing practices. *Journal of Abnormal and Social Psychology, 66,* 261–270.

Roberts, J.M.A. (1989). Echolalia and comprehension in autistic children. *Journal of Autism and Developmental Disorders, 19,* 271–281.

Rodrique, J.R., Morgan, S.B., & Geffken, G.R. (1991). A comparative evaluation of adaptive behavior in children and adolescents with autism, Down syndrome, and normal development. *Journal of Autism and Developmental Disorders, 21,* 187–196.

Ruttenberg, B.A., Kalish, B.I., Wenar, C., & Wolf, E.G. (1977). *Behavior rating instrument for autistic and other atypical children* (rev. ed.). Philadelphia: Developmental Center for Autistic Children.

Rutter, M. (1978). Diagnosis and definition of childhood autism. *Journal of Autism and Developmental Disorders, 8,* 139–161.

Rutter, M., & Schopler, E. (1987). Autism and pervasive developmental disorders: Concepts and diagnostic issues. *Journal of Autism and Developmental Disorders, 17,* 159–186.

Rutter, M., & Schopler, E. (1988). Autism and pervasive developmental disorders: Concepts and diagnostic issues. In E. Schopler & G.B. Mesibov (Eds.), *Diagnosis and assessment in autism* (pp. 15–36). New York: Plenum Press.

Sattler, J.M. (1982). *Assessment of children's intelligence and special abilities* (2nd ed.). Boston: Allyn & Bacon.

Sattler, J.M. (1990). *Assessment of children* (3rd ed.). San Diego: Jerome M. Sattler.

Schopler, E., Reichler, R.J., & Renner, B.R. (1988.). *The Childhood Autism Rating Scale (CARS)*. New York: Irvington Publishers.

Schreibman, L. (1988). *Autism.* Beverly Hills: Sage Publications.

Shah, A., & Frith, U. (1986). An islet of ability in autistic children: A research note. In E.W. Bell (Ed.). *Autism: A reference book* (pp. 22–28). White Plains, NY: Longman.

Shapiro, T., & Hertzig, M.E. (1991). Social deviance in autism: A central integrative failure as a model for social nonengagement. *Psychiatric Clinics of North America, 14*(1), 19–31.

Short, A.B., & Marcus, L.M. (1986). Psychoeducational evaluation of autistic children and adolescents. In P.J. Lazarus & S.S. Strichart (Eds.), *Psychoeducational evaluation of children and adolescents with low-incidence handicaps* (pp. 155–180). Orlando, FL: Grune & Stratton.

Siegel, B. (1991). Toward DSM-IV: A developmental approach to autistic disorder. *Psychiatric Clinics of North America, 14*(1), 53–68.

Sloan, J.L. (1987). Autistic behavior. In C.R. Reynolds & L. Mann (Eds.), *Encyclopedia of special education* (pp. 165–166). New York: John Wiley & Sons.

Smalley, S.L. (1991). Genetic influences in autism. *Psychiatric Clinics of North America, 14*(1), 125–139.

Spitzer, R.L., & Siegel, B. (1990). The DSM-III-R field trial for pervasive developmental disorders. *Journal of the American Academy of Child and Adolescent Psychiatry, 29*, 855–62.

Steffenburg, S. (1991). Neuropsychiatric assessment of children with autism: A population-based study. *Developmental Medicine and Child Neurology, 33*, 495–511.

Steinhausen, H.C., & Erdin, A. (1991a). A comparison of ICD-9 and ICD-10 diagnoses of child and adolescent psychiatric disorders. *Journal of Clinical Psychology and Psychiatry and Allied Disciplines, 32*, 909–920.

Steinhausen, H.C., & Erdin, A. (1991b). The inter-rater reliability of child and adolescent psychiatric disorders in ICD-10. *Journal of Clinical Psychology and Psychiatry and Allied Disciplines, 32*, 921–928.

Szatmari, P., & Jones, M.B. (1991). IQ and the genetics of autism. *Journal of Clinical Psychiatry and Allied Disciplines, 32*, 897–908.

Teal, M.B., Wiebe, M.J. (1986). A validity analysis of selected instruments used to assess autism. *Journal of Autism and Developmental Disorders, 16*, 485–494.

Volkmar, F.R., Cicchetti, D.V., Dykens, E., Sparrow, S.S., Leckman, J.F., & Cohen, D. (1988). An evaluation of the Autism Behavior Checklist. *Journal of Autism and Developmental Disorders, 18*, 81–97.

Volkmar, F.R., Sparrow, S.S., Goudreau, D., Cicchetti, D.V., Paul, D., & Cohen, D.J. (1987). Social deficits in autism: An operational definition using the Vineland Adaptive Behavior Scales. *American Academy of Child and Adolescent Psychiatry, 26*, 156–161.

Walker, H.M., & Fabre, T.R. (1987). Assessment of behavior disorders in the school setting: Issues, problems, and strategies revisited. In N.G. Haring (Ed.), *Assessing and managing behavior disabilities* (pp. 198–243). Seattle: University of Washington Press.

Wenar, C., & Ruttenberg, B.A. (1976). The use of BRIACC for evaluating therapeutic effectiveness. *Journal of Autism and Childhood Schizophrenia, 6*, 175–191.

Wolff, S. (1991). Childhood autism: Its diagnosis, nature, and treatment. *Archives of Disease in Childhood, 66,* 737–741.

World Health Organization: ICD-10. (1990). *Mental and Behavioral Disorder: Diagnostic Criteria for Research.* Geneva: World Health Organization.

Young, J.G., O'Brien, J.D., Gutterman, E.M., & Cohen, P. (1987). Structured diagnostic interviews for children and adolescents. *Journal of the American Academy of Child and Adolescent Psychiatry, 26,* 613–620.

PART II

Instruction and Learning

4

Bilingual Pupils and Special Education: A Reconceptualization

Richard A. Figueroa
Nadeen T. Ruiz

BACKGROUND

In 1933, Reynolds made one of the earliest observations about bilingual children, mental tests, and special education. In a report to the U.S. Department of the Interior she described how the city of Los Angeles, through its "well-organized psychology and educational research division," provided for the needs of Mexican children in "specially adapted . . . environments" (p. 50):

> A *few* Mexican children have had sufficient mental ability to be placed in opportunity A rooms, in which classes for superior children, usually above 125 IQ, are taught. *Many* others are cared for in adjustment and opportunity B rooms, where remedial education is carried on. A number of Mexican children are in development rooms which handle children who are for the most part below 65 IQ. In the words of a member of the research division staff, "The proportion of Mexican pupils in development rooms is probably *higher* than is their relative number in the general (pupil) population." (p. 51, emphasis added)

The three issues of testing, over/underrepresentation, and specialized instruction, however, did not evolve concurrently. By the 1960s and 1970s, testing and overrepresentation in classes for the mildly handicapped took center stage in the courts. The issue of instruction did not receive as much attention until the late 1980s.

This Optimal Learning Environment Project has been funded by the Division of Special Education in the California Department of Education, Dr. Shirley Thornton, Deputy Superintendent.

TESTING

Bilingual children who are referred for special education testing present a rich variety of clinical types: (a) those who remain silent for long periods of time, a condition that educators are tempted to label as a form of aphasia but which in fact is a normal stage in the process of learning a second language; (b) those who learn to say "I don't know" as a strategy to avoid being asked to speak in a language they do not speak well; (c) the Ping-Pong Kids, those who have been exited out of bilingual programs too early, who upon failing in the English-only program go back to the bilingual program, and who upon not doing well there (because of what they missed while in the English-only program) are referred for special education testing; (d) the Gap Kids, those who show up at 10 years of age, who have never or only occasionally been to school in their country of origin, and who seem retarded in their chronological age, fourth-grade placement; (e) the 3–3 Children, those who score in the middle of the proficiency continua (1 to 5) for both English and their native language, whom many consider alingual in terms of school language genres, but whose communicative competence is normal at home; (f) the Hidden Treasure Children, those whose knowledge bases are never reflected or used by their teachers, who forget what they learned yesterday, who don't seem to sequence their ideas, and who perform exceptionally well (cognitively, linguistically, and even academically) in contexts such as sociodramatic play and exceptionally poorly in contexts such as completing worksheets; (g) the Language-Loss Children, those who begin to lose their primary language in school, who then return to their native country and begin to lose their second language, who then return to the United States to again begin to lose their primary language, and who never seem to make any sense of sound–symbol correspondence and never get hooked on phonics; and (h) the Immersion Victims, those who never have a chance to use their primary language in school, who spend large parts of their academic day in decontextualized, rote-driven English-as-a-Second-language classes, and who get further and further behind until special education seems to be the most benign placement possible.

Regretably, tests are insensitive to these linguistic, temporary, and school-based "types." Historically, the net effect has been an overrepresentation of bilingual children in special education.

Since the 1970s, the courts have adjudicated a multiple set of complaints against the placement of bilingual pupils in special education. Three primary solutions have been ordered by the courts: testing (IQ) in the primary language, using bilingual testers, and monitoring for overrepresentation.

Coincidentally, African-American children have also filed similar law suits (*Larry P. v. Riles,* 1979, 1986; *PASE v. Hannon,* 1980) against special education testing (IQ). Here, the call has been for *culturally appropriate* testing and for the removal of IQ testing. In the 1979 decision on *Larry P.,* the court found that IQ tests were culturally biased against African-American pupils and ordered that they not be administered for placement in educable mentally retarded (EMR) classes. This decision was amended in 1986 in a new injunction. Intelligence tests could not be given in California to African-American pupils under *any* special education circumstances, *even* if a parent requested such testing. In 1988, this new injunction was challenged by the parents of African-American pupils in *Crawford v. Honig*. Because of *Crawford*, the bilingual court cases are about to merge with the culturally appropriate court cases in California.

The facts of the *Crawford* case are that the plaintiffs were all recommended for special education testing, which normally includes an IQ test. Because of the 1986 injunction amending the 1979 *Larry P.* decision, however, African-American children could not be given an IQ test even if a parent requested it. The parents of the *Crawford* plaintiffs, under prodding by local school psychologists, became incensed about being "denied the opportunity for the voluntary administration and use of intelligent tests" (p. 9), an opportunity afforded parents of all other ethnic groups. The plaintiffs further noted the inconsistency with regard to testing for the gifted programs in California, since for entrance into those programs IQ tests could be given to black children.

According to the complaint, denying the plaintiffs an IQ test subjects them "to the deprivation of their rights, privileges and immunities . . ." (p. 10). Under the Fourteenth Amendment provisions, the *Crawford* children allege discrimination, deprivation of rights, denial of equal protection, denial of due process, and deprivation of liberty and property interests because of a "racially discriminatory regulation [the 1986 injunction] exceeding the scope of the . . . *Larry P. v Riles*" (p. 10) decision of 1979 and established without a fairness hearing (required to amend). Further, the 1986 injunction does not adequately define "how children are to be classified as 'black'" (p. 11). The 1986 injunction also excludes black children ". . . on the basis of race and color, from benefitting and participating in" (p. 13) special education programs. The 1986 injunction, according to *Crawford*, also violates provisions under P.L. 94–142 ("testing and evaluation materials and procedures . . . will be selected and administered so as to be racially or culturally nondiscriminatory," 20 U.S.C. Sect. 1412(5)(c)) and promotes racial segregation (p. 15, 16).

Crawford, in 1988, asked that the 1986 injunction be declared unconstitutional, that the injunction be removed for the plaintiffs, and that the plaintiffs be given an IQ test.

Crawford never mentions the compelling issues in *Larry P.*: the extreme overrepresentation rates of African-American children in special education classes for the mildly handicapped, or the bitter choice considered in *Larry P.*, that is, that either the IQ tests are biased or that African-American children, as a group, are less intelligent than white children. The *Crawford* case is being litigated on behalf of the plaintiffs by a very conservative legal office, the Landmark Legal Foundation. This organization has been devoted to overturning civil rights cases throughout the country.

In April 1991, Judge Robert Peckham, who wrote the 1979 *Larry P.* decision, held a public hearing on the *Crawford* complaint. New issues surfaced there. The judge broadened the discussion to include the Hispanic bilingual plaintiffs in *Diana v. California State Board of Education* (1970). The *Crawford* children asked to be considered as a class, representing all black children. The question of procedural error (not holding a fairness hearing before issuing the 1986 injunction) kept surfacing. The *Crawford* lawyers turned up the rhetoric by denouncing the 1986 injunction as racist and by comparing it to South Africa's Apartheid laws. Judge Peckham acknowledged a central problem: the possible equal protection problems in the 1986 injunction, that is, treating African-American children differently from all other children. During this public hearing, the point was repeatedly made that the 1979 *Larry P.* decision was about EMR misplacement and that this problem no longer existed because of the virtual disappearance of EMR children and classes. The judge wondered if an equivalent category of "dead end" programs existed in California in 1991.

The most surprising element at this April hearing, however, was California's message to the court: (a) IQ was not a necessary condition for receiving special education services, and (b) the state was considering new regulations to remove IQ testing for *all* children who were referred for special education assessment. Such a move would virtually make all of the *Crawford* complaints moot. It would also dramatically change much of special education.

In December 1991, a second public hearing on *Crawford* was held in Judge Peckham's court. The following issues were addressed, but not resolved, at this hearing: (a) Is misplacement in special education a sentence to dead-end educational programs? (b) Are the *Crawford* children representative of a class (by 1991 there were only two *Crawford* plaintiffs)? (c) Is denying African-American pupils access to IQ tests (found to be biased in *Larry P.*) paternalism or protection? (d) Does parental permission really protect African-American children from being misdiagnosed and misplaced? (e) Are African-American children harmed by denying them access to IQ tests?

An interesting sidelight also emerged at this hearing. A representative from the California Association of School Psychologists (CASP) sat with the *Crawford* attorneys and was ready to testify for them as a representative of CASP, indicating that this professional organization representing school psychologists has decided to take sides in this matter.

Reforming the Assessment Process in California

The California Department of Education, as of April 1992, has embarked on internal discussions about reforming the eligibility criteria for special education placement and on revamping the assessment process. The latter involves two considerations: removing the IQ test and removing the medical model that undergirds the "diagnostic" assessments conducted in special education.

Removing the IQ Test   The rationale for removing IQ tests rests on four types of arguments.

First, there is now evidence of bias in the predictive validity of IQ tests. In examining the historical literature on the testing of linguistic minorities, Figueroa

(1990) found a substantial number of studies showing that when the English language proficiency of linguistic minority groups was controlled, the predictive coefficients were attenuated for those with least proficiency in English. This conclusion was confirmed in a reanalysis of the validity study of the System of Multicultural Pluralistic Assessment (SOMPA) (Mercer, 1979) tests. Hispanic children from Spanish-only homes had 1972 Wechsler Intelligence Scale for Children-Revised (WISC-R) IQs that were consistently less predictive of standardized academic achievement test scores than were those of Hispanic pupils from English-only homes. Ironically, the most hypersensitive IQ score to this form of attenuation was the Performance IQ. It is worth noting that in the past ten years, at least eight similar studies have arrived at the same findings. These are summarized in Valdes and Figueroa (in press).

These data provide strong support to the blanket assertion put forth by the current *Standards for Educational and Psychological Testing* (American Educational Research Association, American Psychological Association, National Council on Measurement, 1985) that in testing linguistic minorities "every test given in English becomes, in part, a language or literacy test" (p. 73) of English. In effect, as Valdes and Figueroa (in press) have comprehensively shown, for bilingual individuals, personality, achievement, vocational, and intelligence tests *in unknown degrees* degenerate into English language–proficiency tests. This means that the removal of IQ tests can be empirically justified for bilingual individuals, concurring with the legal conclusion of bias against African-American students in *Larry P.* and contradicting the Equal Protection argument in the *Crawford* complaint.

Second, IQ tests are consistently misused. Some 22 years after the *Diana v. California Board of Education* court case, bilingual pupils continue to be tested in the wrong language, continue to be overrepresented in new categories of mildly handicapping conditions, and continue to be subjected to special education placement decisions based primarily on IQ test scores (Rueda et al., 1984).

Another body of evidence, in which ethnic children are not the main concern, has documented a unique form of misuse of IQ tests and of tests in general when these are used to determine eligibility for special education. School psychologists test and test until they get the "right" configuration of scores, the one that is required under local eligibility criteria (Mehan et al., 1986; Taylor, 1991). Also, the much touted objectivity of psychometric, individually administered tests may not be so objective. In the study by Mehan and associates (1986), school psychologists were videotaped, and their ability to administer IQ tests according to the test manuals' specifications was empirically evaluated. This is a unique form of measuring reliability. The analyses of the videotaped testing sessions clearly point out that the question–response interactions do not occur in the standardized, required format.

> The administration of tests in practical situations is not routine. The act of testing involves a complex social relationship . . . that makes the uniform and objective measure of intelligence a social activity

(p. 94) . . . testers and students jointly produce answers in individual tests. (p. 100)

Third, IQ testing as used in special education "diagnosis" is essentially a unique form of practicing medicine without a license. The belief has always been that these tests can "diagnose" mental handicaps, that they can differentiate among conditions such as learning disabilities, educable mental retardation, and even some communication handicaps. In fact, data exist documenting how IQ tests fail to do precisely this (Ysseldyke, et al. 1982; Shinn, 1989). One possible effect of this malpractice may well be the capricious fluctuation in national prevalence rates for learning disabilities and mental retardation (U.S. Department of Education, 1989). Whereas the prevalence rates for handicapping conditions with clear medical symptoms and where IQ does not play any role in "diagnosis" (deafness, orthopedic impairments, visual handicaps) remain fairly invariant across different states and throughout the K to 12 grade levels, learning disability rates can vary between 2% and 7% of the K to 12 population.

Fourth, IQ tests, in their wide use and in anchoring the diagnostic assessment practices in special education, inflict a considerable economic hardship on California's public schools, special education instructional programs, and the state's ability to meet the needs of exceptional pupils. Shepard and Smith (1983) estimated that the 21 hours needed to assess a child costs the equivalent of two weeks pay for instructional staff. Poland, Thurlow, Ysseldyke, and Mirkin (1982) estimated that on a national level "diagnostic" testing can cost more than $3,000 per child when the testing is extensive. In California, it is estimated that "diagnostic" testing costs about $1,200 per pupil. Since every one of the 500,000 students in special education must be tested or retested every three years, this "diagnostic" exercise costs some $600,000,000 every three years.

Removing the Medical Model.   Data exist to indicate that substituting IQ tests, in and of itself, will not resolve the issues surrounding the overrepresentation of ethnic children in the mildly handicapped categories. After the *Larry P.* and *Diana* court cases in the early 1970s, the diagnosis of mental retardation began to disappear. Tucker (1980) monitored this phenomenon. As the EMR population declined, the learning-disabled population increased. The irony in this is that whereas EMR "requires" a very low IQ, learning disabled virtually requires an average IQ. This augurs badly for objectivity and suggests that IQ scores serve socially constructed purposes.

Since the 1986 injunction, which effectively banned the use of IQ tests with African-American children, overrepresentation has continued in special education. In other words, even without IQ, other norm-referenced and even criterion-referenced measures carry on the functions of IQ relative to ethnic children. The assessment (medical) model in effect finds new tools for "diagnosing," sorting, and labeling. It continues to "explain" underachievement in terms that do not involve extant curricula and pedagogy and almost exclusively in terms of individual factors. The flaw, like a disease, exists in the pupil.

Under the current medical assessment model, IQ or any other test will serve only the interests of the current special education system, a system significantly influenced by the adults engaged in the process (teachers and psychologists), by their needs relative to underachieving students, and by the bartering of resources among these adults (Mehan et al., 1986). By medicalizing the problem, educational systems are absolved and undefinable handicaps are made real. For children who cannot cope with poor instruction or curricula (more often than not they are ethnic children), the outcome is usually an educational program that is remedial, decelerated, and reductionist.

The California Department of Education, propelled in great part by the intractable issues in the court cases affecting bilingual and African-American pupils, is considering removing IQ testing and also removing the medical model from the public schools. A new model for helping students who are not learning in the regular program may well examine the educational need for having mildly handicapped categories, medical model assessment process and practices, and instruction that assumes that such children learn differently, need a different curriculum, and need to have their educational experiences broken down into small, reductionist drills.

INSTRUCTION

In the late 1980s, studies began to appear that shifted the concerns about bilingual pupils in special education from the debate about testing to the special education classroom (Figueroa et al., 1989a). These studies not only pointed to the historical problem of underutilizing the primary language in the special education classroom, but also noted that instruction was driven by an overemphasis on mechanics. Further, it was underscored that bilingual children did poorly in such settings.

Certainly, at a conceptual level, the typical prepackaged special education curriculum runs counter to much of what researchers on bilingualism had been recommending. That is, for bilingual students, negotiating meaning, working cooperatively, building on cultural knowledge, incorporating home language genres, being in linguistically rich and interactive environments, and having their parents empowered constitute a powerful constellation of factors that positively affect their educational achievement (Cummins, 1989).

The Optimal Learning Environment (OLE) Research Project (Figueroa et al., 1989b) became part of this new literature. This longitudinal study has three phases.

Phase One.   During the first phase, the goal was to define the nature and status of bilingual special education. The results of this first phase (Figueroa et al., 1989b) can be summarized in two conclusions: (a) the bilingual child is far more complex than the current special education "diagnostic" and instructional systems realize; and (b) defining bilingual special education as a modified version of special education may be counterproductive because of the serious criticisms leveled at the special education system, its prevailing paradigm, and its instructional methodology (Poplin, 1988; Coles, 1987; Skrtic, 1991).

Phase Two. This was an ethnographic study of four learning-handicapped classrooms (called resource specialist program [RSP] classrooms) that were heavily overrepresented by Hispanic bilingual pupils. Two of the classrooms were in Los Angeles and two were in rural Northern California. Approximately 120 children were involved.

The goal in this phase of the study was to try to understand the unique culture of these classrooms. Underlying this goal was the assumption that although there were certain modifications unique to these bilingual RSP classrooms (such as having bilingual aides), results from them generalize to RSP classrooms throughout California. The assumption was supported by both a meta analysis of the bilingual special education literature (Ruiz et al., 1992) and a review of RSP training manuals. There was no model for a bilingual RSP classroom.

The theoretical framework for studying the four classrooms was Poplin's (1988a) analysis of the paradigm that has been the foundation for special education for nearly half a century. According to Poplin, despite four distinct emphases in the conduct of special education over the past 50 years (the medical model, the psychological process model, the behavioral model, and the cognitive/learning strategies model), there has been only one paradigm, reductionism. Essentially, reductionism assumes that the whole can be broken into its constituent parts, and that a whole is the sum of its parts. This is the underlying philosophy ascribed to the scientific method and to the scientific study of physical reality. It is also the antithesis to the gestaltist approach to the study of social and behavioral reality; that is, the whole is greater than the sum of its parts. Reductionism in special education assumes that learning occurs best when it is done in small steps and when the curriculum is presented in small pieces. Teaching, accordingly, is mechanistic, controlled by the teacher, and focused on correcting mistakes. Poplin presents a wide array of outcomes that stem from reductionism in special education. In a separate paper (Poplin, 1988b), she also provides the other end of the continuum, the characteristics and outcomes that emanate from a holistic orientation.

The OLE Project used Poplin's paradigmatic continuum to study four RSP classroom sites. Through videotaping of the four RSP classrooms, field observations of the dynamics in these classrooms, interviews with the participants in these classrooms, and analyses of the pupils' cumulative folders and work products, the OLE Project set out to test empirically Poplin's assertion that one paradigm predominates.

Five studies have been produced in the OLE Project summarizing many of the outcomes from phase two of the Project. These studies range in focus from microcontexts of special education, such as lessons in the classrooms, to macrocontexts, such as federal regulations concerning bilingual students identified as handicapped. They also vary along the dimension of time, sometimes focusing on a specific period of observation and data collection, at other times focusing on the historical context. Overall, the studies make a convincing case for looking at multiple layers of context and time to understand, first, the current state of the art of special education for bilingual students in learning-handicapped/learning-disabled programs and, second, what it will take to change the current system.

Ruiz (1990) examined videotapes of classroom interactions from three OLE classrooms taken during the 1988–1989 academic year (a fourth site was added late in that year but the project did not videotape the classroom interaction there until the following academic year). Ruiz was interested in whether or not the pre-intervention OLE classrooms projected a reductionist orientation. This study was one of the first to examine classroom interaction directly for the purpose of gauging the prevailing paradigmatic orientation.

From a total data base of 144 videotaped events (lessons), Ruis randomly selected 22 events for analysis. She devised the Holistic-Reductionist Rating Scale to code the events for evidence of reductionism or holism. The scale was developed from Poplin's work (1988a, 1988b) and also from the instructional principles from Ruiz's OLE Curriculum Guide (1989b). Ruiz provides the theoretical and empirical support for each of the seven holistic features included in the scale (1990). These features are as follows: (a) lessons give students experience with whole texts; (b) lessons link curriculum with students' background knowledge and personal interests; (c) lessons have an authentic outcome or product; (d) lessons emphasize meaning first and form (mechanics, such as spelling) second; (e) lessons promote student activity and interactivity (relatively balanced control of discourse); (f) lessons include and recognize students' personal interpretations and responses; and (g) lessons revolve around choice, that is, student-selected materials or student-originated content.

Two independent raters (interrater reliability coefficient = .91) found that the average number of holistic characteristics, out of a possible seven, was just over two per lesson, clearly indicating a reductionist orientation in instruction. The Holistic-Reductionist Scale also revealed important differences among the three sites. Two of the sites averaged less than one holistic characteristic per lesson, while the third averaged over three. This was explained by the third classroom's incorporation of a number of holistic instructional techniques such as dialogue journals and student's self-selection of reading materials. On the other hand, a closer look at the lessons analyzed from this more holistic classroom revealed that about a third of them received a zero rating, indicating the absence of any holistic characteristics. These classrooms, in effect, expose students to learning experiences that are predominantly segmented, without any link to their experiences, without any authentic purpose, focused on mechanics, requiring their passivity, concerned with the "correct" answer, and focused on teacher-selected content.

The study conducted by Rueda, Betts, and Hammi (1990a) was based on one of the OLE Project's major contextualist assumptions, that depending on the instructional setting, differing pictures of student abilities and disabilities emerge (Ruiz, 1989a). The authors chose to focus on the writing products collected from the OLE sites. The primary goal of this study was to examine these written products for a global picture of the teachers' orientation to literacy as enacted in the literacy activities they chose for their students.

Rueda and associates (1990a) randomly selected two English-speaking and two Spanish-speaking students from each of the four OLE classrooms, for a total of 16 students. The authors created a rating scale for analyzing the student's written products along the holism-reductionism continuum. This scale was similar to that of Ruiz (described earlier). The results showed that there was surprising consistency among the work products collected. Almost all samples fell closer to the reductionist end of the scale.

Rueda and associates (1990a) also presented in their study an example of the powerful effect of context on the writing of one student. In the first writing sample collected, the student had been asked to write about Abraham Lincoln. The teacher assigned one point each (for a total of five possible points) for criteria such as having a title, accurate spelling, and other mechanical considerations. The student's output in this context was minimal and stilted. However, when the student was allowed to write on a topic of great personal relevance, the shooting of his brother who at that time was in serious condition in the hospital, he produced three pages of writing, complete with direct dialogue. Although the second piece had many mechanical errors and some problems with coherence, it provided a very different picture of the writing skills of this student, thereby reaffirming the crucial role of the instructional context for understanding student abilities.

In another study, Beaumont (1990) collected a random sample (n = 38) of individualized education programs (IEPs) from the four OLE sites. Her goal was to analyze the IEPs for what they revealed about the writers' beliefs and expectations regarding instruction. Specifically, she developed ten questions to ask about each IEP. The questions primarily rise from the OLE instructional principles (Ruiz, 1989b) and the research that supports the principles.

Some of Beaumont's major findings regarding the IEPs were: (a) they focus on student deficits with no consideration about context and its impact on performance; (b) they do not identify situations in which the pupils perform optimally; (c) they do not provide data about the curriculum in the regular classroom; (d) they give very little information about bilingual pupils' uses of language or about their bilingual proficiency; (e) they do not include any information on the students' cultural background and its impact on academic achievement; (f) they do not discuss children's learning in contexts outside of school; (g) they do not discuss children's experiences with reading and writing in the home; and (h) they do not consider student interests and how these might inform and affect instruction in the classroom.

Rueda, Ruiz, and Figueroa (1990b) took a broader look at the instructional events in the classrooms. They included such data as interviews with teachers and instructional assistants as to their beliefs regarding learning disabilities, as well as field notes, video recordings, student work products, and data in cumulative folders. They found three major patterns: (a) reductionism in literacy instruction, (b) medicalization of learning problems, and (c) a state of "semi-internalization" of new teaching principles among teachers.

The first pattern has been discussed in the studies cited earlier. The second pattern, couching learning problems in a pseudo medical framework, was of interest primarily because of the differences between the special education teachers (predominantly Anglo) and their instructional assistants (all Hispanic). The teachers explained underachievement as primarily resulting from neurological impairments. Their explanations, it was felt, came directly from the medical model training that they had received. Certainly, the vocabulary and jargon used constitute an educational genre that typically distinguishes and sometimes empowers special educators among their regular peers (Mehan et al., 1986). The assistants tended to view low achievement in terms of home environment problems or poor instruction. What made their explanations compelling was the fact that they usually had a more direct link to the parents, the home, and the challenges confronting the families. Their reactions also tended to be more in line with the National Academy of Science's (Heller et al., 1982) concerns about the impact of poor instruction on the overrepresentation of ethnic children in special education.

The third pattern dealt with the teachers' "partial internalization" of change. As the OLE teachers met with the OLE staff and were exposed to new holistic teaching techniques, some of them began to verbalize new beliefs about how children learn. These new beliefs, however, did not always result in fundamental changes in teaching practices. Alternately, when some change in teaching behaviors occurred, it did not completely replace all reductionist activities. Rather, change was superimposed on them. The question of how special education teachers change out of their reductionist paradigm and practices constitutes one of the most interesting and intriguing research questions in OLE.

The final study by Ruiz and co-workers (1992) examined the history and status of special education for bilingual students identified as mildly handicapped. Specifically, it focused on: (a) the empirical bases for questioning the role of special education in meeting the needs of Hispanic students who either are academically at-risk or are handicapped, (b) the literature on bilingual special education and its underlying assumptions, and (c) the theoretical bases for proposing a new paradigm to meet the needs of bilingual pupils who are diagnosed as learning handicapped. The authors conclude that many of the anomalies that span the macro and micro contexts in the special education of bilingual children (overrepresentation, misdiagnosis, undereducation) can be associated with the reductionist paradigm that has governed special education for much of this century. Unless special educators begin to recognize that these anomalies arise from the flaws of the system and not from the children, their bilingualism, or their culture, the practices in special education will continue to be scrutinized by the courts and disparaged in some of the research and professional literature (Skrtic, 1991; Taylor, 1991).

Phase Three. The last stage of the OLE Research Project entails changing the RSP classrooms into OLE classrooms and changing the reductionist paradigm into a holistic one. The original notions entertained by the OLE research staff framed this reform in terms of creating gifted classrooms (not classrooms for the gifted) and an accelerated educational program for bilingual handicapped pupils. The primary hypothesis has always been that such a setting is far more congruent with what bilingual pupils need and that in such a setting learning handicaps would be shown for what they are: social constructions set up to deal with children with whom the regular education program cannot cope either professionally (monolingual teachers) or politically (bilingual programs).

Quite coincidentally, the second published article by Poplin (1988b) augmented the OLE Curriculum Guide written by Ruiz (1989b) by providing highly congruent and elaborated theoretical foundations (holism, constructivism, structuralism). The unique role played by these theoretical formulations is that they account, accommodate, and legitimize the educational use of children's languages and cultures, the two variables that historically have perplexed special education testing and instruction and have led to so much scrutiny by the courts.

The OLE teachers were trained to use a set of instructional strategies that are antithetical to reductionism. These are literature studies, writers' workshop, dialogue journals, reciprocal teaching, finding out/descubrimiento, DEAR (drop everything and read) time, and portfolio assessment. The OLE classrooms were reconfigured to include a variety of reading materials in English and Spanish (selected on the basis of strong story grammar, celebration of culture, and pupil interest) and technology to support literacy activities (computer, printer, copying machine, etc.). The reductionist, daily pull-out schedule was changed into immersion cycles in which children can come to the OLE classroom for four hours per day for three-week periods. Children off cycle would be returned to the regular classroom where the regular program, with some support from the OLE teacher, would have to re-own the "learning handicapped" pupils.

The OLE classroom will be fully operational during the 1992–1993 academic year. This experiment has several research questions. The primary ones are: Is it possible to "cure" learning-disabled pupils, English-only victims, curriculum casualties, and children who have been subjected to racism? Are holistic strategies more effective than reductionist ones in returning pupils back to the regular program? What are the constraints and facilitators in helping special education teachers for mildly handicapped students move from a reductionist to a holistic paradigm? What is the process of literacy development for bilingual children labeled as learning handicapped? And, does portfolio assessment, conducted by teachers, provide an instructionally valid alternative to the current "diagnostic" assessment practices?

CONCLUSION

Late in the 1991–1992 academic year, the OLE sites began to function like OLE classrooms with full immersion cycles. In one site, after one cycle, two of the children were recommended for decertification out of special education. One of them was a migrant education student who had been in special education for a year and a half. In all the schools where the OLE classrooms began the cycles, the regular education faculties unanimously noted that the learning-handicapped children were performing as they had never done before: they were reading books during recess, they were writing books (trilogies in one instance), they were having their books highlighted in the libraries, and they were dedicating their books to their regular class teachers. In virtually every OLE site, the regular class faculties were asking the special education (OLE) teachers to train them in holistic strategies.

The questions raised by the courts around the issues of assessing and testing minority children in conjunction with the tentative results observed so far in the pre-experiment phase in the OLE classrooms strongly suggest that Poplin (1988) may be right, and, further, that many assumptions that undergird the current special education system may not be valid. The latter include: that it is possible to "diagnose" the mild handicapping conditions; that learning-handicapped children learn differently; that there is a need for a different curriculum for these children; that there are special teaching skills required to teach such children; that there is a need for a special school system within the regular school system to meet the needs of these children; and, that the mildly handicapping conditions, most notably learning disabilities, cannot be "cured" and hence require differential proficiency standards.

As the *Crawford* issues and OLE-like experiments proceed in California and other states (Ortiz et al., 1991), the reform movement in education, particularly as it involves issues of cultural and linguistic diversity, may finally affect special education. There is a certain irony in noting that such a system change is being propelled by pupils who since 1933 have been overrepresented in "development rooms" (Reynolds, 1933), EMR classes, and RSP classrooms.

REFERENCES

American Educational Research Association, American Psychological Association, National Council on Measurement. (1985). *Standards for educational and psychological testing.* Washington, D.C.: American Psychological Association.

Beaumont, C. (1990). *An analysis of IEPs in the OLE classrooms: Baseline phase.* Unpublished manuscript. Davis, CA: University of California.

Coles, G. (1987). *The learning mystique.* New York: Pantheon.

Crawford v. Honig, Complaint for Declaratory Judgment and Injunctive Relief, May 10, 1988.

Cummins J. (1989). A theoretical framework for bilingual special education. *Exceptional Children, 56,* 111.

Diana v. California State Board of Education, C-70 37 RFT (N.D. Cal. 1970).

Figueroa, R.A. (1990). Assessment of linguistic minority children. In C.R. Reynolds & R.W. Kamphuaus (Eds.), *Handbook of psychological and educational assessment of children: Intelligence and achievement.* New York: Guilford Press.

Figueroa, R.A., Fradd, S.H., & Correa, V.I. (1989a). Bilingual special education and this special issue. *Exceptional Children, 56,* 174.

Figueroa, R.A., Fradd, S.H., & Correa, V.I. (1989b). Meeting the multicultural needs of Hispanic students in special education. *Exceptional Children, 56.* (Special Issue).

Heller, K.A., Holtzman, W.H., & Messick, S. (1982). *Placing children in special education: A strategy for equity.* Washington, D.C.: National Academy Press.

Larry P. v. Riles, 495 F.Supp. 926 (N.D. Cal. 1979).

Larry P. v. Riles, 793 F.2d 969 (9th Cir. 1984, as amended, 1986).

Mehan, H., Herweck, H., & Meihls, J. (1986). *Handicapping the handicapping.* Palo Alto: Stanford University Press.

Mercer, J.R. (1979). *The System of Multicultural Pluralistic Assessment (SOMPA).* New York: Psychological Corporation.

Ortiz, A., Wilkinson, C.Y., Robertson-Courtney, P. & Kushner, M.I. (1991). *AIM for the BEST: Assessment and intervention model for the bilingual exceptional student.* Austin: University of Texas.

PASE v. Hannon, No. 74 C 3586 (N.D. Ill. 1980).

Poland, S., Thurlow, M.L., Ysseldyke, J.E., & Mirkin, P.K. (1982). Current psychoeducational assessment and decision-making practices as reported by directors of special education. *Journal of School Psychology, 20,* 171.

Poplin, M.S. (1988a). The reductionist fallacy in learning disabilities: Replicating the past by reducing the present. *Journal of Learning Disabilities, 21,* 389.

Poplin, M.S. (1988b). Holistic/constructivist principles of the teaching/learning process: Implications for the field of learning disabilities. *Journal of Learning Disabilities, 21,* 401.

Reynolds, A. (1933). *The education of Spanish-speaking children in five southwestern states.* Bulletin No. 11. Washington, D.C.: Department of the Interior.

Rueda, R., Betts, B., & Hammi, A. (1990a). *A descriptive analysis of work products in OLE classroom sites: Baseline phase.* Unpublished manuscript. Davis, CA: University of California.

Rueda, R., Cardoza, D., Mercer, J.R., & Carpenter, L. (1984). *An examination of special education decision making with Hispanic first-time referrals in large urban school districts.* Los Alomitos, CA: Southwest Regional Laboratory.

Rueda, R., Ruiz, N.T., & Figueroa, R.A. (1990b). *An ethnographic analysis of instructional events for Mexican-American learning handicapped students.* Paper presented at the meeting of the American Educational Research Association. Boston, MA.

Ruiz, N.T. (1989a). An optimal learning environment for Rosemary. *Exceptional Children, 56,* 130.

Ruiz, N.T. (1989b). *The Optimal Learning Environment (OLE) curriculum guide: A resource for teachers of Spanish-speaking children in learning handicapped programs.* Unpublished manuscript. Davis, CA: University of California.

Ruiz, N.T. (1990). *Instructional events in the OLE classrooms: Baseline phase.* Unpublished manuscript. Davis, CA: University of California.

Ruiz, N.T., Figueroa, R.A., Rueda, R.S., & Beaumont, C. (1992). History and status of bilingual special education for Hispanic handicapped students. In R.V. Padilla & A.H. Benavides (Eds.), *Critical perspectives in bilingual education research.* Tempe, AZ: Bilingual Press/Editorial Bilingue.

Shepard, L., & Smith, M.L. (1983). An evaluation of the identification of learning disabled students in Colorado. *Learning Disability Quarterly, 6,* 115.

Shinn, M.R. (1989). *Curriculum-based measurement: Assessing special children.* New York: Guilford Press.

Skrtic, T.M. (1991). The special education paradox: Equity as the way to excellence. *Harvard Educational Review, 61,* 148.

Taylor, D. (1991). *Learning denied.* Portmouth, NH: Heinemann.

Tucker, J.A. (1980). Ethnic proportions in classes for the learning disabled: Issues in nonbiased assessment. *Journal of Special Education, 14,* 93.

U.S. Department of Education. (1989). *Annual report to Congress on the implementation of the Education of the Handicapped Act.* Washington, D.C.: U.S. Government Printing Office.

Valdes, G., & Figueroa, R.A. (in press). *The nature of bilingualism and the nature of testing.* New York: Ablex.

Ysseldyke, J.E., Algozzine, B., Shinn, M.R., & McGue, M. (1982). Similarities and differences between low achievers and students labeled learning disabled. *Journal of Special Education, 16,* 73.

5

Direct Instruction: A Research-Based Approach for Designing Instructional Programs

Craig Darch

"I don't know why I can't do better in school. I don't organize things like I need to. I just wish that I could do better." (John, fourth-grade student)

A question facing many educators, particularly those who teach students who are at risk for school failure, is "How can instructional programs be designed so that even the lowest performing student can achieve his/her potential?" It is possible for teachers to determine whether an approach is effective by considering its characteristics and its research support. An effective instructional model will (a) have evidence that the model is effective for students in regular and special education, (b) be designed in a manner to ensure that teachers can implement programs in a reliable fashion, and (c) be versatile enough to be applied to various content areas. The premise of this chapter is that direct instruction is such a research-based model.

The purpose of this chapter is to provide the reader with a clear definition of direct instruction and then to evaluate research that has investigated the effectiveness of this curriculum design and teaching approach. First, a discussion of the various definitions of direct instruction is presented. Research evidence on larger-scale studies, studies that have investigated the effectiveness of the direct instruction model, follows. A review of research that has investigated the effectiveness of specific teaching techniques is also presented. Finally, a review of direct instruction academic research is provided.

DEFINING THE DIRECT INSTRUCTION TEACHING MODEL

Rosenshine (1976) first introduced the term *direct instruction* into the arena of educational research. As he used this term, *direct instruction* was the series of teaching behaviors that were correlated with increased levels of achievement, as well as classroom organization, and how teachers use instructional time. The specific teaching functions associated with this conceptualization of direct instruction are generic activities that can be applied to most instructional programs used by classroom teachers. The emphasis of this approach is on general teaching techniques, such as increased teaching time, use of reinforcement, and organizational structures for classrooms. The majority of studies used to determine this list of teaching techniques were completed with elementary students. This conceptualization of direct instruction, although important, is not comprehensive because it does not directly address the issues of curriculum design, instructional content, and teacher training.

Rosenshine's direct instruction teaching model is based, in part, on the results of the following noteworthy experimental studies: the Direct Instruction Follow Through Program (Becker, 1977), the Texas Elementary School Study (Emmer et al., 1982), and the Missouri Mathematics Effectiveness Study (Good & Grouws, 1979).

Another conceptualization of *direction instruction,* the one that is the focus of this chapter, emphasizes the design and implementation of curriculum. Direct instruction is a comprehensive model that dictates how a teaching program should be organized and implemented. There are two principles that guide all direct instruction classrooms: the first is to teach more academic content in less time, the second is to control all the details of instruction (Engelmann et al., 1988). In this model, no instructional detail is left to occur by chance.

Direct Instruction programs are designed to provide lower-performing students an opportunity to "catch up" to their peers. Gersten, Woodward, and Darch (1986) defined direct instruction as ". . . a comprehensive model that covers the details of curriculum design, teaching techniques for low-performing students, implementation policy, and teacher training" (p. 18). The components of the direct instruction model are (a) the curriculum materials, which include the DISTAR programs in reading, arithmetic, and language; (b) efficient use of teaching time; (c) scripted presentation of lessons; and (d) use of specified teaching techniques (e.g., pacing, reinforcement, corrections). Teachers who use this model look carefully at *what* is taught to students, as well as at the instructional design of each teaching sequence. For example, in a direct instruction program that teaches students to read critically, a problem-solving strategy is developed, and each step in the reading strategy is explicitly taught to the students.

When teaching problem-solving strategies, teachers must consider the six critical features of direct instruction teaching sequences. These features are the (a) presentation of an explicit problem-solving strategy, (b) mastery teaching of each step in the strategy, (c) development of specific correction procedures for student errors, (d) a gradual switch from teacher-directed work to independent work, (e) systematic practice activities, and (f) built-in cumulative review of previously taught concepts. Students who are taught with a direct instruction program would also be given carefully sequenced practice examples. This structured practice would help the student to develop mastery of the strategy. In essence, nothing is left to chance in a direct instruction teaching program.

This model of direct instruction is based on the work of Sigfried Engelmann and his colleagues at the University of Oregon (Engelmann et al., 1988) and was implemented in Project Follow Through in the late 1960s and 1970s. One major application of the direct instruction model is that it can be used as a guide by teachers when they are constructing curriculum materials. This model does not focus exclusively on one content area; rather, the curriculum design guidelines can be applied to most teaching situations and have application to all of the major instructional areas in elementary and secondary classrooms. This model is often used with students who are at risk for school failure or are in programs for the mildly handicapped. In the remainder of this chapter, research that has looked at the major components of the direct instruction model will be summarized and discussed with a particular emphasis on those studies that have been completed with handicapped students.

RESEARCH ON THE DIRECT INSTRUCTION MODEL: EVALUATION OF PROGRAM IMPACT

Studies have investigated the impact of the direct instruction model on the performance of low-income students who were taught reading, math, and language using the DISTAR programs. These studies do not look at individual components, but rather they evaluate the entire direct instruction model. These studies can be categorized as (a) those that investigated the short-term effects of direct instruction (student performance was evaluated at the end of third grade) and (b) those that looked at long-term effects (student performance was evaluated at the end of ninth and twelfth grades).

Short-Term Effects. The major research that evaluated the short-term effects of the direct instruction model was an independent evaluation of Project Follow Through conducted by Stanford Research Institute and Abt Associates (Stebbins et al., 1977). The effectiveness of eight different instructional models, including direct instruction, was investigated. The model's impact on economically disadvantaged students in the elementary grades was the focus of these investigations.

This evaluation showed that, in general, the direct instruction model had a beneficial effect on the achievement levels of those children who participated in the program for a full four years, kindergarten through third grade. Results indicated that, in the major academic areas tested, students taught by direct instruction performed near the national median in reading, math, spelling, and language. These results suggest that direct instruction is an effective educational intervention in the content teaching areas for elementary-aged students who are functioning below expected levels.

One study evaluated the effects the direct instruction model has on the performance-handicapped students. Gersten, Becker, Heiry, and White (1984) conducted a secondary analysis of the Project Follow Through data and looked at the effect of the direct instruction model on students with low IQs. The results of their investigation indicated that (a) significant achievement gains are made for students with IQs below 80, and (b) significant IQ gains are found in this sample of students. Engelmann and associates (1988) elaborated on these findings: "Students with IQs below 71 gain 17 points in the entering kindergarten sample and 9.4 points in the entering first grade sample; gains for the children with IQs in the 71–90 range are 15.6 and 9.2 respectively" (p. 312).

Long-Term Effects. Studies have been conducted to determine whether the performance gains made by students taught with direct instruction persist beyond the third grade. These longitudinal studies are important to consider in light of the fact that some educators suggest that academic gains made by students taught with direct instruction will deteriorate once the instructional program is withdrawn. If longitudinal studies were to show that the academic gains made by low-performing students in the primary grades remained throughout their school years, then the importance of the direct instruction model as an intervention program for students would be greatly enhanced.

Gersten, Keating, and Becker (1988b) reported the results of a follow-up study of fifth- and sixth-grade students who had received a direct instruction program in the primary grades. The study was designed so that the performance of the students taught with direct instruction was compared to the performance of local control subjects who did not receive this type of structured teaching in the primary grades. This method allowed the researchers to compare the performance of students who were in direct instruction programs to students who received instruction with traditional teaching methods typically used in these school districts (Gersten et al., 1988a). This study was conducted at five diverse Project Follow Through sites: Dayton, Ohio; East St. Louis, Illinois; Tupelo, Mississippi; Smithville, Tennessee; and Uvalde, Texas. The results showed that, in most of the content areas evaluated and across each of the five project sites, the students who had received direct instruction in the primary grades outperformed local control-group students at the end of the fifth and sixth grades. This study provides strong evidence of the persistent effects of the direct instruction model once students leave elementary grades.

Becker and Gersten (1982) completed a study that evaluated the performance of ninth- and twelfth-grade students who had received direct instruction during their primary grades. As was the case with the study reported above, students who had received direct instruction in the primary grades were compared to local control-group students at three separate sites, East St. Louis, Illinois; Flint, Michigan; and New York City. Briefly, the results from the ninth-grade reading and math analysis consistently favored the direct instruction groups. In addition to achievement measures, this study used two other outcome measures: (a) graduation/dropout rates and (b) college applications/acceptances. The effects of the direct instruction model on graduation rates and college acceptance rates were not as consistent as the ninth-grade achievement results. However, at the New York site, students taught in the direct instruction program graduated at higher rates than comparison students (60% versus 38%), and college acceptance rates were higher for direct instruction students at both the New York and Flint sites. Gersten and co-workers (1988b) summarized these high school effects by stating, "These results give a clear indication that intensive intervention in the primary grades can have long-term benefits for at-risk students" (p. 326). For a detailed and thoughtful discussion of these results, the reader is directed to papers by Meyer, Gersten, and Guttin (1983) and Gersten and Keating (1987).

Weisberg (1988) reported the effects that a direct instruction preschool program can have on low-income children after they complete first and second grades. In this program, prekindergarten children, all living below poverty level and considered at high risk for school failure, attended a preschool that used direct instruction programs in reading, language, and math. Students who received two years of the direct instruction preschool program were compared with (a) those who received only one year of the direct instruction preschool program and (b) a local control group who did not receive instruction in the direct instruction preschool program. The results of this program evaluation demonstrated that children who received the two-year direct instruction program (prekindergarten and kindergarten) performed at significantly higher levels than did children who received just one year of the program. In addition, each of these groups significantly outperformed local control children on two standardized reading measures, the California Achievement Test and the Stanford Achievement Test, when tested at the end of the first and second grades. The largest effect was found in first grade. Weisberg reported that 90% of the children who received two years of the direct instruction program achieved at or above the 50th percentile, whereas 84% of the students who received the program for one year scored above the 50th percentile. Local control children, those who did not receive this program, performed much lower: only 15% of these children scored beyond the 50th percentile. A similar pattern of results was found when students were tested at the end of second grade. Weisberg's (1988) results, when linked to the other reports of the long-term effects of the direct instruction model, present compelling evidence that early, intensive direct instruction can have a continuing impact on the performance of the students even after the program has been withdrawn.

RESEARCH ON DIRECT INSTRUCTION TEACHING TECHNIQUES

Proponents of direct instruction (Engelmann & Carnine, 1982) suggest that teachers implement their instructional programs using several specified teaching techniques. It is argued that these techniques are closely tied to the success of direct instruction academic programs. Teachers who are trained to develop or modify academic programs according to direct instruction guidelines are also trained to use these teaching techniques in many teacher training programs (Darch et al., 1991). The five teaching techniques most frequently mentioned by proponents of the direct instruction model are (a) pacing, (b) signals, (c) frequent oral responding, (d) monitoring, and (e) teacher praise. A review of the relevant research on each of these teaching techniques follows.

Pacing. Instructional pacing is defined as the speed with which a teacher presents the tasks in a lesson (Carnine, 1976). Pacing is considered important for several reasons. First, it is postulated that pacing of instructional tasks reduces management problems. It is assumed that the rapid succession of instructional tasks increases the interest and motivation of the students. It is also suggested that rapid pacing results in greater achievement levels for students because it reduces the memory demands of the students during small group instruction.

Several researchers have investigated the effects that rapid pacing has on the attending behavior and academic performance of elementary students. In these studies, the rate of presentation of academic content is altered and then evaluated. In one study, Carnine (1976) investigated rapid-pacing effects on the performance of low-performing first graders by alternating rapid and slow pacing of lessons. Rapid pace was operationally defined as the presentation of a new task every 5 seconds. The results of this investigation indicated that fast pacing resulted in (a) higher attending rates and (b) more frequent correct responding when rapid pacing was compared to slower-paced instructional presentations. More specifically, during the fast-paced condition, students were on task approximately 90% of the time and responded correctly to content-oriented questions 80% of the time. However, when presented similar content with slow-paced instruction, these same subjects were on task only about 30% of the time and responded correctly to only about 30% of the questions. It should be pointed out that both of the subjects who participated in this study had been placed in the low-achieving first-grade classrooms and were significantly behind their classmates in reading-decoding skills.

In a more recent study, Darch and Gersten (1986) evaluated the effects of rapid pacing on student performance in a study of the isolated and combined effects of pacing and teacher praise. The two teacher presentation variables evaluated were (a) teacher presentation rate and (b) teacher praise. Four elementary students served as subjects. Each subject was identified as learning disabled by school psychologists, whose assessment included a history of difficulty in basic word decoding. Students were placed in the DISTAR Reading I Program (Engelmann & Bruner, 1974). Experimentation lasted 25 school days, which was longer than the Carnine (1976) study. The teacher systematically varied the pace of instructional presentation (rapid pace vs. slow pace), as defined by Carnine's study, and varied the use of teacher praise (praise vs. no praise). A modified reversal design was used to evaluate both the isolated and combined effects of pacing and praise.

The results of this investigation indicated instruction was most effective during the fast-paced teaching format when compared to the slower format. This effect was pronounced on two measures: percentage of correct responding and percentage of on-task behavior. For example, the mean percentage increase in on-task behavior for all subjects was approximately seven percentage points when compared to the students' performance during the slow-paced condition. It is interesting to note that the most pronounced effect of rapid pace was on the academic measure, the percentage of correct responding. The average increase in correct responding during this condition was 11 percentage points when compared to the slow-paced instructional presentation. It should be pointed out that although the rapid-pacing effects were demonstrated, the changes in on-task and correct responding were not as pronounced in this study. Student performance was highest on both measures during the combined rapid pace and praise condition. These results were similar to Carnine's (1976) findings with nonhandicapped beginning readers, but are quite different from the results of the study by West (1981). West found that rapid pacing was more effective than praise in decreasing off-task behavior, but that the accuracy rate actually decreased during the rapid-pacing phases.

The results of these experimental studies suggest that rapid pacing is an instructional technique that is useful to teachers who are working with young elementary-aged students learning basic skills. The rather powerful effects of rapid pacing can help students be successful in the initial stages of a remedial program. As teachers who work with special education and other low-performing students have come to realize, it is critical to help students get off to a good start in early academic instruction. Therefore, it is a promising finding that rapid pace has an impact on correct responding and on-task behavior. It is still to be determined whether these results extend to older students who are receiving instruction in more advanced content. Future research should therefore replicate these findings with other populations and with different academic content.

Teacher Signals. Because direct instruction is often implemented in small groups, signals are used to elicit unison responding. In direct instruction teaching, group unison responding serves several purposes. Signaling (a) keeps all students actively engaged in the instructional lesson, (b) allows for efficient group testing, and (c) increases the time students are actively engaged in learning activities. In direct instruction training programs, a considerable amount of time and effort is devoted to helping teachers master the art of using instructional signals. Given this, it is important to determine whether studies have demonstrated the positive effects of using signals during direct instruction teaching.

A study conducted by Cowart, Carnine, and Becker (1976) assessed the effects of signaling during direct instruction. The experimental design allowed for the researchers to compare the performance of students during teacher signaling with their performance when teachers taught with traditional methods. The researchers were able to control instructional content; that is, students were taught similar content in each instructional condition. Cowart and associates found that signaling resulted in higher rates of responding and attending. When the teacher used signals to elicit group responses, the students were attentive 55% of the time and responded 80% of the time. Conversely, when the teacher did not use signals, students attended less, about 35% of the time, and responded only

60% of the time. The authors also reported that the positive effects of signaling were found during whole-class instruction. For example, in one classroom when the teacher used signals to elicit unison responding, attending averaged approximately 54% of the time. However, when this teacher did not use signals, attending averaged approximately 30% of the time. Similar effects were found when percentage of responding was assessed. The responding percentage was 77% when signals were used and 57% when they were not used. No other studies that have investigated the effects of signaling have shown strong positive effects. Future research should be conducted to replicate these findings as well as to determine whether signals are useful. These studies need to determine whether teachers using signals can expect consistent, reliable effects.

Praise. Although there are many investigations that have shown that teacher praise can have a positive effect on the performance of students, it is interesting to note that there are only a few studies that have been reported that have evaluated the effects of teacher praise during direct instruction. Of these, earlier studies looked at the effects of teacher praise during large group instruction. For example, Thomas, Becker, and Armstrong (1968) and Madsen, Becker, and Thomas (1968) showed that teacher attention to appropriate student behavior in the form of praise was more effective than either rules or teacher reprimands. In similar fashion, Hall, Lund, and Jackson (1968) and Cossairt, Hall, and Hopkins (1973) found that teacher praise coupled with positive physical contact effectively increased students' study behaviors in a large-group instructional context.

Other studies have investigated the effects of praise during small-group, direct instruction. In a single subject design study by Kryzanowski (1976), systematic use of praise during instructional activities was found to be effective in increasing the level of on-task behavior in each of the subjects. There was no academic measure used in this investigation. However, Darch and Gersten (1986) looked at the effects of praise on academic performance as well as on-task behavior during small-group direct instruction. This study, discussed in an earlier section of this chapter, used four elementary students as subjects and evaluated the isolated and combined effects of instructional pacing and praise. The results showed that praise was a more powerful instructional tool than rapid pacing on both performance measures, percentage of on-task behavior and percentage of correct responding. However, the results also indicated that the combination of the two variables, rapid pacing and praise, had the most powerful effect on the performance of elementary-aged students with learning disabilities. In summary, for pronounced increases in achievement and improvements in the manageability of students, the teacher should consider combining pacing and praise techniques.

Frequent Oral Responding. Direct instruction programs are designed so that students are actively participating during instruction. One method that direct instruction programs use to accomplish this objective is to require that students engage in frequent oral responding. In a direct instruction activity, the students spend a significant amount of their time responding orally during individual or group turns. The quote below, taken from the teacher's guide for the *Corrective Reading Series* (Engelmann, 1988), a popular direct instruction program for teaching low-performing students decoding skills, gives the reader a sense of the prominent role oral responding plays in this model:

> When tasks calling for group answer are presented, the entire group should respond on signal. By listening carefully to the responses, the teacher can tell both which students make mistakes and which ones respond late. . . . As a result, the teacher will be able to correct specific mistakes, maximize the amount of practice and evaluate the performance of each student. (p. 24)

Low-performing students often are reluctant to respond during instructional activities (Brophy & Evertson, 1976). Group responding is one method that teachers can use to facilitate the participation of reticent students. Even though not many studies have looked at the effects of frequent oral responding, a few have been completed that suggest the significance of this teaching technique (Darch, 1990). Durling and Schick (1976) and Blank and Frank (1971) reported that oral responding resulted in improved performance when compared to instructional conditions that did not require overt responding. Abramson and Kagen (1975) reported similar findings. Students who responded orally to material outperformed other students who were required only to read material. These results suggest that oral responding can improve the learning of low-performing students.

There are several possible reasons why frequent oral responding is an important teaching technique to use during small-group direct instruction. Oral responding allows the teacher to monitor more carefully the performance of the students. Rather than allowing students to study independently and rarely requiring students to respond directly to questions, teachers who require frequent student responses are in a better position to determine if reteaching a concept is necessary. This is particularly important with the lower-performing students in the group. In addition, some research suggests that learning-disabled students may have a tendency to be passive learners, which, in part, may account for some of their performance problems. Frequent oral responding helps the teacher more effectively engage this type of student during the instructional activity.

RESEARCH ON CURRICULUM DESIGN FEATURES IN DIRECT INSTRUCTION

Another way to determine the effectiveness of the direct instruction model is to look at studies that have evaluated the curriculum design principles that govern the construction of materials. The major principles that have received attention are (a) teaching students explicit learning strategies, (b) careful sequencing of concepts, and (c) providing strategy corrections in response to students' errors (Darch, 1989). The outcomes of these studies provide guidelines on how instructional programs can be constructed to have the greatest impact on student learning. These studies, rather than being comprehensive like the research discussed earlier, are smaller in scale and singular in focus. In these studies, the researcher asks questions like, "What is the best sequence of letter introduction when students are first taught sound–symbol relationships?" or, "What is the most effective spelling instruction sequence when teaching students entry-level spelling skills?" This research provides some answers to practical questions about how we can teach most effectively.

Reading Research.   Two important curriculum design features found in all of the direct instruction entry-level reading programs are the careful sequencing of the introduction of letters when teaching students how to sound out words and the use of cumulative review procedures. Carnine (1976) investigated the effects of each of these principles by evaluating (a) the effectiveness of separating similar-sounding letters (e.g., e and i) during early reading instruction and (b) the effects of using cumulative review procedures to enhance mastery of previously learned information. The subjects for this study were first graders who were being taught decoding skills. The results of this study showed that students who were taught from a letter-introduction sequence that separated auditorily similar letters learned considerably more than they did from a sequence that did not control this variable (51% correct vs. 33% correct).

Teaching students to sound out words is an important design feature in direct instruction reading programs. A substantial body of research supports this teaching approach with elementary students. Studies by Carnine (1977) and Vanderever and Neville (1976) demonstrated the superiority of the sounding-out strategy as opposed to a whole-word teaching approach. In the study by Carnine, students were also taught how to blend sounds together to form words. A very effective strategy with low-skilled readers has been to teach them blending after they have been taught sound–symbol relationships.

There is also a considerable body of research on teaching students comprehension skills using direct instruction procedures. In one study, Baumann (1986) tested a strategy approach that was designed to teach students how to identify the main idea of reading passages. Sixth grade students were taught with a direct instruction program, an instructional program that taught main ideas using traditional basal procedures, or one that used vocabulary development. The results of this study showed that students who were trained to use a five-step direct instruction procedure outperformed students from each of the other experimental groups. Other reading areas where direct instruction strategy teaching has proven to be effective are in (a) metacognition (e.g., Baumann et al., 1987), (b) inferences (e.g., Carnine et al., 1982), and (c) using context (e.g., Carnine et al., 1984).

Direct Instruction procedures have also been shown to be effective in teaching learning-disabled students critical reading skills (e.g., identifying faulty arguments, determining the trustworthiness of an author, and discriminating evidence from opinion). Patching, Kameenui, Carnine, Gersten, and Colvin (1983) evaluated three approaches for teaching critical reading: (a) a direct instruction strategy, (b) a workbook with teacher-feedback approach, and (c) a no-intervention condition. The results of this investigation showed that students who were provided direct instruction that taught the application of strategies outperformed students from the other groups on a series of critical reading measures. Darch and Kameenui (1987) replicated and extended these results to learning-disabled students by investigating direct instruction teaching that included the use of strategy corrections. In this study, if students were unable to apply one of the critical reading strategies that were taught to them, the teacher provided explicit, step-by-step strategy corrections. Results favored the direct instruction approach that used strategy corrections. These corrections helped the student understand the application of the strategy rather then merely teaching them to blindly follow steps. This type of correction procedure is quite different from the procedures usually found in traditional materials. In these programs students are often just supplied the correct answer in the complete absence of a strategy correction.

Math Research. Teaching students to use explicit strategies is a design feature of the direct instruction curriculum that has been demonstrated to be effective in several math skill areas. Whether the area is instruction in addition or subtraction (Kameenui et al., 1986) or in more advanced areas such as analyzing fractions (Carnine, 1977) or instruction in word-problem solving (Darch et al., 1984; Wilson & Sindelar, 1991), students, particularly those who are low performers, benefit from strategy instruction.

Kameenui, Carnine, Darch, and Stein (1986) investigated whether a traditional teaching approach that used pictures and manipulatives was more effective in teaching elementary students subtraction than was a direct instruction counting strategy. This study used 26 first-graders as subjects. These students were randomly assigned to either the direct instruction group who were taught a counting strategy or to the traditional instruction group, an instructional program based on a composite of several basal mathematics programs. The results of this study indicated that students who were taught to implement a direct instruction counting strategy outperformed those students who were taught using pictures and manipulatives.

Many students, particularly low-performing students, have difficulty learning how to solve word story problems. There is a body of descriptive research that indicates that how story problems are constructed can add to their difficulty. For example, the order of information that is presented in the story, the placement of the unknown factor, the complexity of the operations required, and whether the problem requires the student to use classification skills contribute to the difficulty of story problems. Rosenthal and Resnick (1974) have demonstrated that when the unknown came first and the events in the problem were presented in reverse order, the problem was more difficult to solve. Also, Blankenship and Lovitt (1976) have shown that the inclusion of extraneous information made story problems more difficult to solve. Low-performing students are particularly affected by complex story problems. Research has been reported that has evaluated the effects of direct instruction in teaching students to solve story problems.

Darch and co-workers (1984) evaluated the effects of using an explicit strategy training program that put considerable emphasis on teaching students to identify the correct operation, as opposed to teaching students to translate story problems directly into an equation. The direct instruction strategy did not focus on computational issues, but rather focused on how students should determine the correct operation to solve the problem. Other researchers have presented results that support the technique of teaching students to use strategies systematically when learning how to solve word problems (e.g., Fleishner et al., 1987).

Wilson and Sindelar (1991) demonstrated the effectiveness of using direct instruction strategies when teaching math word problems to learning-disabled students in the elementary grades. In this study, learning-disabled students were taught to solve math word problems. The study was designed to evaluate the relative significance of (a) an explicit problem-solving strategy and (b) use of carefully controlled teaching and practice examples. The results of this study indicated that students who were taught to use a problem-solving strategy from a series of carefully controlled teaching and practice examples performed at significantly higher levels than did students who were not taught an explicit strategy. These results are consistent with the findings of Darch and colleagues (1984).

Science and Social Studies Research. Instruction in most classrooms conveys information through texts, films, lectures, and discussions. The manner in which texts are structured is related to the ability of students to comprehend (Geva, 1983; Goetz & Armbruster, 1980; Marshall & Glock, 1978; Mayer, 1978). The principles of direct instruction have recently been applied to the area of advanced organizers in science and social studies content. Advanced organizers are materials and preteaching activities that a teacher uses to highlight and preview important concepts that will be presented in either lecture or text reading.

One particularly useful format for organizing information is through the application of visual–spatial displays. Visual displays attempt to facilitate the initial introduction of material by using lines, arrows, and spatial arrangements that highlight text content, structure, and key concepts (Engelmann & Carnine, 1982). Students are given a preview of a lesson by the teacher carefully presenting the visual–spatial representation of the critical concepts. Providing students such an overview, it is postulated, will enhance the comprehension of the material.

Darch and Carnine (1986) looked at the effectiveness of visual–spatial displays in a study with learning-disabled students. This study examined two approaches to teaching learning-disabled students literal comprehension during a social studies unit. An approach that utilized a visual–spatial display was contrasted to a traditional teaching approach where the teacher introduced the unit with a lecture and student learning activities that were designed to increase motivation. For both learning conditions, students studied content in groups. Twenty-four fourth-, fifth-, and sixth-grade students with learning disabilities were randomly assigned to one of the two instructional groups. Daily instructional sessions lasted 50 minutes and continued for 9 consecutive school days. The results indicated that students who were provided an overview of the content with a visual–spatial display learned more than did students who were provided traditional instruction. The learning differences were present on several daily probe tests as well as on a unit post-test. However, no differences were found on a transfer test. The reason for the failure of students with learning disabilities to transfer these skills is fairly obvious. Learning-disabled students probably need extensive practice using visual displays before transfer can be expected.

The use of visual–spatial displays with high school students with learning disabilities during science instruction has also been investigated (Darch & Eaves, 1986). Students in grades 9 to 11 served as subjects. One group of students was taught by presenting key concepts with a visual–spatial display of information while the other group was taught the same content, except that teaching was done primarily with text and lecture. The results of this study replicated previous findings. The outcomes favored the group taught with the visual–spatial display on the short-term recall tests, but no differences were found on the transfer test. These studies suggest that short-term recall of critical concepts is enhanced by explicitly detailed instruction, intensive practice of key concepts, and a schema to help students to organize important concepts in the unit. Text approaches that use semistructured discussion, with time allotted for students to read from a text individually, will probably be less helpful to students, particularly students with learning disabilities.

Visual–spatial displays are not the only type of advanced organizers that can be used during comprehension instruction. A study reported by Darch and Gersten (1986) demonstrated the effectiveness of using an advanced organizer in the form of a detailed outline. In this study two types of preteaching activities were evaluated among high school students with learning disabilities. One group of students was taught with a prereading activity patterned after the approach used in some basal programs to foster attention. The major focus of this condition was on (a) developing student interest and motivation, (b) highlighting the importance of the passage to the students' past experiences, and (c) offering a general introductory discussion. The second group in this study was provided direct instruction using an advanced organizer in the form of a text outline designed to help students process and organize information from the text. The results of this study showed that high school learning-disabled students who were taught with a combination of direct instruction and advanced organizers outperformed students taught with the basal approach.

Spelling Research. Teaching spelling to students in the elementary grades is an instructional area that has received a considerable amount of attention in recent years. This interest has been fueled by the awareness that many mildly handicapped students experience difficulty in this area of written expression. However, there are a few experimental studies that have validated the effectiveness of specific instructional approaches. That is not to say that there are no articles that discuss the merits of one spelling instruction approach over another, but few of these papers provide the reader with data that validate the author's position. There have, however, been two studies that investigated the effectiveness of two spelling programs, *Spelling Through Morphographs* and the *Spelling Mastery Program,* programs that incorporate direct instruction curriculum design principles.

Robinson and Hess (1981) evaluated the differential effectiveness of the *Spelling Through Morphographs* with low-, average-, and high-performing seventh-grade students. This program is designed to teach students generalizable spelling skills through the application of teaching morphographs and explicit rule-based instruction. Overall, the results of this study indicated that students taught with *Spelling Through Mastery,* a direct instruction program, displayed significant achievement gains in spelling when compared to controls. The instructional program was less successful with the high-performing students. The results clearly indicated the beneficial effects of the direct instruction design principles with teaching average- and low-performing students spelling.

In another study, Darch and Simpson (1990) evaluated the effectiveness of the *Spelling Mastery Program,* a direct instruction curriculum used for teaching entry-level spelling skills. The subjects for this study were 28 learning-disabled students who attended a university-based summer-school program. The purpose of this study was to investigate the relative effectiveness of two approaches for teaching spelling. One group of students was taught spelling with a visual imagery mnemonic, a popular teaching approach in many special education classrooms. The other group was taught spelling using rule-based teaching strategies developed from direct instruction curriculum design principles (the *Spelling Mastery Program*). Instructional procedures lasted several weeks for this investigation. Three measures were used to evaluate each of the teaching approaches: (a) a 10-item unit test, administered every ten lessons; (b) a post-test comprised of randomly selected words from all lessons in each instructional program; and (c) the Test of Written Language, a standardized spelling test that allowed for the evaluation of phonetically regular and irregular words. The results of this study showed that the students who were taught spelling with the direct instruction program outperformed the students who were taught with the visual-imagery program on each of the measures used. This study adds support to the notion that learning-disabled students learn most during rule-based strategy teaching.

The explicit, rule-based spelling strategies that were used in each of the direct instruction programs described above facilitated successful learning. Research in memory performance of low-performing students has shown that these students often exhibit retrieval, organizational, and/or selective-attention deficits (Tarver et al., 1976). Teaching these students rule-based strategies enhances their ability to perform memory tasks. Strategies provide students an organized and efficient way to analyze and solve new learning tasks.

WHY DIRECT INSTRUCTION PROGRAMS ARE EFFECTIVE

The driving force behind the direct instruction model was put simply but forcefully by Engelmann and Carnine (1982):

> If we are humanists, we begin with the obvious fact that the children we work with are perfectly capable of learning anything that we have to teach. We further recognize that we should be able to engineer the learning so that it is reinforcing, perhaps not "fun," but challenging and engaging. (p. 376)

In this chapter, research has been reviewed that supports the use of direct instruction procedures in a variety of content areas. Considered together, this body of work provides evidence that there exists a set of research-based teaching techniques and instructional design principles that can be used in both regular and special education classrooms. The major components of the direct instruction model that contribute to this kind of success are listed and discussed below.

The Details of Instruction Are Controlled.   An important factor that contributes to the success of direct instruction programs is that all the important details of instruction are carefully controlled. Gersten and co-workers (1986) stated why this is important when working with low-performing students: "The key principle in the design of Direct Instruction programs is deceptively simple: For all students to learn, both the materials and the teacher presentation of these materials must be clear and unambiguous" (p. 18). For example, lesson scripts provide the teacher with precise instructional wording. The scripted lessons ensure that teachers introduce concepts to students in an orderly and efficient manner. The scripted presentations provide teachers with specific teaching examples, a sequence of teaching activities, and an array of test examples. Because these important details are controlled by the instructional programmer, the teacher can focus his or her effort on efficiently using instructional time.

Explicit Strategies Are Taught to Students.   An important characteristic of direct instruction programs is that students are taught explicit, step-by-step strategies. As the research reviewed in this chapter has shown, strategy instruction is effective in each of the major content areas. Unlike the approach taken in many traditional programs, where students are sometimes left to their own devices to complete new learning tasks, students are provided intensive instruction in the application of specified learning strategies. These carefully crafted instructional sequences help students to attack new learning tasks systematically. The use of strategy instruction with low-performing students is particularly important as research has shown that many of these students have tremendous difficulty in developing learning strategies on their own. When these students are left to their own devices, they resort to guessing or, sometimes, not responding at all. Strategies also allow for mastery teaching of subskills. By teaching the component parts of the strategy, students have an opportunity to learn complex strategies gradually in relatively easy learning contexts. Because students are carefully guided by the teacher, it is easier to ensure that the students are applying the strategy correctly. Future research will help to identify what are the most effective and efficient strategies for specific skills in the various content areas.

Students Are Monitored and Corrections Are Provided. Direct instruction programs use continuous testing procedures to ensure that the teacher can monitor the performance of all the students in the instructional group. By closely monitoring students, the teacher is in an excellent position to make instructional adjustments when needed. Because explicit strategies are taught to students, mistakes can be corrected immediately and precisely. Rather than just providing students with correct answers, direct instruction correction sequences focus on the process for determining the correct answer. This is quite different from the approach taken in many traditional instructional programs. In basal programs teachers will often overlook students' errors because correction procedures are not specified by the program.

Success Rate of Students. The underlying theme of the direct instruction model is to design and implement programs that ensure the success of all students. It is the emphasis on success that is perhaps the most important feature of the direct instruction model. Teaching students explicit problem-solving strategies with carefully designed instructional sequences allows even low-performing students to experience success. Once these students learn that they too can compete successfully in a learning environment, improvement occurs in their attitudes toward learning and in their self-concept. Engelmann and Carnine (1982) have commented on the importance of providing students a powerful teaching program that leads to success: "Let's recognize the incredible potential for being intelligent and creativity possessed by even the least impressive children, and with unyielding passion, let's pursue the goal of assuring that this potential becomes a reality" (p. 376). Direct instruction is a model that educators can use to realize the potential of all students. Perhaps with the implementation of effective instructional programs, we will not hear a student like John say, "I wish I could do better."

REFERENCES

Abramson, T., & Kagan, E. (1975). Familiarization of content and differential response modes in programmed instruction. *Journal of Educational Psychology, 67,* 83–88.

Baumann, J.F. (1986). The direct instruction of main idea comprehension ability. In J.F. Baumann (Ed.), *Teaching main idea comprehension* (pp. 133–178). Newark, DE: International Reading Association.

Baumann, J.F., Seifert-Kessell, N., & Jones, L.A. (1987). *Effect of think aloud instruction on elementary students' ability to monitor their comprehension.* Paper presented at the 37th Annual Meeting of the National Reading Conference, St. Petersburg, FL.

Becker, W.C. (1977). Teaching reading and language to the disadvantaged: What we have learned from field research. *Harvard Educational Review, 47*, 518–543.

Becker, W.C., & Gersten, R. (1982). A follow up of Follow Through: The later effects of the Direct Instruction Model. *American Education Research Journal, 19*, 27–55.

Blank, M., & Frank, S.M. (1971). Story recall in kindergarten children: Effect of method of presentation on psycholinguistic performance. *Child Development, 42*, 229–312.

Blankenship, C., & Lovitt, T. (1976). Story problems: Merely confusing or downright befuddling? *Journal for Research in Mathematics Education, 7*, 290–298.

Brophy, J.E., & Evertson, C.M. (1976). *Learning from teaching: A developmental perspective.* Boston: Allyn & Bacon.

Carnine, D. (1976). Two letter discrimination sequences: High-confusion alternatives first versus low-confusion alternatives first. *Journal of Reading Behavior, 12*, 41–47.

Carnine, D. (1977). Phonics versus look-say: Transfer to new words. *Reading Teacher, 30*, 636, 640.

Carnine, D., Kameenui, E., & Coyle, G. (1984). Utilization of contextual information in determining the meaning of unfamiliar words. *Reading Research Quarterly, 19*, 188–204.

Carnine, D., Kameenui, E., & Wolfson, N. (1982). Training of textual dimensions related to text based inferences. *Journal of Reading Behavior, 14*, 182–187.

Cossairt, A., Hall, V., & Hopkins, B.L. (1973). The effect of experimenter's instructions, feedback, and praise on teacher praise and student attending behavior. *Journal of Applied Behavior Analysis, 6*, 89–100.

Cowart, J., Carnine, D., & Becker, W.C. (1976). The effects of signals on attending, responding, and following in direct instruction. In W.C. Becker & S. Engelmann (Eds.), *Technical Report 1976-1, Appendix B.* Eugene, OR: University of Oregon.

Darch, C. (1989). Comprehension instruction for high school learning disabled students. *Research in Rural Education, 5*, 43–49.

Darch, C. (1990). Research on direct instruction. In Carnine, D., Silbert, J., & Kameenui, E. *Direct instruction reading* (pp. 23–33). Columbus, OH: Merrill Publishing Co.

Darch, C., & Carnine, D. (1986). Teaching content area material to learning disabled students. *Exceptional Children, 53*, 240–246.

Darch, C., Carnine, D., & Gersten, R. (1984). Explicit instruction in mathematics problem solving. *Journal of Educational Research, 77*, 350–359.

Darch, D., & Eaves, R. (1986). The use of visual displays during content instruction to increase comprehension of high school LD students. *Journal of Special Education, 20*, 309–318.

Darch, C., & Gersten, R. (1986). Direction-setting activities in reading comprehension: A comparison of two approaches. *Learning Disabilities Quarterly, 9*, 235–243.

Darch, C., & Kameenui, E. (1987). Teaching critical reading skills to learning disabled children. *Learning Disabilities Quarterly, 10*, 82–92.

Darch, C., Rabren, K., & Dyas, J. (1991). Preparing teachers of learning disabled students to work in rural settings: A direct instruction model. *California Journal for Supervision and Curriculum Improvement, 5*, 16–24.

Darch, C., & Simpson, R. (1990). Effectiveness of visual imagery versus rule-based strategies in teaching spelling to learning disabled students. *Research in Rural Education, 7*, 61–70.

Durling, R., & Schick, C. (1976). Concept attainment by pairs and individuals as a function of vocalization. *Journal of Educational Psychology, 68*, 83–91.

Emmer, E.T., Evertson, C., Sanford, J., & Clements, S. (1982). *Improving classroom management: An experimental study in junior high classrooms.* Austin, TX: Research and Development Center for Teacher Education, University of Texas.

Engelmann, S. (1988). *Corrective reading series.* Chicago: Science Research Associates.

Engelmann, S., Becker, W., Carnine, W., & Gersten, R. (1988). The Direct Instruction Follow Through Model: Design and outcomes. *Education and Treatment of Children, 11,* 303–317.

Engelmann, S., & Bruner, E. (1974). DISTAR Reading Series. Chicago: Science Research Associates.

Engelmann, S., & Carnine, D. (1982). *Theory of instruction: Principles and applications.* New York: Irvington Publishers.

Fleishner, J.E., Nuzum, M.B., & Marzola, E.S. (1987). Devising an instructional program to teach arithmetic problem solving skills to students with learning disabilities. *Journal of Learning Disabilities, 20,* 214–217.

Gersten, R., Becker, W.C., Heiry, T.J., & White, W.A.T. (1984). Entry IQ and yearly academic growth of children in direct instruction programs: A longitudinal study of low SES children. *Educational Evaluation & Policy Analysis, 6,* 109–121.

Gersten, R., Darch, C., & Gleason, M. (1988a). Effectiveness of a direct instruction academic kindergarten for low-income students. *Elementary School Journal, 89,* 227–240.

Gersten, R., & Keating, T. (1987). Improving high school performance of "at-risk" students: A study of long-term benefits of direct instruction. *Educational Leadership, 44,* 28–31.

Gersten, R., Keating, T., & Becker, W. (1988b). The continued impact of the direct instruction model: Longitudinal studies of Follow Through students. *Education and Treatment of Children, 11,* 318–327.

Gersten, R., Woodward, J., & Darch, C. (1986). Direct instruction: A research based approach to curriculum design and teaching. *Exceptional Children, 53,* 17–31.

Geva, E. (1983). Facilitating reading comprehension through flowcharting. *Reading Research Quarterly, 18,* 384–404.

Goetz, E.T., & Armbruster, B.B. (1980). Psychological correlates of text structure. In B.J. Spiro, B.C. Bruce, & W.F. Brewer (Eds.), *Theoretical issues in reading comprehension.* Hillsdale, NJ: Erlbaum, 1980.

Good, T.L., & Grouws, D.A. (1979). The Missouri mathematics effectiveness project. *Journal of Educational Psychology, 71,* 355–362.

Hall, V., Lund, D., & Jackson, D. (1968). Effects of teacher attention on study behavior. *Journal of Applied Behavior Analysis, 1,* 1–12.

Kameenui, E., Carnine, D., Darch, C., & Stein, M. (1986). Two approaches to the development phase of mathematics instruction. *Elementary School Journal, 86,* 633–650.

Kryzanowski, J. (1976). Praise effects on on-task behavior during small group instruction. In W.C. Becker & S. Engelmann (Eds.), *Technical Report 76–1, Appendix B, Formative Research Studies.* Eugene, OR: Follow Through Project, University of Oregon.

Madsen, C., Becker, W.C., & Thomas, D.R. (1968). Rules, praise, and ignoring: Elements of elementary classroom control. *Journal of Applied Behavior Analysis, 1,* 139–150.

Marshall, W., & Glock, M. (1978). Comprehension of connected discourse: A study into the relationships between the structure of the text and information recalled. *Reading Research Quarterly, 13,* 10–56.

Mayer, R.E. (1978). Advanced organizers that compensate for the organization of text. *Journal of Educational Psychology, 70,* 880–886.

Meyer, L., Gersten, R., & Gutkin, J. (1983). Direct instruction: A project follow through success story in an inner-city school. *Elementary School Journal, 84,* 241–252.

Patching, W., Kameenui, E., Carnine, D., Gersten, R., & Colvin, G. (1983). Direct instruction in critical reading skills. *Reading Research Quarterly, 18,* 406–418.

Robinson, J.W., & Hess, K.D., (1981). A morphemically based spelling program's effect on spelling skills and spelling performance of seventh grade students. *Journal of Educational Research, 75,* 56–62.

Rosenshine, B. (1976). Classroom instruction. In L. Gage (Ed.), *The psychology of teaching methods: The seventy-fifth yearbook of the National Society for the Study of Education.* Chicago: University of Chicago Press.

Rosenthal, D.J.A., & Resnick, L.B. (1974). Children's solution processes in arithmetic word problems. *Journal of Educational Psychology, 66,* 817–825.

Stebbins, L., St. Pierre, R.G., Proper, E.C., Anderson, R.B., & Cerva, T.R. (1977). *Education as experimentation: A planned variation model* (Vols. IV A-D). Cambridge, MA: Abt Associates.

Tarver, S., Hallahan, D., Kaufman, J., & Ball, D. (1976). Verbal rehearsal and selective attention in children with learning disabilities: A developmental lag. *Journal of Experimental Child Psychology, 22,* 375–385.

Thomas, D.R., Becker, W.C., & Armstrong, J. (1968). Production and elimination of disruptive classroom behavior by systematically varying teacher's behavior. *Journal of Applied Behavior Analysis, 1,* 35–45.

Vanderever, T.R., & Neville, D.D. (1976). Transfer as a result of synthetic and analytic reading instruction. *American Journal of Mental Deficiency, 30,* 498–503.

Weisberg, P. (1988). Direct Instruction in the preschool. *Education and Treatment of Children, 11,* 349–363.

West, R.P. (1981). *The effect of two levels of teacher presentation rate and reinforcement rate on classroom disruptions, performance accuracy, and response rate.* Unpublished doctoral dissertation. Salt Lake City: University of Utah.

Wilson, C., & Sindelar, P. (1991). Direct instruction in math word problems: Students with learning disabilities. *Exceptional Children, 57,* 512–520.

6

Translating Research: Classroom Application of Validated Instructional Strategies

Susan Fister
Karen Kemp

Educational researchers and others have been deeply concerned over the past several years that the knowledge base for school improvement has often been ignored. This has resulted in the application of practices that have not been based on empirical evidence. Additionally, teachers do not always know how to translate effectively available research into practical classroom activities (Everston, 1987). Ultimately, the student becomes the victim of ineffective teaching practices. There have been numerous attempts to interpret research to the classroom teacher; most approaches have not been successful. Although researchers have pleaded with teachers to consider educational research, the fact remains that the knowledge on teaching and learning is not systematically integrated into classroom practice (Goodlad, 1983). Barbara Bateman, writing on academic child abuse, contends that the biggest problem with educational leaders and decision makers is their lack of respect for data. There *are* approaches that work much better than others. Yet teachers within the system are influenced by decision makers and continue to be naive about instruction. In fact, teachers "are denied access to effective instruction and the facts about what works and what doesn't" (Bateman, 1991).

A variety of reasons account for the delays from research discovery to practical involvement: failure to hold decision makers accountable for the performance of students (Bateman, 1991), failure to communicate research findings and data in ways that are "user friendly," failure to field-test practices adequately in classroom settings, failure to consider implementation costs realistically, failure to consider research findings on effective staff-development procedures, and failure to establish model sites for the demonstration of proven innovations.

The gap between research and classroom practice has been of particular concern in the area of strategy instruction. Too often educators assume that

107

students automatically acquire effective strategies. Therefore, teachers do not devote direct instructional time to this area. Furthermore, teachers are frequently not aware of validated strategies that are necessary for student success in classroom situations and in daily life (Palloway & Patton, 1989).

A collaborative effort began in 1986 when researchers at the University of Washington and practitioners from the Utah Learning Resource Center (ULRC) attempted to bridge gaps between research and practice in the area of strategy instruction. The purpose of the project was to determine if strategies that had been proven in research studies could be effectively implemented by teachers. During the course of the 4-year Research Translation and Demonstration Project, a variety of strategies were validated in classroom settings, revalidated, and then disseminated to teachers. Products from the grant included a series of teacher training video tapes on strategy instruction entitled *Translating Research into Practice* (TRIP).

DEFINITIONS

For the purpose of the study, the term *strategy* was defined as a careful plan or method, or the act of employing a specific plan or method, designed to achieve a goal. Strategies were examined in two areas: teaching and learning. *Teaching strategies* were defined as methods or techniques that are developed, controlled, and managed by the teacher. These strategies include the use of systematic plans and require decisions on the part of the teacher regarding *what* information is presented, *when* it is presented, and *how* it is presented to students (Lovitt et al., 1990). For example, a teacher may use an overhead transparency of a graphic organizer to assist in the presentation of information so that students will be better able to organize and retain the important concepts. *Learning strategies* were defined as methods or techniques the student uses, controls, and manages in order to promote effective processing, storage, and retrieval of information. Both teaching and learning strategies are considered unique in that they facilitate memory, problem solving, and independent learning (Alley & Deshler, 1979).

The research project targeted four major themes: adapting materials, study skills, social skills, and self-management. Table 6.1 outlines the specific strategies that were researched within each theme. Upon validation, video training tapes were developed on eight strategy topics: graphic organizers, study guides, vocabulary practice sheets, self-monitoring, classwide peer tutoring, social skills, reading strategies, and cooperative learning. The intent of this chapter is to address five of these strategies: vocabulary practice sheets, study guides, cooperative learning, self-management, and graphic organizers. These represent teaching and learning strategies that had the greatest impact on student performance as well as those that were easily blended into instructional settings for a variety of content areas and grade levels.

Table 6.1 Research themes and topics

Themes	Year 1 1987–1988	Year 2 1988–1989	Year 3 1989–1990	Year 4 1990–1991
Adapting materials	Study guides* Graphic organizers*	Study guides* Graphic organizers* Precision teaching vocabulary practice sheets*	Precision teaching vocabulary practice sheets*	
Study skills	Key words	Scanning for information*	Scanning for information* Note taking	Classwide peer tutoring*
Social skills		Compliance	Social skills* One-minute teaching interaction	Cooperative learning*
Self-management			Self-monitoring*	Self-monitoring*
Number of participants	1,353	1,128	436	924

*Available on video training tape.

GENERAL PROJECT METHODS

The purposes of all investigations were to (a) determine if teachers, after attending a 1-day training session, were able to implement the approach with their students; (b) demonstrate the usefulness of the approaches as shown by the degree to which the intervention influenced student performance; and (c) gather teacher and student reactions to the approach. A brief definition of the intervention, discussion of research methods and results, and procedures for classroom application are provided for each strategy.

It should be noted that for all research projects conducted over the 4-year period, teachers and facilitators participated on a volunteer basis. Local district directors and principals often identified possible participants. Established statewide communication networks such as the Special Education Consortium meetings, Mentor Academy trainings, and the *Utah Special Educator* newsletter were also used to inform teachers of the upcoming training on a selected strategy. A pre-training session was scheduled and conducted in each district to explain general study procedures and participant responsibilities. A local district facilitator or a ULRC staff member presented this information to potential participants. Additionally, for all research projects, teachers were informed that they would receive a small stipend (between $50 and $100) for carrying out the project. At the completion of the orientation session, teachers agreeing to participate signed a commitment form. A 1-day training session was then held for teachers who had signed up to conduct the classroom research on a designated strategy. This training explained the strategy, outlined procedures for collecting and recording data, and provided practice in developing the strategy for classroom implementation. Training materials were provided to all participants, along with all of the materials necessary for classroom implementation. (Materials included a training notebook, computer software for developing quizzes, student and teacher data forms, questionnaires, transparencies, etc.). After training, teachers returned to their classrooms, introduced the approach to students, and monitored their performance. Participants also had the opportunity to register for three credit hours from a local university. Requirements included carrying out the classroom research, submitting data from their study, and writing summaries of their experiences.

PROJECT DESIGN AND PROCEDURES

Experimental designs for each of the studies described in this chapter are illustrated in Table 6.2. The design was selected partly in consideration of teachers' instructional schedules and partly in an attempt to standardize the implementation of the strategy across several teachers.

Table 6.2 Experimental designs used in the research project

Study	Design	Independent Measure(s)	Dependent Measure(s)
Precision teaching vocabulary practice sheets	10 days of baseline 10 days of intervention 5 days of rest 2 days of retention-baseline 2 days of retention-intervention	Precision teaching practice sheets were scheduled	Rate of correct/incorrect responses on quizzes
Study guides	10 days of baseline 10 days of intervention 5 days of rest 2 days of retention-baseline 2 days of retention-intervention	Study guides were scheduled	Rate of correct/incorrect responses on quizzes
Cooperative learning	10 days of baseline 15 days of intervention (5 days of training in the model) 5 days of rest 2 days of retention-baseline 2 days of retention-intervention	Jigsaw and SMARTS methods were scheduled	Rate of correct/incorrect responses on quizzes Comparison of social behavior across phases
Self-management	10 days of baseline 10 days of intervention A 10 days of intervention B 5 days of rest 5 days of retention	A = self-monitoring B = self-monitoring plus reinforcement	Count of correct/incorrect behavior across an instructional period
Graphic organizers	10 days of baseline 10 days of intervention 4 days of retention-baseline 4 days of retention-intervention	Graphic organizers were scheduled	Rate of correct/incorrect responses on quizzes

GENERAL PROJECT RESULTS

Workshop evaluations were completed by the participating teachers at the conclusion of the 1-day training. Overall ratings for the inservice training sessions ranged from 3.25 to 5.0 on a Likert-type scale, with 5 being the most favorable. Some questions elicited free responses. Comments expressed a general excitement about the use of the techniques. For the most part, respondents agreed to carry out the intervention. However, in a few cases, teachers felt that they could not take on a project of this magnitude but indicated that they would use the technique with their students.

The onset of the classroom research procedures usually occurred within 1 to 3 weeks of the initial training session. Teachers' implementations of the research procedures were assessed during telephone conversations (which usually occurred on the first Friday of implementation), classroom visits by the ULRC project staff, and classroom visits by district facilitators who had attended the training. Copies of teacher-generated materials, quizzes, and student data sheets were collected at the conclusion of the study. Teachers who elected the university credit option either submitted an audio tape of their instructions to students regarding the strategy that was used during the intervention phase and/or a write-up of their research. Although teachers demonstrated the procedures during the training, no specific records were kept regarding how the procedures were used by individual teachers throughout the study.

The evaluation of student performance involved one or more of the following analysis methods: mean rate, average percent correct, and performance change. Additionally, both students and teachers were asked to respond to Likert-type scale surveys regarding the success of the strategy, ease of implementation, and likelihood of using the strategy on completion of the study.

The five strategies, vocabulary practice sheets, study guides, cooperative learning, self-management, and graphic organizers, are discussed separately. Each strategy includes a definition along with a description of design and procedures, results, and classroom application procedures specific to the procedure.

Precision-Teaching Vocabulary-Practice Sheets

Definition. A precision-teaching vocabulary-development strategy was defined as a rate-based drill activity consisting of key vocabulary and definitions from selected course content. This teaching strategy required students to practice a specified number of definitions, which were paired with the associated key vocabulary and repeated over a specified time period. Figure 6.1 illustrates one of three formats used in the vocabulary-development strategy: (a) boxes with words and corresponding definitions/answers on reverse side; (b) folded sheets with words and corresponding definitions, and (c) sets of index cards with words on one side and corresponding definitions on the back side.

The vocabulary-development strategy was researched twice during the 4-year grant. A total of 35 general and special educators made a commitment to participate in the investigations, which included a total of 694 students, 125 of whom were students with learning disabilities.

Design and Procedure.   Following the 1-day training workshop for this strategy, teachers returned to their classrooms, constructed necessary materials like quizzes and vocabulary sheets, and then began the research. During a 10-day baseline period, teachers instructed in their typical fashion and students were allowed from 5 to 10 minutes to study key vocabulary from the daily presentation independently. The independent study time was unstructured in terms of the use of any specific study procedures. Following that study time, computer-generated quizzes were

Materials of the Earth's Crust

See/Say Vocabulary Words

1. The weight of the mineral compared to the weight of an equal volume of water.	1. Specific Gravity
2. How easily a mineral can be scratched.	2. Hardness
3. The characteristic shape of a mineral.	3. Crystal Form
4. The color left by a mineral when rubbed against a streak plate.	4. Streak
5. How a mineral splits or breaks.	5. Cleavage/Fracture
6. The ability of a mineral to reflect, bend or absorb light.	6. Luster
7. The object color as seen by the eye.	7. Color
8. How easily a mineral can be scratched.	8. Hardness
9. How a mineral splits or breaks.	9. Cleavage/Fracture
10. The weight of the mineral compared to the weight of an equal volume of water.	10. Specific Gravity
11. The color left by a mineral when rubbed against a streak plate.	11. Streak
12. The object color as seen by the eye.	12. Color
13. The characteristic shape of a mineral.	13. Crystal Form
14. The ability of a mineral to reflect, bend or absorb light.	14. Luster

(Fold down the middle on the vertical line)

Start Over   Start Over

Figure 6.1   Precision teaching vocabulary practice sheet—materials of the earth's crust.

administered covering 10 days of material, and students were allowed 3 minutes to respond to as many items as possible. Students exchanged papers for correcting (some teachers chose to do all the correcting), during which time they counted the number of correct and incorrect responses and recorded those figures onto the data sheets. Items that were not attempted were not counted in either total.

The precision-teaching vocabulary-development strategy lasted for a period of 10 days. Vocabulary presented during this phase was different from the baseline phase. Following teacher instruction, students were assigned to practice in pairs and were given 2 or 3 minutes to say the vocabulary words/concepts and corresponding definitions, using one of the suggested formats (boxes, folded paper, or index cards). The vocabulary words to be practiced were taken from the current lesson, and when time permitted, shorter 30-second or 1-minute timings were conducted on previous days' vocabulary.

The following procedure was used during intervention: one member of each pair looked at a vocabulary item and supplied the definitions; the checking partner scored the responses. The checking partner was instructed to give immediate positive feedback for correct answers. A simple error-correction procedure was used for incorrect responses ("No, the answer is _____ ."). Halfway through the practice period, partners reversed roles and the review timings continued. At the conclusion of the partner practice timings, computer-generated quizzes covering the vocabulary words for the entire 10-day unit were administered and scored, and the rates were recorded using the same method used during baseline.

A period of rest from the study was arranged for the next 5 days. During this time, teachers introduced new material. Neither the timed practice strategy nor the quizzes were scheduled for those 5 days.

Finally, a 10-day retention phase was arranged. During the first week of retention, two quizzes were administered that represented items from the baseline period. During the second week, two quizzes from the intervention set of items were administered. No accompanying instruction on these items nor any practice timings occurred during this phase. However, teachers were free to present new material during this phase.

Results. Student performance data were analyzed in three areas for this study. Group mean performance rates for each phase of the study were calculated, and comparisons were made across phases. The second analysis focused on performance accuracy as measured by average percent correct for the group within each phase. A change-score technique was used for the third area to determine individual performance change across baseline and intervention phases. These procedures enabled individual student performances to be quantified and the following questions to be addressed: (a) to what degree did the intervention influence students' average rates of responding; (b) to what extent did students' average percentages of correct responding change; (c) what percentage of students improved, stayed the same, or worsened in performance across the first two phases; and (d) did students with learning disabilities in mainstream or special education classrooms benefit more from the strategy.

Results for the first question indicated dramatic changes between the rate of correct responses, with all comparisons achieving significance. The use of precision-teaching practice sheets significantly increased the correct rate of responding of all students, including those with learning disabilities. The incorrect rates significantly changed for the overall and general education groups during the first two phases, but not for the remaining comparisons.

The analysis of performance accuracy demonstrated that all groups improved in accuracy during the intervention phase, with each group gaining between 8 to 21 percentage points. Percentage correct scores during the retention-intervention phase were also higher for all groups when compared with the retention-baseline scores. This also indicated that the average correct percentages were influenced by implementing the vocabulary practice sheets.

The third analysis demonstrated that between 65% and 68% of all students participating in the study improved from baseline to intervention, and 13% worsened. A similar pattern was revealed for the general education and special learner groups. These outcomes indicate that the majority of students improved in performance across the first two phases of the study (Stump & Lovitt, 1990).

In response to the final question regarding performance across mainstream and special education classrooms, similar numbers of students improved, stayed the same, and worsened in each placement. The majority of students with learning disabilities were placed in mainstream settings and improved in performance. The majority of general education students enrolled in these mainstream classes also improved. In terms of the performance of the general education students attending mainstream settings, there was a slight decrease in the percentage of students improving as the number of students with learning disabilities increased.

Classroom Application. Precision-teaching vocabulary practice sheets can be developed for a variety of subject areas, content areas, and grade levels. The information contained on a practice sheet should be closely aligned not only with the daily lesson but also with the critical information contained in the unit objectives. The practice sheets are best used as reinforcement and fluency-building activities that follow the presentation of new information by the teacher. The following steps can be used when developing practice sheets:

1. Select key vocabulary/concepts for the entire unit.
2. Construct lists of five to eight items to correspond with daily lessons.
3. Format the five to eight items using one of the methods illustrated (boxes, folded sheet, or cards).
4. Repeat the five to eight items at least two or three times if using the box format. (During the timed practice, students should have multiple opportunities to practice each item. Students can start over when they finish the list or pile of cards.)
5. Practice new concepts and review each day, individually, or with a partner, for short, timed sessions (i.e., 1 to 3 minutes).

Students can be taught how to make their own practice sheets or sets of cards, which can be stored in student folders or card files. Response modes can be varied (oral, written, performance, etc.). Additional ideas and training information can be obtained by viewing the TRIP Strategies Video program on Vocabulary Practice Sheets (1990).

Study Guides

Definition. Study guides are defined as outlines, abstracts, or questions that emphasize important information from textbooks or lectures (Lovitt & Horton, 1987). For purposes of this research project, study guides were implemented as a *teaching* strategy. All participating teachers were requested to develop written outlines for the students to complete as important information was presented. The purpose of using a study guide was to focus the students' attention on the critical components of the lecture and to enhance their overall comprehension of the content material.

The study-guide strategy was researched twice during the grant period. Each time, 12 to 15 teachers participated in the study, most of whom were general educators. Their content specialties included history, English, health, and psychology. A total of 401 students participated in the research. The majority of these (60%) had disabilities and were mainstreamed in regular education classes.

Design and Method. A baseline phase, which ran for 2 weeks, included a teacher lecture each day. The method for acquiring the critical information was determined by the student, and a 50-item quiz was administered to students three times a week. Next, an intervention phase was introduced. During this 2-week phase, teachers provided a study guide for each student, instructed pupils on how to use it, and requested the completion of the study guide during the lecture. Again, the students responded three times a week to a 50-item quiz. A rest week followed intervention. No activities or quizzes related to the project were scheduled, and no data were collected. A 2-week retention phase completed the study. In the first week of retention, students responded to a quiz covering material from the baseline phase. The second week of retention covered information from the material presented during the intervention phase.

Results. To determine whether a student's performance improved, remained the same, or worsened as a result of the instructional strategy, changes in correct and incorrect rate averages across baseline and intervention phases were examined. Students' average correct rates increased from 7.77 in baseline to 9.52 in the intervention phase. At the same time, overall average incorrect rates decreased from 3.57 to 2.62. Across all groups the data indicated that mean correct rates increased, with 55% of the students improving their performance, 23% remaining the same, and 22% worsening when making comparisons between baseline and intervention (Stump & Lovitt, 1990). Teachers and students also completed follow-up surveys. The majority of teachers reported that they liked using study guides, and 50% reported that they would continue to use the study-guide strategy with their students; 61% of the students felt that the study guides helped them prepare for tests and to remember material better than taking notes did.

Classroom Application. Study guides can be written for various ability levels, from a simple list of sentences to more involved outlines with questions that promote higher-order thinking. The information on a study guide should represent the content material for an entire chapter or unit. In that way, a study guide differs from a daily worksheet. A four-step procedure can be used to develop a study guide.

1. Select an appropriate scope of content material. Remember that a study guide is similar to a chapter or unit outline.
2. Determine the objective of the study guide and the *most* important facts and concepts from the selected material. The final product may vary according to the students' ability levels and the amount of material to be completed.
3. Arrange the chosen facts and concepts logically and sequentially.
4. Produce copies of the study guide for students.

The standard format of a study guide can be adapted or modified depending on the instructional method to be used. Some examples of different formats include (a) a study guide with margins that allow students to expand on given information by taking additional notes in the margins; (b) a study guide with prompts, such as page numbers, to help students locate the correct information; and (c) a study guide with a word bank to assist students in choosing the correct response. Teachers have reported improvement in both student attention during lecture and student performance on tests as a result of implementing this strategy in the classroom. Additional information regarding study guide use and development can be obtained be viewing the TRIP Study Guide videocassette (1990).

Cooperative Learning

Definition. This study introduced teachers to a combination of cooperative learning formats. Specific cooperative approaches were chosen based on their ease of implementation and opportunity for student involvement. Teachers applied the key characteristics of cooperative learning while integrating a modified Jigsaw format (Aronson et al., 1978), with a modified SMARTS (Self-Motivational and Recreational Teaching Strategies) format (Buchanan, 1989) to conduct a daily lesson. The purposes of cooperative learning were twofold: first, to encourage cooperation and positive interdependence among students, and second, to improve overall student performance on tests. The Jigsaw approach involved the completion of a study guide by each team. Every team member was given a portion of the study guide and required to locate the answers and teach the information to the rest of the group. This created the positive interdependence required for cooperative learning. The SMARTS approach also involved teams but included an active review, with the teacher posing the questions. To play SMARTS the material is presented and discussed (in this case a study guide was used), the class is divided into teams, the teacher selects each team captain, additional team roles are assigned, the scoring system and rules of the game are discussed, a sample round is played, and play begins. This format proved effective for building students' comprehension and critical-thinking skills.

A total of 194 students participated in this research project, 22 (11%) of whom were identified as learners at risk for academic failure. They represented boys and girls from middle schools, junior high schools, and high schools in four districts.

Design and Method. Four phases comprised the study (see Table 6.2). During the 10-day baseline phase, teachers instructed in their usual manner, and students individually completed study guides, reviewed the main ideas of the lesson, and completed timed quizzes that lasted 3 minutes. During the first week of the 15-day intervention phase, teachers trained students in the Jigsaw and SMARTS procedures when completing the study guides and reviewing the material. The next 2 weeks of intervention involved implementation of the methods. On completion of teacher-directed instruction, the students were instructed to complete the study guide using the Jigsaw method and prepare for the SMARTS review with their teams. The review was followed by a 3-minute timed quiz. The third phase of the study was a rest week. No procedures were scheduled, and no data were collected. During the final phase, maintenance, quizzes from the baseline and intervention phases were alternately readministered.

Results. The data collected indicated that students significantly improved in the number of correct and incorrect responses made on the timed quizzes. During baseline, the mean rates of student responses were 19.67 for correct items and 2.34 for incorrect items. During intervention these rates were 22.8 for corrects and 1.58 for incorrects. An analysis of the mean rates for students identified as "at risk" denoted a significant change from baseline to intervention. Baseline rates were 17.41 for corrects and 2.97 for incorrects; during intervention these rates were 21.34 for correct items and 1.97 for incorrect items (Stump & Lovitt, 1991).

Surveys were administered to all participating students and teachers to examine the effects of cooperative learning on the social behavior and academic performance of the students. The teacher survey was rated on a Likert-type scale of 1 to 5, with 5 being the most favorable. Teachers thought the approach improved the social behavior of the children ($M = 3.89$), enhanced academic performance ($M = 4.22$), and was an effective instructional technique ($M = 4.44$). Students also rated the approach. They indicated that cooperative learning had improved their grades in the class ($M = 3.59$) and had helped them learn the material better ($M = 3.77$).

An additional student survey was completed at the end of the study that included 20 questions on a Likert-type scale with a rating of 1 to 3, with 3 indicating the most favorable response. The questions on this survey were grouped into three cluster areas. Cluster one examined the students' reactions to cooperative learning in the classroom ($M = 2.26$), cluster two looked at the impact the approach had on building relationships with others in the classroom ($M = 2.12$), and cluster three included statements about student reactions to the various components of the strategy ($M = 2.18$) (Stump & Lovitt, 1991).

Classroom Application. Cooperative learning is an approach that can be used in any subject area and at any grade level to provide students with an alternative teaching arrangement in which peers serve as instructional agents. The following steps represent a starting place for using Jigsaw and SMARTS in the classroom:

1. Teacher-directed instruction occurs.
2. Small heterogeneous teams are formed to complete a study guide.
3. Teacher provides instruction for student roles and responsibilities.
4. Each team member is accountable for all information studied.
5. Teacher allows 15 minutes for study guide completion.
6. Teacher uses study guide for SMARTS questions.
7. Rules are reviewed for team play and scoring.
8. Teacher announces performing team and opposing teams.
9. Play begins with a round including two segments of questions. See Figure 6.2 for a complete description of each segment in a SMARTS round of play.
10. Administer quizzes individually for student accountability.

More information regarding the implementation of the procedure described in this chapter can be obtained from the TRIP Cooperative Learning video (1992).

Self-Management Strategy

Definition. For this study, self-management was defined as the ability of individuals to take on responsibility for changing personal behavior. Additionally, it involved the personal and systematic application of behavior-change strategies that resulted in the desired modification of one's own behavior.

Design and Procedure. Teachers were trained in a 1-day workshop in the application of a student self-monitoring checklist. The checklist developed for this study was completed by students each day and included five target behaviors: arrived on time to class, brought materials to class, turned in assignments, contributed to class, and gained teacher's attention appropriately.

Segment 1

Part I:

1. Performing team captain confers with teams and selects questions from chart and answers after 1 minute.

Who/What	When/Where	How/Why
1.	1.	1.
2.	2.	2.
3.	3.	3.

2. Opposing team gets a chance to respond if performing team answers incorrectly.

3. Two team points are awarded for each correct answer.

Part II:

4. Performing team must spell or define a designated word or term that is in or related to the original word or question.

5. An opposing team responds if the performing team is incorrect.

6. Points are awarded for each correct answer.

Segment 2

1. Teacher requests information about the segment 1 question from performing and opposing teams.

2. Teams write answers on paper (optional chalkboard) in 1 minute.

3. Performing team reads their answers aloud.

4. Points are awarded for each correct answer.

5. Opposing team can earn points for appropriately correcting performing team errors.

- Score keeper adds score for first round and records on a score sheet.
- The team turn changes to a new performing team.
- Other teams are opposing teams. Continue play until all teams have completed a round as a performing team. (Play may be extended into next day)

Figure 6.2 Cooperative learning game.

A total of 25 teachers, representing 7 districts, attended the workshop and later submitted data. Each teacher selected to work with two target students. The study was carried out over an 8-week period.

During baseline, teachers observed and recorded data on the target behavior of five or six potential students in their classrooms. At the end of the week, teachers selected two of these students for continuation in the project. The behavior of these two students was then recorded for an additional week.

Following the baseline period, teachers carried out the intervention phase of the project, which lasted for 4 weeks. During this time, teachers taught students the first level of using the self-monitoring checklist. Explanations and demonstrations were provided for students to teach (a) checking if target behaviors had or had not been performed, (b) counting the number of yes/no marks each day, and (c) charting the total yes counts. When students improved their behavior, they moved through the following different levels of intervention:

Level 1: Students' behavior was counted and charted by both teachers and students, daily points were awarded, and reinforcement was provided by teachers.

Level 2: Students set goals for improving their behavior and, at the end of each session, compared their performance ratings with that of the teacher. Bonus points were earned for matched ratings.

Level 3: Ratings were randomly compared by teachers and students. Students chose their own reinforcers for meeting goals and matching ratings.

Level 4: If the student was performing all five target behaviors on a regular basis, an optional behavior was selected by the teacher or student and added to the self-monitoring checklist. All other procedures remained in place.

A period of rest was arranged for the next phase of the study. Student behaviors were not counted or recorded during this time. Finally, a retention phase was arranged where teachers collected student performance data in the same manner as during the baseline period. Self-monitoring checklists were made available to the students if desired.

Results.   Summary data from the project indicated that students were performing between two and three target behaviors during the baseline phase and between three and four target behaviors during the intervention and follow-up phases. Survey responses indicated that both teachers and students found the project to be quite useful. Teachers rated six survey responses (rated on a Likert-type scale of 1 to 5, with 5 indicating the most favorable response). Mean ratings were (a) 3.79 on helping students improve their behavior, (b) 3.50 on improving the behavior of other students, (c) 3.93 on reminding students to continue using the approach, (d) 4.29 on recommending the approach for inservice training, (e) 4.14 on their continued implementation of the technique, and (f) 4.57 on their principal's support for attempting new projects. Students' mean responses were 3.89 for the approach improving their behavior and 4.14 for how well they liked using the approach (Stump & Lovitt, 1991).

Classroom Application.   There are at least five areas that can be considered when beginning a self-management program: self-selecting the target behaviors, self-determining performance standards, self-counting behaviors, self-charting behaviors, and self-decision making, including self-delivered consequences. Each of these areas can be used alone or in combination with another area depending on the individual's needs. The following steps should be addressed when setting up a self-management program in a classroom:

1. Introduce the procedure to the student by discussing the rationale and the anticipated outcomes. Gain the student's support of the program (e.g., "It's important that you be able to monitor the way in which you gain the teacher's attention. When you get my attention in appropriate ways, you will get my help immediately. I need your support and cooperation so that you can be in charge of your own behavior. Do I have your support?").

2. Define and model the behavior to be increased and the behavior to be decreased, using several explicit examples and nonexamples of the behavior. Provide the student with multiple opportunities to demonstrate the behavior (e.g., "Here is one way that you can give me a quiet hand raise when you want to get my attention. Here is a way that would not work when you want to get my attention [demonstrate a noisy hand raise].). The examples can be written or illustrated on the self-management card as shown in Figure 6.3.

3. Teach the student how to use the self-monitoring instrument: where, how, and when to record accurately, and so forth.

4. Determine the period in which the student will be self-monitoring. This could be as short as 1 minute or as long as the entire day, depending on the target behavior.

5. Monitor the student's use of the system, and provide prompts, check points, and continuous reinforcement for appropriate use of the procedure.

6. Chart the daily counts of behaviors at the end of each counting period. The behavior to be increased as well as the behavior to be decreased should be charted as illustrated in Figure 6.3.

7. Decide if additional contingencies are necessary to achieve behavior change after several days of data. In some instances, a group contingency may be appropriate if peer support is maintaining behavior. In other cases, increased teacher praise or a simple contract may be required. Additional classroom application information may be obtained by viewing the TRIP strategies video program, Self-Management (1991).

Graphic Organizers

Definition. Graphic organizers are visual displays of information (facts, ideas, and concepts) that are connected in a meaningful way. This study investigated the use of graphic organizers as a teaching strategy. Teachers were requested to design and develop graphic organizers to correspond with their weekly or daily lessons. In addition, teachers were required to use the organizers during whole-group instruction. It was hypothesized that if teachers presented their lesson with the aid of a graphic organizer, students would improve their performance on quizzes. The design of the graphic organizer could include one or a combination of the following types: top down or bottom up (to organize information that has main ideas followed by supporting details); compare and contrast (to relate key attributes of various items or situations); sequence (to illustrate a progression of events); or diagram (to display information in the form of sketches, maps, and pictures).

The use of graphic organizers was researched twice during the grant period. A total of 46 teachers participated in the studies. They instructed 813 students in middle schools, junior high schools, and high schools from seven school districts.

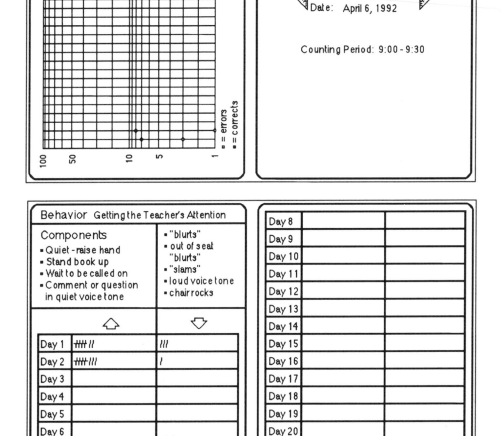

Figure 6.3 Self-management: student tracker card.

Design and Method. The design for carrying out these studies included three phases: baseline, intervention, and retention. The baseline phase ran for 2 weeks, during which time teachers were asked to present information to students in their usual manner while obtaining scores from quizzes three times a week. The intervention phase, which also lasted 2 weeks, followed the same procedures with the addition of a graphic organizer. During this phase, teachers instructed students on the use of graphic organizers. They also required students to complete the graphic organizer with the teacher as the material was presented. The week following intervention was considered a rest week. Activities unrelated to the study were conducted and no data were collected. A 2-week retention phase completed the study. In the first week students responded to a quiz on two occasions based on material that had been introduced during baseline. In the second week of retention students were again quizzed twice; this time the material covered information presented during the intervention phase.

For this study, teachers were given the option to develop the quizzes on a MECC microcomputer program (Study Guides, 1984). To use this program, teachers identified 50 items from the information presented during baseline and another 50 items from the material to be covered during the intervention phase. These items formed pools of test items. The program could print out different test versions for the quizzes administered during each phase of the study.

Results. Three analyses were used to judge student performance. These included mean rate, average percent correct, and performance change. When data from the baseline and intervention phases were compared, significant changes for both correct and incorrect rates were noted. Significance was also found for correct responses across the two retention phases. The average correct percentage improved across all phases, increasing from 82% to 88%. Overall, performance of 48% of the students improved from baseline to intervention, 23% remained the same, and 30% worsened. Percent correct per phase indicated that learners with special needs made the most dramatic change, moving from a baseline of 65% to an intervention level of 71% correct. A subgroup of students with behavior disorders demonstrated a gain of 13 percentage points across those phases.

Classroom Application. A five-step procedure can be used to develop graphic organizers for classroom use.

1. Select an appropriate scope of content material. A graphic organizer should contain enough information to cover one or two days of lecture or discussion.
2. Identify the objectives from the selected content area. The objectives should represent the outcomes to be achieved by completing the graphic organizer. The objectives will then lead to the selection of the most appropriate graphic organizer format.
3. Determine the facts, concepts, and vocabulary related to the objectives.

These will become the visually displayed components of your graphic organizer.

4. Arrange the facts and concepts in a logical manner. Boxes, circles, lines, arrows, and other icons are used to display the relationship between all elements of information. Some tips to consider when sketching the graphic organizer include the following: (a) include no more than 16 to 18 major facts or concepts; (b) make efficient use of space, but do not overcrowd the page; and (c) include reference points for each shape or icon so students can follow along with the teacher and remain focused during the presentation. This is the major difference between graphic organizers and other forms of semantic maps or flowcharts.

5. Prepare copies of the graphic organizer for the students. It is often useful to prepare a blank copy of the final product as well as a partially filled-in copy, and a completed copy of the graphic organizer. Different types of graphic organizers can be applied to each component of a lesson such as teacher-directed activities (lecture), guided practice (review with the teacher or a peer), and independent practice or final measurement (homework or quiz). For additional information on developing and implementing graphic organizers, see Horton and Lovitt (1989) and the TRIP Graphic Organizer video tape (1990).

SUMMARY

Results from specific classroom research projects on these teaching and learning strategies have been promising in terms of gains in student performance, ease of implementation, and teacher and student satisfaction. These data support the viability of the techniques and procedures for assisting teachers in bridging the gap between research and practice. Preliminary data from longitudinal studies indicate that teachers are continuing to blend the strategies into their instruction several months and years after the classroom research has been completed.

Generally, the use of "teacher" strategies promoted better results than the "learner" strategies studied throughout the 4-year project. Some possible explanations may include the following: teacher strategies required less time to implement, learner strategies required at least an additional week to teach the procedure to the students, the design of the learner-strategy studies did not allow adequate time to see the potential growth and changes, procedures for implementing "teacher" strategies were more controlled and explicit in terms of step-by-step instructions and allowed for less variability in teaching method, and teacher strategies could be more easily blended into the teacher's ongoing instructional program. Further classroom research on these issues would be recommended to provide clarification on these variables.

The staff development materials that have resulted from this project are in constant demand and continue to receive local validation. The Utah Learning Resource Center staff are using and disseminating the products in conjunction with ongoing agency personnel development plans, the Utah Mentor Teacher Academy, the 40 school districts in Utah, state-operated programs, the Utah Parent and Information Center, and state institutes of higher education. Staff developers in Utah are also finding that teachers have effectively integrated these strategies with other promising practices and models such as co-teaching, building-based support teams, direct instruction procedures, precision teaching procedures, and mastery learning principles. This research represented an initial attempt to explore methods for facilitating the implementation of validated practices into the classroom. Further study will be necessary and additional questions will need to be addressed in order to resolve the dilemma of bridging the research gap.

REFERENCES

Alley, G., & Deshler, D. (1979). *Teaching the learning disabled adolescent: Strategies and methods.* Denver: Love Publishing Company.

Aronson, E., Blaney, N., Stephan, C., Sikes, J., & Snapp, M. (1978). *The Jigsaw classroom.* Beverly Hills, CA: Sage Publications.

Bateman, B. (Chair). (1991). *Academic Child Abuse (The Study Group).* Eugene, OR: International Institute for Advocacy for School Children.

Buchanan, L. (1989). *S.M.A.R.T.S. – Self Motivational and Recreational Teaching Strategies.* Waco, TX: Recreational Education Enterprises.

Cooperative Learning videocassette. (1992). Distributed by Sopris West, Inc., 1140 Boston Ave., Longmont, CO 80501.

Everston, C.M. (1987). Creating conditions for learning: From research to practice. *Theory Into Practice, XXVI* (1).

Goodlad, J.L. (1983). A study of schooling: Some findings and hypotheses. *Phi Delta Kappan, 6,* 465–470.

Graphic organizer videocassette. (1990). Distributed by Sopris West, Inc., 1140 Boston Ave., Longmont, CO 80501.

Horton, S.V., & Lovitt, T.C. (1989). Construction and implementation of graphic organizers for academically handicapped and regular secondary students. *Academic Therapy, 24,* 625–640.

Lovitt, T.C., Fister, J.L., Kemp, K., Moore, R.C., Schroeder, B., & Bauernschmidt, M. (1990). Using precision teaching techniques: Translating research. *Teaching Exceptional Children, 22*(II), 16–19.

Lovitt, T.C., & Horton, S.V. (1987). How to develop study guides. *Reading Writing and Learning Disabilities, 3,* 333–343.

Palloway, E.A., & Patton, J.R. (1989). Study skills: Introduction to the special issue. *Academic Therapy, 24,* 379–381.

Self-management videocassette. (1991). Distributed by Sopris West, Inc., 1140 Boston Ave., Longmont, CO 80501.

Study guide videocassette. (1990). Distributed by Sopris West, Inc., 1140 Boston Ave., Longmont, CO 80501.

Study Guides. (1984). Minnesota Educational Computing Corporation (MECC), 3490 Lexington Avenue North, St. Paul, MN 55126.

Stump, C., & Lovitt, T.C. (1990). *Vocabulary practice sheets, study guides & graphic organizers, results of Utah studies.* Unpublished data.

Stump, C., & Lovitt, T.C. (1991). *Self-management and cooperative learning, results of Utah studies.* Seattle, WA: University of Washington. Unpublished data.

Vocabulary practice sheets videocassette. (1990). Distributed by Sopris West, Inc., 1140 Boston Ave., Longmont, CO 80501.

7

A Model for Noncategorical Service Delivery for Students with Mild Disabilities

William N. Bender
Kris Scott
Phillip J. McLaughlin

The idea of noncategorical placement for children with mild handicaps is not new (Belch, 1979; Hallahan & Kauffman, 1977; Phipps, 1982; Reynolds & Balow, 1972). Numerous states developed plans for noncategorical placement for all or most children with mild handicaps over 20 years ago, and of those states that developed such a model, none has done away with it. In 1985, Chapey, Pyszkowski, and Trimarco surveyed state directors of special education and reported that 25 states certified teachers in some type of noncategorical certification, and 35 states indicated that such a certification was desirable. Yet many other states are still "stuck" in the same categorical service-delivery patterns of 10, 20, or 30 years ago.

It should be clear that the status quo for service delivery cannot be maintained. The current economic squeeze is forcing some type of restructuring of service-delivery patterns, as the recent debate over the regular education initiative indicates (Wang & Zollers, 1990). Administrators in special education have become concerned with the inaccurate labeling practices for many handicapping conditions, with the financial costs of assessment and service, and with the research that seems to suggest that special education pull-out programs are not notably effective.

There are some reasons to suppose that this pressure for restructuring special education may lessen somewhat if current service-delivery systems for children with mild handicaps could be shown to be effective and efficient. For example, if the funds currently spent on extensive normative assessments used to differentiate various mildly handicapped groups could be used for educational programming expenditures, a substantial savings would result. This could conceivably lessen the pressure to end all pull-out special education programs. While no responsible practitioner argues against assessment that is useful for

127

instructional planning, practitioners have known for years that many of the current eligibility assessments are wasteful (Coles, 1978). As concerned professionals, we are unwilling to see the entire edifice of special education crumble at the altar of economic necessity simply because a few practitioners are wedded to the dated and superfluous use of extensive norm-based assessment. Likewise, the field should not be so myopic as to remain embedded in a service-delivery system that research has suggested may be grossly inefficient.

Some restructuring of special education service delivery will probably result, given the deficits in national and state budgets, and special educators must be prepared to defend their practices (Jenkins et al., 1988). Put simply, it is easier to defend an efficient service-delivery system than to defend an inefficient one, and noncategorical service delivery is more efficient than a categorical model.

In our presentation, we have made several assumptions that the reader should bear in mind. First, most of the states that have moved to a noncategorical model of service delivery have included only children in the high-incidence handicapping conditions. The high-incidence conditions typically include students with educable mental handicaps (EMH), learning disabilities (LD), or behavioral disorders (BD). Hawaii is typical of these states, in that separate teaching certifications are maintained for low-incidence conditions such as physically/multiply handicapped, severely/profoundly developmentally disabled, visually handicapped, and hearing impaired, whereas a single teacher certification is used for teachers of the high-incidence conditions (Chapey et al., 1985). When we say noncategorical service delivery in this chapter, we mean a system in which the low-incidence handicaps continue to be categorically identified and students with mild handicaps in the high-incidence conditions are not differentiated.

Second, we wish to point out that we are speaking merely of a service-delivery change; we do not intend to advocate for the abolition of currently recognized handicaps. At the severe end of the continuum, there is a great deal of difference between a child with a LD, a BD, and mental retardation. We merely suggest that most of the children presently identified as children with LD, EMH, and BD should be served in a noncategorical framework.

Next, eligibility decisions currently involve two determinations: (a) the distinction of children with handicaps and those without, and (b) discrimination among children with different handicaps to determine placement. A noncategorical service-delivery model makes the second determination unnecessary, and substantial savings result. Also, state-of-the-art practice in special education suggests that the first discrimination may be accomplished much more economically.

Service delivery must include all elements of the current system, as well as recent knowledge that impacts on service delivery. The service-delivery system currently in use was founded on Deno's (1970) cascade of services. That model focused exclusively on instructional settings and was silent on certain other issues that impact significantly on service delivery, including teacher certification and differentiations between the handicapping conditions. This silence is, in some sense, understandable because most special educators in 1970 assumed that the problems in differentiation of various handicapped groups were solvable. Likewise, most practitioners in 1970 assumed that the different handicapping conditions required different instructional programming, and that teachers would continue to be certified according to the different instructional requirements of the children they served. Because many of these assumptions were incorrect, a modern service-delivery model must address these issues. At a minimum, learner characteristics, instructional programming concerns, teacher certification issues, and instructional setting needs must be included in any service-delivery model. Our goal is to provide a comprehensive model that addresses these issues.

Finally, the law of parsimony suggests that simpler is better, and that a service-delivery system should attempt to accomplish its goals in the most efficient way possible, so long as the demonstrable needs of its clients are met. We accept this maxim, and we do not feel that we have to prove that a noncategorical system is better than a categorical model. We merely seek to demonstrate that there is no rationale for a categorical service-delivery system, and that a noncategorical system as described herein is more efficient — more parsimonious, if you like — and thus preferable.

THE CATEGORICAL MODEL

One method to facilitate discussion on a difficult issue is through examination of the chain of assumptions on which the issue rests. If any one of the sequential assumptions is invalid, that perspective on the issue becomes invalid. The initial assumption of proponents of categorical placement is that the learning characteristics of children with LD, EMH, and BD vary a great deal. A further assumption is that different learning characteristics require different educational programming and curricula. A final assumption suggests that differential educational programming requires different certifications for teachers as well as different special education classes for the group. Today, each of these assumptions is challenged by research.

Cognitive Learning Characteristics

On consideration, it seems clear that learning characteristics vary in importance when decisions about educational placement, services, and teaching methods are made. For example, IQs among the three groups — LD, EMH, and BD — may vary somewhat simply by the definition of each category. However, no evidence exists to suggest that minor differences in IQ indicate major differences in the way children learn a specific task, nor do they necessitate major variations in the way the children are taught.

There is evidence today that certain characteristics, which have not been historically considered, are, in fact, more educationally relevant than the standard norm-based IQ measures in determining instructional needs (Chandler & Jones, 1983). Some of these characteristics may also be important in placement decisions.

For example, recent evidence suggests that adaptive behavioral characteristics may impact the academic environment and instruction of children with mild handicaps (Epstein & Cullinan, 1984; McKinney & Forman, 1982; Pullis, 1985). Emotional and personality characteristics may also be very influential in academic learning (Carroll et al., 1984; Gajar, 1980; Luchow et al., 1985; Pullis, 1985). As is clear from these studies, comparisons between mildly handicapped groups on each of these characteristics would be desirable prior to differential placement decisions. Only some of this research has been conducted, but the available evidence implies that significant differences relating to learning characteristics do not exist among children currently identified as having mild LD, EMH, or mild BD. Differences that do exist do not appear to be sufficient to justify separate educational programs.

Research comparing the IQs of mildly handicapped groups is consistent; certain IQ differences do exist among the groups (Gajar, 1979, 1980; Webster & Schenck, 1978). However, the evidence suggests that these differences are not as large as one would assume, given the definitions of the various groups. For example, Gajar (1980) investigated cognitive variables, including intelligence, underachievement in reading, and subtest scatter. Participants in the study included 198 elementary school children: 63 children with EMH, 75 children with LD, and 60 children with BD. These groups demonstrated average IQ scores of 70.0, 93.3, and 91.0, respectively, on the *Wechsler Intelligence Scale for Children* (WISC) (Wechsler, 1949). While one may anticipate that the IQs of children with LD and BD are normal, this study indicates average IQs for these groups that are well below the mean of 100. These means suggest that the overall IQ differences, which many would assume to be two standard deviations, are, in reality, about one and one-half standard deviations.

In addition to intelligence, researchers have examined differences in IQ and academic characteristics of the mildly handicapped, using sophisticated statistical techniques (Gajar, 1979, 1980; Webster & Schenck, 1978). Test data of children with LD, BD, EMH, and multiple handicaps were the focus of a study by Webster and Schenck (1972). Subjects included 1,524 children ages 6 to 17 years. All participants in the study had been labeled by a special education diagnostic team as LD, BD, EMH, multiple-handicapped, or other (no clear diagnostic label). Test scores on the WISC-R and the *Wide Range Achievement Test* (Jastak & Wilkinson, 1984) were taken from the children's cumulative folders. A series of discriminant function analyses was performed on the data in an effort to identify group membership based on assessment results. Results showed that it was possible to differentiate only the EMH group, resulting in an accuracy of 52%. Needless to say, this accuracy is quite low. Another finding revealed that 77.76% of the children not labeled as LD by the special education diagnostic team were identified as LD by the discriminant analysis. The results from the analyses failed to differentiate children with LD and children with BD. This study, like the others, failed to reveal any important differences in learning characteristics among the three groups. With the exception of some minor IQ differences, IQ and achievement scores failed to discriminate among the mildly handicapped.

Other researchers have directly compared children with LD, BD, and EMH on several other cognitive variables, and none has demonstrated educationally relevant differences (Becker, 1978; Keogh et al., 1973). When minor differences were found on certain characteristics in these studies, no attempt was made to document the educational relevance of these differences. For example, O'Grady (1974) looked at psycholinguistic abilities in children with LD and BD and non-handicapped children. The children were tested on the *Illinois Test of Psycholinguistic Abilities* (McCarthy & Kirk, 1963). Results showed that children with LD and BD differed significantly from normal children but did not differ significantly from each other on total scores.

Intelligence quotients can be used to make gross distinctions in placement, such as distinguishing between children with severe mental handicaps and those with mild mental handicaps. Numerous studies have indicated that certain other cognitive differences exist among the various groups of children with mild handicaps. However, these differences are minimal, and there is no evidence to suggest that minor differences in any of these cognitive characteristics require fine distinctions in educational programming for the three mildly handicapped groups.

Behavioral Characteristics

Research on the behavioral characteristics of children with BD, LD, and EMH has been conducted recently. Some authors believe that no evidence suggests the necessity for differential placement and programming (Bender et al., 1984; Candler et al, 1984). For example, Candler and co-workers (1984) investigated the behavioral differences among various children with learning problems. Elementary school children ages 8 to 11 years participated in the study. Fifteen children were drawn from each of three groups: mentally handicapped, LD, and Chapter I programs for children with reading delays. Each child's behavior was rated on an unpublished behavior-rating scale by the teacher. Results demonstrated no significant difference among the groups on this measure. The authors suggested that since the groups appeared to be much the same, similar teaching strategies could be implemented.

When researchers include children with BD in their designs, differences in behavior begin to emerge among the mildly handicapped groups (Barr & McDowell, 1972; Epstein & Cullinan, 1984; Gajar, 1980; McCarthy & Paraskevopoulos, 1969; McKinney & Forman, 1982; Sherry, 1981). In a study that compared all three mildly handicapping conditions, Sherry (1981) examined the frequency of nontask-oriented behaviors in the regular classroom as well as in the special education resource room. Observers counted the frequency of gross motor behavior, disruptive noise with objects, disturbing others directly/aggression, orienting responses, blurting out/commenting/vocal noise, talking, other, and improper position in children with LD, BD, and EMH. Significant differences among the groups were found regarding frequency of nontask behavior in the regular classroom. However, the groups were not found to be different when observed in the special education resource room. In addition, although the frequency of the nontask behaviors may not have been the same, the behaviors exhibited by the children in each handicapped group were the same.

While a number of these behavioral studies have been criticized on methodological grounds, the weight of the evidence suggests that certain behavioral differences do exist among the mildly handicapped groups. Where differences are found, they seem to be most apparent between children with BD and other children with mild handicaps. However, some of the studies that suggest the children with BD behave differently may be biased because of the use of different teachers to complete the ratings. Teachers certified exclusively to teach children with BD may perceive behavioral problems in a different way. Further, most of the studies indicated that the demonstrable differences are, in fact, differences in severity of behavior problems as opposed to typography. Finally, none of the studies has suggested explicit educational planning differences based on the measurable differences in behavior among these groups. As in the area of cognitive characteristics, there seems to be no justification for categorical programming related to behavioral differences between the mildly handicapped groups.

In addition to cognitive and behavioral characteristics, researchers have examined the affective traits of children with mild handicaps, although no research to date has directly compared all three groups on any affective variable. Some research has found no differences on affective characteristics between some of the mildly handicapped groups (Candler et al., 1984). Other research, however, has revealed some differences among the groups (Carroll et al., 1984; Luchow et al., 1985).

Two studies have compared students with LD and students with EMH on self-concept (Candler et al, 1984; Carroll et al., 1984). Candler and associates (1984) investigated the self-esteem of children with EMH, LD, and reading problems. Results revealed no significant differences among the three groups; in fact, mean *T* scores for each group were all approximately 50. The authors believe that their results support the assertion that the categorical groups do not possess unique characteristics.

Another comparison of self-concept was conducted by Carroll and co-workers (1984). Participants in this study included high-functioning EMH children (IQs from 60 to 69), low-functioning EMH Children (IQs from 50 to 59), children with LD, and nonhandicapped children. Two measures of self-concept were administered: the *Student Self Evaluation* (SES) and the *How I See Myself*. Results demonstrated that differences were found between the group with LD and the groups with EMH on the SES; no differences were observed on the other measure.

Luchow and colleagues (1985) examined learned helplessness among children with BD and children with LD/BD. The *Intelligence Achievement Responsibility Questionnaire* (Crandall et al., 1965) was administered individually to each subject. Children with BD and children with LD/BD did not exhibit differences in attributions of academic success to internal factors. However, differences were found in their attributions of academic failure. Students with BD attributed failure to lack of effort and lack of ability; students with LD/BD attributed failure to lack of effort only.

It has been shown that some differences in affective variables among the mildly handicapped groups do exist. However, too little information relating to affective variables is available to draw conclusions regarding the necessity of differential planning and programming. First, no study directly compared the three groups. Second, when differences between the groups were found, the differences were minimal (Candler et al., 1984; Carroll et al., 1984; Luchow et al., 1985). Finally, none of these studies specifically showed how observed differences in affective variables could be influential for educational planning and placement decisions.

Categorical Fluctuations

The notion that the mildly handicapped groups can be meaningfully differentiated on the basis of learner characteristics remains unconvincing. With this in mind, it seems prudent to investigate the stability of the categorical designations for children who are classified as mildly handicapped. In the only study available, Wolman, Thurlow, and Bruininks (1989) accessed the school records of 523 students with mild handicaps, including students with LD, BD, EMH, and speech impairment. The records were collected for all of the students who received special education in grades 10, 11, and 12 in three high schools in a suburban district. The number of times that a student was reclassified into a different category was noted. Overall, 24% of the sample ($n = 126$) had been classified into at least two categories during their school years. Of those students who were reclassified, 83% ($n = 105$) were reclassified once and 16% ($n = 20$) were reclassified twice. Specifically, 18% of the children who were initially classified as LD were classified into at least one other category. The comparable figures for EMH and BD are 13% and 4%, respectively. This instability of categorical designations — like the evidence on learner characteristics — suggests that the categorical distinctions currently used may not be valid.

In reviewing the literature on learner characteristics, little evidence supports the assumption that learner characteristics vary greatly among the mildly handicapped groups. The only tentative conclusions that can be drawn indicate (a) children with EMH may be differentiated from other groups by IQs, although the differences are not as large as one may expect; (b) children with BD may be differentiated from the other groups based on maladaptive behavior; (c) behavioral differences that do exist appear to be differences in severity rather than type; and (d) none of the studies in any area that found differences explicitly stated how these learning characteristic differences should be related to differences in educational programming. It seems relatively clear that the evidence on learner characteristics does not provide a meaningful rationale for continued use of the present categorical service-delivery system.

Instructional Programming

Research on instructional programming indicates a few differences in the instruction provided for groups with mild handicaps (Morsink et al, 1987). Reynolds and Balow (1972) provided the early suggestion that differential curriculum needs should be the focus of the classification system and, by extension, the types of training that teachers receive. These scholars recommended a trait-by-treatment interaction model as one method to use regarding service-delivery issues. According to that model, if trait-by-treatment research suggested that children in different categories (i.e., different traits) respond differentially to educational treatments, then the rationale for categorical programming would be established.

As scholars through the years have pointed out, every curriculum developed for one handicapped group has been used successfully with each of the other groups (Reynolds & Balow, 1972; Morsink et al., 1987). In addition, no trait-by-treatment evidence exists to support differences of curriculum needs among the handicapped groups. If anything, consideration of the trait-by-treatment interaction model in a discussion of service-delivery issues leads to the conclusion that noncategorical service-delivery models are more appropriate (Jenkins et al., 1988).

Instructional Teacher Behaviors

Another method by which instructional programming needs have been investigated is the comparison of categorically trained teachers and noncategorically trained teachers. In a survey, Carri (1985) examined the skills that special educators viewed as necessary to teach specific categories of children with mild handicaps. The views of teachers of children with LD and with EMH were similar, whereas teachers of children with BD held different views about crucial teacher skills. The BD teachers differed in their views on assessing and evaluating student behavior and curriculum design and use. However, these results must be interpreted in light of the potential bias discussed previously. When one trains teachers differently in categorical training programs, they may perceive different needs even when they do not exist.

A number of studies on the instruction received by children with different handicaps and the instruction provided by teachers from categorical preparation programs seem to suggest the appropriateness of noncategorical programs (David & Fairchild, 1976; Idol-Maestas et al, 1981; Mayer & Scheffelin, 1975). Researchers have investigated the issues relating to both instructional practices and teacher certification, and results consistently demonstrate a lack of any rationale for categorical service delivery (Algozzine et al., 1986; O'Sullivan et al., 1987; Sindelar et al., 1986; Ysseldyke et al., 1989a; Ysseldyke et al., 1987).

Ysseldyke and associates (1989a) examined the differences in reading and math instruction offered to students with mild handicaps. Subjects included students with LD, BD, and EMH, and nonhandicapped students. *The Instructional Environment Scale* (Ysseldyke et al., 1986) was administered in each teacher's classroom. Examiners completed two classroom observations, a student interview, and a teacher interview. Students with LD or BD were observed in the regular and special education classrooms, whereas the nonhandicapped students and students with EMH were observed only in their respective self-contained classrooms. No significant differences were found to exist in the instruction received by the handicapped groups on four factors: instructional planning, instructional presentation, practice, and feedback when comparing the qualitative nature of reading and mathematics instruction.

Several recent studies involved observations of instructional behaviors of categorically trained teachers and failed to find major differences among teachers certified to teach children with BD, LD, and EMH (Algozzine et al., 1986; Sindelar et al., 1986; Ysseldyke et al., 1989a). Further, Marston (1987) examined student achievement outcomes when students were trained by teachers certified by category versus teachers certified in another category. No achievement differences were noted.

The evidence on instructional programming seems to support the noncategorical approach to teacher certification, training, and instruction. First, no trait-by-treatment research has demonstrated the need for children in different categories to be exposed to different instructional treatments or curricula (Morsink et al., 1987). Next, noncategorical certification programs have been shown to be just as effective as categorical certification programs (David & Fairchild, 1976). Third, no differences in student achievement related to differential teacher certification or training have been shown (Marston, 1987; O'Sullivan et al., 1987). Fourth, few differences have been found among teacher beliefs of competency skills needed to teach each of the mild handicapping categories (Carri, 1985). Finally, categorically trained teachers were found to be consistent across categories in time allocation for instruction, instructional arrangements, student–teacher ratios, and general teaching behaviors (Algozzine et al., 1986; Sindelar et al., 1986; Ysseldyke et al., 1989a, Ysseldyke et al., 1987; Ysseldyke et al., 1989b).

THE NONCATEGORICAL MODEL

Because no rationale for continued use of a categorically based service-delivery model has been found, exploration of noncategorical service delivery seems in order. Figure 7.1 presents the proposed model. The central goal of the model is achievement growth and social/emotional development of the handicapped child. It is our belief that all aspects of the system must focus on achieving these goals in the most efficient way possible. As is apparent, the cascade concept that was originally discussed by Deno (1970) is still a component of the model, but the instructional setting comprises only one aspect of the model. Other key components include learner characteristics and how those characteristics impact on instructional programming and curriculum needs and instructional setting needs to enhance the achievement and social/emotional development of the child.

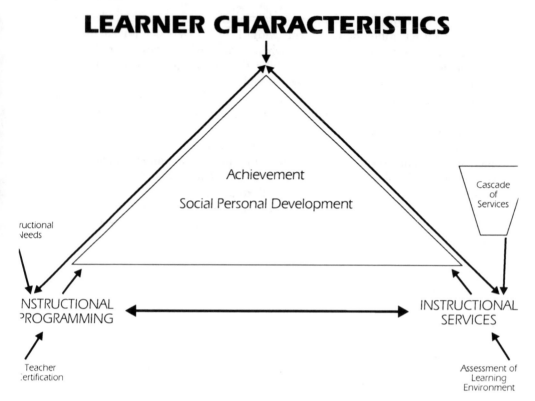

Figure 7.1. Comprehensive service-delivery model.

As the arrows on Figure 7.1 indicate, each of the three components of the model — learning characteristics, instructional programming needs, and instructional setting needs — interact to foster achievement and social/emotional growth. However, the demand for efficacy and parsimony inherent in this model suggests some modifications in the traditional approaches to these components.

Learning Characteristics

Learner characteristics include characteristics that affect the growth of the child. Practitioners have historically been free to assess any characteristic judged important for achievement or social/emotional growth. However, the demand for parsimony within this model suggests the need for additional criteria. First, only characteristics that are direct measures of these growth outcomes or characteristics that research has shown to be causally related to those growth outcomes are considered for measurement under this model. Assessment of other characteristics is a waste of resources (Coles, 1978; Galagan, 1985). Second, only those causal characteristics that are amenable to educational treatment should be routinely measured. Bloom (1980) first suggested the emphasis on measurement of alterable variables, rather than static cognitive variables and that suggestion is economically prudent today.

Based on the recommended reduction of norm-based assessment, we may need to decrease assessment positions related to cognitive ability assessment and increase other professional positions such as special education teachers and consultation personnel (Fuchs et al., 1990; Jenkins et al., 1988). Such a shift would result in more direct assistance to children.

Instructional Programming

As the earlier review demonstrated, there are no instructional strategies that are differentially effective for any particular mildly handicapped group. Consequently, teachers of the mildly handicapped should be trained in the same instructional strategies — as they already are in 23 states (Chapey et al., 1985). Such training would avoid the redundancy in courses in categorically oriented states such as Georgia that require separate methods courses for LD, BD, and mild MH, in order to obtain the noncategorical certification. When students of education realize that the same methods work for all mildly handicapped, college faculty are placed in the ridiculous position of having to justify these redundant courses. Such certification requirements are inherently unfair to pre-service and in-service teachers and may help to create the shortage of special education teachers nationally.

Instructional Setting

The instructional setting component of the model refers to placement in the least restrictive environment in which the child can be successful. This component incorporates the most modern versions of Deno's (1970) cascade of services, but also includes two additional considerations. First, some objective mechanism is required for making instructional setting decisions. In determining the level of placement within the cascade, we recommend decisions based on the level of severity of the handicap, as explained below.

Second, our understanding of effective instructional practice allows us to go further than Deno (1970) did 23 years ago. Rather than merely specifying the particular type of class a child should be placed in, our current knowledge allows us to make some recommendations for specific instructional strategies to which a child should be exposed, based on ecological assessment of the strategies used in the class and the learner's specific needs. Further elaboration of this concept follows.

Underlying Principles of the Model

Internal Integrity.   This principle suggests that service-delivery systems should be logically consistent. The assessment of learner characteristics should be based on program planning needs and the determination of the least restrictive setting. According to this principle, if the handicapping conditions are believed to be important enough to require different labels, then both educational programs and special educators should be identified by handicapping condition in order to maintain the internal integrity in the service-delivery system. Conversely, if the categorical distinctions between groups of mildly handicapped students have no relationship to either instructional programming or instructional setting needs, those distinctions should be dropped from consideration for service delivery.

After examination of research relevant to specific components of the model, we accept the latter premise. Consequently, we are compelled to advocate a shift to a noncategorical model for the mildly handicapped. Further, we do not see that such a shift represents the major service-delivery change that many professionals fear, simply because we know of no states with categorically based service-delivery systems that demonstrate internal integrity. For example, in Georgia, West Virginia, and North Carolina, children are identified categorically, and teachers are trained and certified categorically, but the children are often placed in the same noncategorical resource room and in some cases in the same noncategorical self-contained class. These placements assume that the categorically certified teacher in a noncategorical class has the competency to meet the needs of all of the children, regardless of the presumed differences in the children's handicaps or the certificates that teacher holds.

Forty-eight states have noncategorical/multicategorical resource room placements available to handicapped children (Morsink et al., 1987), while only 12 states certify teachers for the mildly handicapped exclusively along noncategorical lines (Chapey et al., 1985). These data seem to suggest that large numbers of categorically identified children are placed in noncategorical special education. This type of service delivery seems, at best, somewhat inconsistent.

Other states also demonstrate inconsistencies. In New Jersey, a state that certifies teachers noncategorically (Chapey et al., 1985), students are identified in the traditional categories, even though the students, once identified, are often placed in the same programs as students with other handicapping conditions. Like the inconsistencies discussed above, this pattern of service delivery makes little sense.

The comprehensive service-delivery model recommended here incorporates the following recommendations: (a) students should be labeled as demonstrating some form of mild learning handicap (California uses the term *educationally handicapped*), (b) teachers should be certified noncategorically (New Jersey uses the term *teacher of the handicapped*), (c) special educational programs should be undifferentiated for the majority of children now considered mildly impaired, and (d) for teachers who wish to teach children who are more severely impaired, the noncategorical certification should be required as a basic certification, with additional course work leading to endorsement for the low-frequency handicaps. The recommended model is thus structured to be internally consistent — each of the major components of the model informs and regulates the other components.

Fluidity of Placement

The concept of fluid, flexible placements was a cornerstone of Deno's cascade of services (Deno, 1970), although this cornerstone has not been realized. Under that model, the possibility of brief placements of several weeks' or several months' duration in special education resource programming was emphasized. However, experience tells us that the door to the special education class tends to be a one-way door — once students are classified, they rarely are released from special education placement.

One principle of the recommended model is the assumption of fluid placements. In order to facilitate fluid placements, students should initially be placed in a short-term special education setting (we envision one grading period, or 6 to 9 weeks). Such placement should be based on assessment of adaptive behavior by the mainstream teacher, failure of prereferral interventions, review of the child's mainstream class work by the child study team, and parental permission. If improvement is not demonstrated during that time in the academic and/or behavioral problems, placement should be changed, adapted, or terminated. Likewise, if the presenting problems can be alleviated by such a short-term intervention, the child would then move back into the mainstream class, with consultation services as necessary.

There are at least two reasons to be optimistic about our ability to establish and maintain a more fluid service-delivery system today than was possible when Deno (1970) conceived of the cascade of services. First, a service-delivery system that is not categorically dependent is inherently more flexible than a system that is dependent on categories, because professionals will not be troubled by vague distinctions that must be emphasized in categorical service-delivery systems.

Second, we know a great deal more today about curriculum-based assessment (Lindsley, 1990; Wesson, 1991). Because of recent advances in research, a daily portrait of growth on academic and behavioral skill may be completed in a single grading period in the resource room placement. Such data are highly sensitive to change, which means that more responsive educational programming decisions may be made more quickly. Further, Peterson, Heistad, Peterson, and Reynolds (1985) demonstrated that curriculum-based assessment data could be collected by microcomputer, which makes obtaining a charted portrait of a child's progress fairly easy in the one grading period. At the end of that grading period, if the presenting problems can be alleviated by such a short-term intervention, the child would then move back into the mainstream class. The mainstream teacher could then take responsibility for continuation of the curriculum-based assessment project on a daily basis. Further, informed support services could also be provided as necessary.

Functional Assessment.   Assessment devices should be used only if they are functional in answering questions that arise from within this model. The model does include several decisions that must be made based on assessment data. The two assessment measures that were suggested to facilitate short-term placement can be the basis for long-term eligibility decisions. First, there is precedent for using measures of adaptive behavior to differentiate children with handicaps and those without (Walker, 1983; Weller & Strawser, 1981). Children who suffer from mental handicaps are routinely assessed on adaptive behavioral functioning; these measures are used to help determine both the disability and the level of severity. Further, current practices in assessment of children with LD and BD also depend on measures of adaptive behavior, as rated by the teachers, to determine both the existence of a handicap and the level of the severity. The *Walker Problem Behavior Identification Checklist* (Walker, 1983) is a rating of behavior that is currently used in assessment of children with behavioral problems. The manual for that teacher rating device includes a cut-off score to be used as a screening measure to differentiate children who may have a handicap from those who do not. Weller and Strawser (1981) recommended use of an adaptive behavior measure for students with LD to determine the level of severity of the handicap. That measure involves ratings of pragmatic language skills, social coping skills, relationships, and work prediction. Like measures used for children with EMH and BD, the assessment is based on mainstream teacher ratings of adaptive behavior.

The teacher ratings that would be collected prior to the short-term placement could be used again at the end of that placement in the long-term eligibility decision. However, if a major change resulted, the teachers may wish to fill out a new rating at the end of the grading period.

Another measure of adaptive behavior that should be collected during the first grading period placement is observation of on-task behavior in the mainstream classroom (McKinney & Feagans, 1983). On-task behavior is a variable that is causally related to achievement (Hoge & Luce, 1979). Research suggests that each of the mildly handicapped groups has problems attending to task (McKinney & Feagans, 1983; Sherry, 1981). Also, various instructional procedures have demonstrated that this attention characteristic is manipulable within the context of the classroom, and that certain educational treatments result in both increased attention and increased achievement productivity (Hallahan & Sapona, 1983; Snider, 1987). For these reasons, this may be a variable that should be measured for every child in the system.

Another procedure that would facilitate long-term placement decisions is assessment of the learning environment (Bender, 1986, 1988). Under current practice, assessment resources have been directed almost exclusively at learner characteristics. However, researchers have recently recommended evaluation of the instructional settings that handicapped children attend (Bender, 1986, 1988; Ysseldyke & Christenson, 1987). From an ecological point of view, learning must be interpreted in terms of its setting. Practically speaking, an ecological perspective suggests the importance of a long-neglected need — the need to assess how the child with the suspected handicap is taught. An understanding of the types of instructional strategies offered in the current instruction program assists the child-study team in determining what types of instructional practices may or may not work in the future. For example, there is no need to try a behavioral contract in the special education placement if such an approach has been rigorously attempted and has not succeeded in the mainstream class. This model encourages assessment of the instructional strategies used in the mainstream setting. Hopefully, such assessment conducted during the short-term placement period would prompt many mainstream teachers to carefully evaluate their instructional strategies that may facilitate success in mainstream classes (Bender, 1988).

Finally, long-term eligibility for services could also be based on the curriculum-based assessment data collected during the short-term placement (Lindsley, 1990; Marston & Magnusson, 1985; Marston et al., 1984). Galagan (1985) indicated that, from a legal viewpoint, eligibility decisions based exclusively on curriculum-based assessment were at least as defensible as current practices. Also, the functional productivity of using daily data charts of student progress to determine eligibility has been demonstrated elsewhere (Peterson et al., 1985).

With these measurement devices in mind, the child-study team should carefully follow the progress of the child during the short-term placement and determine during that period if additional assessment is necessary. If so, the team members, such as the psychologist or educational consultant, would observe the child's on-task behavior over (at least) a 3-day period for 20 minutes each day. Data of this sort can lead directly to suggestions for intervention to increase on-task behavior.

During the short-term placement, mainstream teachers would be expected to keep data for use in the long-term placement decisions. A critical incidents log of behavioral problems, as recommended by Sugai (1986), would certainly help. Additional worksheets could be collected in the mainstream class, and errors could be analyzed. The teacher should also be expected to evaluate the mainstream instructional environment using the procedures discussed previously.

The team would then meet at the end of the short-term grading period to consider additional placement based on a wide array of data. The data would include (a) several curriculum-based assessments that present a daily portrait of a child's academic and behavioral growth, (b) teacher ratings of adaptive behavior, (c) observations of on-task behaviors in the classroom, (d) additional documentation from the mainstream teacher, and (e) an instructional environment evaluation.

At that point several types of decisions are possible. First, the team may determine that the interventions that have been implemented can be conducted in the mainstream, either with consultation or without. Early research results on efficacy of consultation services, in combination with direct special education services, suggest impressive positive effects for this service-delivery model (Schulte et al., 1990). In either case, the mainstream teacher would assume primary responsibility for the education of the child.

Next, should the team decide that a longer-term placement is necessary, they could choose to continue the present special education/mainstream combination or even increase the time that the student spends in the special education program. The professional team should be allowed to place a child in any mainstream/special education combination based on the data that have been collected in the 9-week grading period.

Finally, should the team feel that special education services would be necessary in a more restrictive setting (i.e., a self-contained class, a special school, or an out-of-district placement), then the team would have to assess the child in considerable depth. Only if this level of restrictiveness is necessary would the team use the traditional battery of norm-referenced testing and apply the traditional labels for handicapping conditions (i.e., BD, LH, MH).

Application of this decision-making process should reduce assessment time for 70% of those children who are presently served in mainstream and special education combinations (Danielson & Bellamy, 1988). Beck and Weast (1990) have stated that assessment of one student in the Great Falls Public Schools costs $400.00. Using this figure, in a moderate-sized school district (which we define as having 300 referrals or 3-year reevaluations per year) would save $84,000 in assessment alone. Obviously, this noncategorical model would result in impressive savings. Not only does this model represent state-of-the-art practices, it is much more efficient.

CONCLUSION

The comprehensive model discussed herein represents, in our view, the only service-delivery system that incorporates each of the innovative strategies developed within the last two decades. We strongly feel that the current service-delivery system — appropriate though it has been for the first two decades of public school special education service — has outlived its usefulness. We have shown how some of the assumptions made in 1970 and incorporated into Deno's cascade have been challenged by research and experience. We have shown how our current categorical models are wasteful of assessment resources and preservice teacher training resources. We have carefully maintained those aspects of current service-delivery models that work for the child in need — multiple flexible placements, team-based decision making — and we have incorporated numerous innovative strategies such as precision teaching, curriculum-based assessment, adaptive behavioral assessment, and assessment of the instructional environments.

We believe that our nation should enter the next millennium using a service-delivery system that demonstrates internal integrity, fluid placements, and functional assessment. The current debates, stemming from the current budgetary concerns, represent only the tip of the iceberg in challenges to an outdated and inefficient service-delivery system. We believe that the comprehensive noncategorical model of service delivery represents the most straightforward and efficient model of service delivery available to meet the needs of handicapped children in the next century.

REFERENCES

Algozzine, K.M., Morsink, C.V., & Algozzine, B. (1986). Classroom ecology in categorical special education classrooms: And so, they counted the teeth in the horse! *Journal of Special Education, 20,* 209–217.

Barr, K.L., & McDowell, R.L. (1972). Comparison of learning disabled and emotionally disturbed children on the three deviant classroom behaviors. *Exceptional Children, 38,* 60–62.

Beck R., & Weast, J. (1990). Project RIDE: A staff development program for assisting "at risk" students in the regular classroom. *Journal of School Research and Information, 8*(3), 9–16.

Becker, L.D. (1978). Learning characteristics of educationally handicapped and retarded children. *Exceptional Children, 44,* 502–511.

Belch, P.J. (1979). Toward noncategorical teacher certification in special education — myth or reality? *Exceptional Children, 45,* 129–131.

Bender, W.N. (1986). Effective educational practices in the mainstream setting: Recommended model for evaluation of mainstream teachers' classes. *Journal of Special Education, 20,* 475–487.

Bender, W.N. (1988). The other side of placement decisions: Assessment of the mainstream learning environment. *Remedial and Special Education, 9*(5), 28–33.

Bender, W.N., Wyne, M.D., Stuck, G.B., & Bailey, D.B. Jr. (1984). Relative peer status of learning disabled, educable mentally handicapped, low achieving, and normally achieving children. *Child Study Journal, 13,* 209–216.

Bloom, B. (1980). The new direction in educational research: Alterable variables. *Phi Delta Kappan, 61,* 382–386.

Candler, A.C., Johnson, D.L., & Green, C. (1984). The differences among children with learning problems. *Education, 104,* 219–223.

Carri, L. (1985). Inservice teachers' assessed needs in behavioral disorders, mental retardation, and learning disabilities: Are they similar? *Exceptional Children, 51,* 411–416.

Carroll, J.L., Friedrich, D., & Hund, J. (1984). Academic self-concept and teachers' perceptions of normal, mentally retarded, and learning disabled elementary students. *Psychology in the Schools, 21,* 343–348.

Chandler, H.N., & Jones, K. (1983). Learning disabled or emotionally disturbed: Does it make a difference? Part 1. *Journal of Learning Disabilities, 16*(7), 8–10.

Chapey, G.D., Pyszkowski, I.S, & Trimarco, T.A. (1985). National trends for certification and training of special education teachers. *Teacher Education and Special Education, 8,* 203–208.

Coles, G.S. (1978). The learning disabilities test battery: Empirical and social issues. *Harvard Educational Review, 48,* 313–340.

Crandall, V.C., Katkovsky, W., & Crandall, V.J. (1965). Children's beliefs in their own control of reinforcements in intellectual-academic achievement situations. *Child Development, 36,* 91–109.

Danielson, L.C., & Bellamy, G.T. (1988). State variation in placement of children with handicaps in segregated environments. *Exceptional Children, 55,* 448–455.

David, W.J., & Fairchild, M.R. (1976). A study of noncategorical teacher preparation in special education: A self realization model. *Exceptional Children, 42,* 390–397.

Deno, E. (1970). Special education as developmental capital. *Exceptional Children, 37,* 229–237.

Deno, S.L., Mirkin, P.K. (1977). *Data Based Program Modification.* Reston, VA: Council for Exceptional Children.

Epstein, M.H., & Cullinan, D. (1984). Behavior problems of mildly handicapped and normal adolescents. *Journal of Clinical Child Psychology, 13*(1), 33–37.

Fuchs, D., Fuchs, L., & Bahr, M.W. (1990). Mainstream assistance teams: A scientific basis for the art of consultation. *Educational Children, 57,* 128–139.

Gajar, A.H. (1979). Educable mentally retarded, learning disabled, emotionally disturbed: Similarities and differences. *Exceptional Children, 45,* 470–472.

Gajar, A.H. (1980). Characteristics across exceptional categories: EMR, LD, and ED. *Journal of Special Education, 14,* 165–173.

Galagan, J.E. (1985). Psychoeducational testing: Turn out the lights, the party's over. *Exceptional Children, 52,* 288–299.

Hallahan, D.P., & Kauffman, J.M. (1977). Labels, categories, behaviors: ED, LD, and EMR reconsidered. *Journal of Special Education, 11,* 139–149.

Hallahan, D.P., & Sapona, R. (1983). Self-monitoring of attention with learning-disabled children: Past research and current issues. *Journal of Learning Disabilities, 16,* 616–620.

Hoge, R.D., & Luce, S. (1979). Predicting academic achievement from classroom behavior. *Review of Educational Research, 49,* 479–496.

Idol-Maestas, L., Lloyd, S., & Lilly, M.S. (1981). A noncategorical approach to direct service and teacher education. *Exceptional Children, 48,* 213–220.

Jastak, S., & Wilkinson, G.S. (1984). *Wide Range Achievement Test – Revised.* Wilmington, DE: Jastak Associates.

Jenkins, J.R., Pious, C.G., & Peterson, D.L. (1988). Categorical programs for remedial and handicapped students: Issues of validity. *Exceptional Children, 55,* 147–158.

Keogh, B.K., Wetter, J., & McGinty, A. (1973). Functional analysis of WISC performance of learning-disordered, hyperactive, and mentally retarded boys. *Psychology in Schools, 10,* 178–181.

Lindsley, O.R. (1990). Precision teaching: By teachers for children. *Teaching Exceptional Children, 22,* 10–15.

Luchow, J.P., Crowl, T.K., & Kahn, J.P. (1985). Learned helplessness: Perceived effects of ability and effort on academic performance among EH and LD/EH children. *Journal of Learning Disabilities, 18,* 470–474.

Marston, D. (1987). Does categorical teacher certification benefit the mildly handicapped child? *Exceptional Children, 53,* 423–431.

Marston, D., & Magnusson, D. (1985). Implementing curriculum-based measurement in special and regular education settings. *Exceptional Children, 52,* 266–276.

Marston, D., Tindal, G., & Deno, S.L. (1984). Eligibility for learning disability services: A direct and repeated measurement approach. *Exceptional Children, 50,* 554–556.

Mayer, C.L., & Scheffelin, M. (1975). State-wide planning for special education in California. *Journal of Learning Disabilities, 4,* 50–54.

McCarthy, J.J., & Kirk, S.A. (1983). *The construction, standardization, and statistical characteristics of the Illinois Test of Psycholinguistic Abilities.* Urbana: University of Illinois Press.

McCarthy, J.M., & Paraskevopoulous, J. (1969). Behavior patterns of learning disabled, emotionally disturbed, and average children. *Exceptional Children, 36,* 69–74.

McKinney, J.D., & Feagans, L. (1983). Adaptive classroom behavior of learning disabled students. *Journal of Learning Disabilities, 16,* 360–367.

McKinney, J.D., & Forman, S.G. (1982). Classroom behavior patterns of EMH, LD and EH students. *Journal of School Psychology, 20,* 271–279.

Morsink C.V., Thomas, C.C., & Smith-Davis, J. (1987). Noncategorical special education programs: Process and outcomes. *Handbook of Special Education Research and Practice, 2,* 287–312.

O'Grady, D.J. (1974). Psycholinguistic abilities in learning-disabled, emotionally disturbed, and normal children. *Journal of Special Education, 8,* 157–165.

O'Sullivan, P.J., Marston, D., & Magnusson, D. (1987). Categorical special education teacher certification: Does it affect instruction of mildly handicapped pupils? *Remedial and Special Education, 8*(9), 13–18.

Peterson, J., Heistad, D., Peterson, D., & Reynolds, M. (1985). Montevideo individualized prescriptive instructional management system. *Exceptional Children, 52,* 239–243.

Phipps, P.M. (1982). The merging categories: Appropriate education or administrative convenience? *Journal of Learning Disabilities, 15,* 153–154.

Pullis, P.M. (1985). Temperament characteristics of LD students and their impact on decisions made by resource and mainstream teachers. *Learning Disability Quarterly, 8,* 109–122.

Reynolds, M.C., & Balow, B. (1972). Categories and variables in special education. *Exceptional Children, 38,* 357–366.

Schulte, A.C., Osborne, S.S., & McKinney, J.D. (1990). Academic outcomes for students with learning disabilities in consultation and resource programs. *Exceptional Children, 57,* 162–172.

Sherry, L. (1981). Non-task oriented behaviors of educable mentally retarded, emotionally handicapped and learning disabled students. *Educational Research Quarterly, 6,* 19–29.

Sindelar, P.T., Smith, M.A., Harriman, N.E., Hale, R.L., & Wilson, R.J. (1986). Teacher effectiveness in special education programs. *Journal of Special Education, 20,* 195–207.

Snider, V.E. (1987). A response to Hallahan and Lloyd. *Learning Disabilities Quarterly, 10,* 157–159.

Sugai, G. (1986). Recording classroom events: Maintaining a critical incidents log. *Teaching Exceptional Children, 18,* 98–102.

Walker, H.M. (1983). *Walker Problem Behavior Identification Checklist Manual.* Los Angeles: Western Psychological.

Wang, M.C., & Zollers, N.J. (1990). Adaptive instruction: An alternative service delivery approach. *Remedial and Special Education, 11*(1), 7–21.

Webster, R.E, & Schenck, S.J. (1978). Diagnostic test pattern differences among LD, ED, EMH, and multi-handicapped students. *Journal of Educational Research, 72,* 75–80.

Wechsler, D. (1949). *Wechsler Intelligence Scale for Children.* New York: The Psychological Corporation.

Weller, C., & Strawser, S. (1981). *Weller-Strawser Scales of Adaptive Behavior for the Learning Disabled.* Navote, CA: Academic Therapy.

Wesson, C.L. (1991). Curriculum-based measurement and two models of follow-up consultation. *Exceptional Children, 57,* 246–257.

Wolman, C. Thurlow, M.L., & Bruininks, R.H. (1989). Stability of categorical designations for special education students: A longitudinal study. *Journal of Special Education, 23,* 213–222.

Ysseldyke, J.E., & Christenson, S.L. (1987). Evaluating students' instructional environments. *Remedial and Special Education, 8,* 17–24.

Ysseldyke, J.E., Christenson, S.L., McVicar, R., Bakewell, D., & Thurlow, M.L. (1986). *Instructional Environmental Scale: Scale development and training procedures* (Monograph No. 1). Minneapolis: University of Minnesota, Instructional Alternatives Project.

Ysseldyke, J.E., O'Sullivan, P.J., Thurlow, M.L., & Christenson, S.L. (1989a). Qualitative differences in reading and math instruction received by handicapped students. *Remedial and Special Education, 10*(1), 14–20.

Ysseldyke, J.E., Thurlow, M.L., & Wotruba J.W. (1989b). Special education student-teacher ratios for mildly handicapped children. *Journal of Special Education, 23,* 95–106.

Ysseldyke, J.E., Thurlow, M.L., Christenson, S.L., & Weiss, J. (1987). Time allocated to instruction of mentally retarded, learning disabled, emotionally disturbed, and nonhandicapped elementary students. *Journal of Special Education, 21,* 43–55.

8

Artificial Intelligence and Expert Systems: What Have We Learned?

Cleborne D. Maddux

In the field of educational computing, it sometimes seems as if every issue produces a controversy. Yet none of the controversial issues in this new field is as controversial as that of determining the appropriate role for artificial intelligence and expert systems in helping professions such as special education and rehabilitation.

ARTIFICIAL INTELLIGENCE

The very term *artificial intelligence* is capable of producing a visceral reaction in many people. A rose by any other name may be a rose, but the choice of this particular term is a monument to semantic provocation. The term *artificial intelligence* evokes emotional responses because it implies that what many people regard as uniquely human can be created scientifically and bestowed on a machine. As Weizenbaum (1976) has said, the term leads to consideration "about nothing less than man's place in the universe" (p. 8).

Obviously, it is beyond the scope of this Chapter to provide a comprehensive discussion of the philosophical issues inherent in the concept of artificial intelligence. Although there are many excellent books and papers related to such issues, the reader is especially encouraged to read the works by Weizenbaum (1976) and Dreyfus and Dreyfus (1988).

One reason that the term *artificial intelligence* is controversial is that it reflects an underlying world view that is itself highly controversial. This world view is that of *man as a machine,* and this theme has engendered decades of bitter invective in many disciplines. The debate is pertinent to the field of artificial intelligence because, if a human is merely a specialized machine, then it is logical and theoretically possible that a machine could be produced that is intelligent. A colleague recently displayed a sign on his door that read, "The human brain is a sophisticated computer made of meat." This slogan takes the "man as a machine" orientation to its extreme! Although the "man as a machine" world view has had a profound influence on the field of artificial intelligence, it did not originate there. Most recently, it caused one of the most divisive controversies in the history of psychology by providing the basis for the debate between cognitive and behavioral psychologists. For an excellent discussion of the mechanistic view of man in psychology and in computer science, see Reese and Overton (1970) and Shanker (1989).

Some of the controversy concerning artificial intelligence is probably due to ambiguity of the terms *artificial* and *intelligence*. After all, psychologists have struggled (unsuccessfully) for years to achieve consensus on a definition of "intelligence." There are also various meanings for the word *artificial*. McFarland and Parker (1990) have acknowledged this ambiguity: "The terms 'artificial' and 'intelligence' are plainly central concepts of AI. These concepts are not easily defined or described. The concept 'artificial' may be used in differing ways. For example 'artificial' light is a useful source of illumination that is similar to natural light, but 'artificial' flowers (although potentially useful) are only related to natural flowers in appearance" (pp. 9–11).

Artificial Intelligence: A New Discipline Is Founded

The field of artificial intelligence is a subspecialty within computer science and owes its roots to a 1956 conference held at Dartmouth University (Born & Born-Lechleitner, 1987). This conference was planned by John McCarthy, who is often credited with coining the term *artificial intelligence* and with developing LISP, the first artificial intelligence programming language (McFarland & Parker, 1990). Other key individuals who attended this early conference and who went on to do important work in artificial intelligence were Allen Newell and Herbert Simon, from Carnegie-Mellon, and Marvin Minsky, from MIT (Dreyfus & Dreyfus, 1988).

Defining Artificial Intelligence

What exactly is meant by *artificial intelligence*? The term is difficult to define and means different things to different people. McFarland and Parker (1990) agree and suggest that "Artificial intelligence has complex connotations as well as an ill-defined denotation" (p. 12). Van Horn (1991) defines it as "the attempt to create machines that mimic intelligent human behavior" (p. 176). Other authorities forsake words such as *mimic* or *simulate* and refer to the goal of producing intelligent machines, or machines that can learn (Lockard et al., 1990).

An example is Barr and Feigenbaum's (1981) often-quoted definition stating that artificial intelligence is concerned with the design of intelligent computers that "exhibit the characteristics we associate with intelligent human behavior — understanding, language, learning, reasoning and problem solving" (p. 3). Similarly, Winston (1984) suggests that artificial intelligence is "the study of ideas that enable the computer to be intelligent" (p. 4).

Searle (1989) describes artificial intelligence by dichotomizing its activities into *weak AI* and *strong AI* categories. According to Searle, *weak AI* seeks to provide a tool for study of the human mind, whereas *strong AI* strives to create computers "that can be literally said to *understand* and have other cognitive states" (p. 18). Most of the controversy about AI has been sparked by goals from *strong AI*. Weizenbaum's (1976) objections are characteristic of critics of this approach. He articulates two goals for AI researchers: one he calls the "grand vision;" and the other the "grandiose fantasy." Both of these are *strong AI* goals and are, respectively, (a) ". . . the building of machines whose range of thought is to be coextensive with that of humanity itself" (p. 197); and (b) ". . . to build a machine on the model of a man, a robot that is to have its childhood, to learn language as a child does, to gain its knowledge of the world by sensing the world through its own organs, and ultimately to contemplate the whole domain of human thought" (pp. 202–203). It would be surprising, to say the least, if goals such as these did *not* provoke controversy and skepticism.

Special education and rehabilitation are applied disciplines. Professionals in these fields are practitioners who interact with students and clients, and therefore most of the applications that are available to such professionals are designed not to help *study* intelligent behavior (*weak AI*), but to engage in intelligent behavior in order to accomplish some practical task. They are, in other words, applications that are products of *strong AI*, and they are designed to mimic, simulate, or replicate intelligent human behavior.

Applications of Artificial Intelligence

As mentioned earlier, AI is different things to different people. Even experts in this field do not agree on exactly which computer applications should be subsumed under the general rubric of AI. To give the reader a feel for the ambiguity in the literature concerning what specific applications are part of AI, it might be helpful to look at a representative sample of opinion regarding this matter.

Dear (1986) suggests that AI applications include those that deal with *vision systems, robotics, speech and natural language systems, knowledge representation and expert systems, intelligent tutoring systems,* and *problem-solving systems.* Schorr (1989) asserts that *expert systems* are applications most rapidly coming into widespread use, but that artificial intelligence also includes *robotics, neural networks,* and *natural-language processing.* Merrill and co-workers (1992) list *intelligent computer-assisted instruction (ICAI)* (also known as *intelligent tutoring systems,* or *ITS*), *intelligent authoring tools, expert systems,* a variety of *intelligent psychological and educational assessment tools,* and the *Logo computer language.* Van Horn (1991) includes *expert systems, robotics, speech processing, natural language processing (written), theorem proving, general problem solving, pattern recognition, game playing, machine learning, machine vision,* and *neural network simulation.*

The above lists are characteristic of those who define AI very broadly. Consequently, their lists of applications are long. There are others, however, who define AI more narrowly. For example, Yin and Moore (1987) define AI as "The use of the computer to conduct the types of problem solving and decision making faced by human beings in dealing with the world" (p. 62). These authors differ from others who use a broad definition of AI in that they treat robotics, for example, not as a subcategory of AI but as a category separate from AI and computer simulations, the other two categories addressed in their article. Similarly, many other authorities use a narrow definition and refer to *expert systems* as if they are the only application of AI. Some even treat expert systems as a category of its own, completely separate from AI.

Regardless of the way that AI is defined or which applications are listed as examples, nearly all authorities agree that *expert systems* have become the most common application. McFarland and Parker (1990), for example, suggest that AI problem-solving processes "are only beginning to enter the marketplace" and that "expert systems and knowledge representations are presently the most active areas of practical problem solving" (p. 12). Wilson and Welsh (1986) emphasize the expanding interest of business and industry and suggest that many large businesses are investing heavily in AI in general, and that "about half of the companies in the Fortune 500 are actively pursuing one area of AI, expert system development" (p. 7). Lockard and associates (1990), in discussing AI in education, call expert systems the "most concrete application of artificial intelligence" (p. 337), and Ferrara, Parry, and Lubke (1985) suggest that "Much of the current interest in AI has been a result of the practical success of computer-based expert systems" (p. 39).

Most of the early work on expert systems was carried out outside the field of education for use in business and industry. However, expert systems are beginning to be implemented in public school settings.

As we have seen, the field lacks consensus about exactly which applications should be classed as AI. Some authorities define the term quite broadly, whereas others use a narrower definition. The one application that is classed as an AI application by nearly everyone, however, is expert systems. Expert systems are also the most common AI application, both outside and inside education.

This chapter briefly reviews some of the other applications of AI in special education and rehabilitation and then returns to devote considerable space to a discussion of expert systems and their roles in these two fields. The applications chosen for this review are those that appear to be the most common or to hold the most promise for use in special education and rehabilitation.

Throughout the following discussion, the reader should keep in mind that a major obstacle to implementation of these new technologies (perhaps the only *significant* obstacle) is cost. This is a barrier that cannot be solved solely by operation of a free market economy. The problem is that the market for this technology is comparatively small, given the cost of research and development. To solve this problem, government will have to become involved. Some preliminary progress has been made through passage of the Technology-Related Assistance for Individuals with Disabilities Act of 1988. Although funding is relatively modest, passage of the bill signals that the nation is at least aware of the problem.

Robotics

Robots are reprogrammable devices that can manipulate their environment (Post et al., 1988). Robots have been in existence for many years, and industrial robots have been serving successfully on assembly lines for some time. According to Van Horn (1991), there are about 100,000 industrial robots in the world, including 16,000 in the United States and 60,000 in Japan. However, robots have only recently begun appearing in schools.

A good indicator of the limited extent to which robots have been put to use in education is the meager space devoted to them in introductory computer education textbooks. Until recently, most such textbooks devoted no more than a page or two to robotics, and many books included only a paragraph or two or omitted discussion of robotics entirely. The Geisert and Futrell (1990) text is a case in point. This 346-page book devotes a total of only two paragraphs to robotics and concludes that "robots do not currently have broad curricular applicability, and so they are unlikely to make a very profound impression on most teachers" (p. 53).

This situation appears to be changing, however. It is noteworthy that a recent new book by Van Horn (1991) mentions robotics in its subtitle, devotes an entire chapter to the uses of robots in education, and includes an appendix on the anatomy of two commercially available robots suitable for classroom use. Van Horn goes on to suggest five educational uses for robots, including (a) the study of robotics as a significant technology, (b) uses in a wide variety of problem-solving activities, (c) aids for teaching traditional curriculum topics such as physics, (d) robot-assisted instruction to teach content directly, and (e) motivation leading to intensified learning.

Although robotics has yet to exert a broad influence in education, special education and rehabilitation are two educational specialties that have recognized the *potential* of robots and have already begun research and development efforts. One of the greatest potential uses for robots in these two fields is as prosthetic aids for physically disabled individuals.

Post and associates (1988) refer to such uses as the most exciting of all educational applications of robotics and suggest that "Research and development work done throughout the U.S. has demonstrated the utility of the robot as a physical prosthetic device for use by the orthopedically handicapped" (p. 44). These researchers reviewed the literature and concluded that the greatest benefit appeared to be for individuals with *spinal cord injury,* with *cerebral palsy,* and for *disabled geriatric patients.* They report that the technology has been demonstrated to be useful to stimulate walking in individuals with paralysis (Petrofsky & Phillips, 1983; Marsolais & Kobetic, 1986) and to manipulate objects for individuals who lack fine motor control (Hoseit et al., 1986).

Robotics appears to have the potential to play an important role in special education and rehabilitation, provided that one difficult problem can be solved. That problem is the high cost of the technology and finding a way to pay for it. Studies reported by Moore, Yin, and Lahm (1986) and Yin and Moore (1987) show that special educators with technological expertise agree with this assessment. The researchers concentrated on investigating the future special education applicability of three new technologies: robotics, AI, and computer simulations. These technologies were chosen because they satisfied the following criteria: "(a) technological advances in fields other than the target field (e.g., special education) are perceived to be in place, (b) there appear to be potential payoffs from these technologies for the target field, but (c) the applications of these technologies have not yet been directed at the target field" (Yin & Moore, 1987, p. 60).

After a review of the literature and interviews with experts, the researchers identified 59 current, successful, non-education applications of the three technologies, including 26 applications in robotics, 20 in AI, and 13 in computer simulation. These 59 applications were then screened for apparent promise in special education and to confirm their existence in a practical setting. Seventeen of the applications met these criteria and became the subjects of in-depth study consisting of visits to the sites and interviews with key individuals. A panel of 10 experts was then chosen from a pool of 42 persons judged to be experts in both special education and technology. This panel rated the non–special education applications for their applicability in special education and created special education scenarios for them. The panel then rated the applications for the type of special education student likely to benefit, the number of years before 10%, 50%, and 90% of the special education population would benefit, factors inhibiting implementation, and amount of money needed for implementation.

For robotics, major non-education applications were found in which robots were used for assembly, including welding and painting, and for tasks that would be repetitive or dangerous for humans. Also reviewed was a robot with an artificial vision system used to identify and select parts on a conveyor belt.

The panel concluded that physically disabled students were most likely to benefit from robotics, although they suggested that AI and computer simulation applications were more promising for use in special education in the foreseeable future. They identified potential special education applications including "an object- and mechanical-device-manipulating robot, which could be used by handicapped students to move objects and manipulate mechanical devices" (Moore et al., 1986, pp. 74–75). They also identified the robot with machine vision as having potential as a "multiple environment assistive robot that could be attached to a wheelchair and used to identify and manipulate various objects" (Moore et al., 1986, p. 75).

The researchers found that implementation of robotics in special education will require solving many problems. Specific technical problems include refinement of existing vision and voice-control systems and a need to make robots sufficiently flexible for use in everyday situations. The panel also suggested that technical and cost barriers of all three technologies are not likely to be overcome solely for special education applications, and that success will depend on the need for solving these problems in other, commercial settings where demand is high. They caution that implementation will require investigation into the cognitive impact of robotics use by disabled individuals, and that researchers have focused almost exclusively on development of the physical parameters of the robots.

The authors conclude that all three applications (robotics, AI, and computer simulations) face major cost barriers and significant time periods before implementation can benefit substantial numbers of special education students. Further, they suggest that the robotics applications will require the longest time and the most money, since current uses are almost always found outside education, primarily in manufacturing environments.

Voice Synthesis and Language Processing

Both of these applications hold great promise but have not been widely used in education. The technology necessary for *voice synthesis* has improved greatly in the last few years, and some applications are so good they can hardly be distinguished from real speech. Unfortunately, however, the price that must be paid for highly accurate synthesized speech is often beyond the resources of the public school classroom. Although dollar costs for the hardware are declining sharply, the amount of *memory* required for excellent voice synthesis may not be available. For example, digitized speech, the most accurate type of synthesized speech, requires 7,000 to 8,000 bytes of memory on an Apple IIGS (Anderson-Inman et al., 1990). This requirement places limited digitized speech in reach only if the computer is equipped with a hard drive. Few school computers are so equipped. Even then, digitized speech is not usually a school option, since the $700 to $800 cost of the required expansion board is approximately equivalent to attaching a videodisc player and a controller card (Hannafin & Peck, 1988). According to Hannafin and Peck, "Since the initial hardware price is comparable and disc mastering fees have come down significantly in price, more and more designers faced with an audio need are considering installing video hardware and using only the audio tracks. That way, if a video application arises at a later date, the equipment will have already been purchased" (p. 351).

Encoded speech and synthesized speech are the other two methods of voice synthesis, and these are not as memory intensive as is digitized speech. However, even for these two methods, which are not as accurate as digitized speech, the quality is directly related to memory used.

We can only conclude that use of voice synthesis in education is promising but still experimental. One problem is that very little research has been carried out, and what does exist varies greatly in voice quality and intelligibility across studies (Anderson-Inman et al., 1990).

Anderson-Inman and co-workers (1990) reviewed the research and concluded that the use of talking word processors is supported and leads to (a) increased editing, (b) more collaboration, (c) greater motivation (especially for less skilled writers), and (d) increased language acquisition for developmentally delayed children. When these authors examined research on reading instruction in which students can elect to have the computer read unknown words, they concluded that (a) poor readers will read material that is more difficult than they would ordinarily read, (b) word-recognition test scores increase, and (c) disabled readers profit from having words broken down into very small, sub-syllable components.

Anderson-Inman and associates (1990) made several recommendations for using voice synthesis with special populations. These included (a) the need for speech to be very accurate and supplemented with graphics when used with young students and nonreaders, (b) an emphasis on problem sounds when used with students studying English as a second language, and (c) the need for emphasis on speed rather than quality when used with visually impaired individuals. These authors also include an excellent appendix listing a large number of computer programs that use speech synthesis.

Speech synthesis has been successful when used with visually impaired students. The Kurzweil Reading Machine allows a reading rate as fast as human speech by using a computer to convert print into synthesized speech. The original machine was so expensive ($50,000) that it was generally found only in state schools, colleges, and libraries (Bullock, 1992). A smaller version, the Kurzweil Personal Reader, is now available for less than $10,000 (Brody, 1989).

Speech synthesis has also been successfully used in augmentative communication systems such as communication boards, which are often flat surfaces on which words and pictures are placed. Students who have speech disabilities and motor problems prohibiting keyboarding point to the symbols. This input is transferred to a computer, and the computer then synthesizes the speech that has been "ordered."

Although the technology for speech synthesis is available to those who can afford to purchase it, the same cannot be said for true, flexible, and unlimited *language processing,* which remains beyond our technological reach at any cost.

Language processing refers to the ability of a computer to recognize and respond to natural language commands such as those given in English. Although some effort has been put into language processing of written language, most applications are devoted to developing programs that can respond to oral commands. Such programs suffer from many problems such as restricted vocabulary and the need to pause unnaturally between words.

Wetzel (1991) reviewed available systems and discusses the potential for complete language recognition in the future. Wetzel asks "Will schools have an affordable speech processing system within 10 years?" (p. 29). His answer is "probably not" if such systems must include unlimited vocabularies, although optimists predict $500 cards with very limited vocabularies (2,000 to 10,000 words) within that time frame. In fact, Wetzel conducted interviews with executives of leading commercial developers and suggests that "no one asserts that speech recognition with unlimited vocabulary will be available within 10 years" (Wetzel, 1991, p. 20). Merrill (Twitchell, 1991), in a published interview, suggests that "the pursuit of a natural language interface is to pursue the Holy Grail" (p. 35).

Wetzel (1991) is slightly more optimistic than is Merrill about the future of this technology. He discusses its application to special education and rehabilitation:

"Some physically handicapped populations are already affected by this technology. For example, those without use of limbs, but who have consistent voice patterns, can use the commercial speech recognition technologies described earlier. Access to the technology, that is, the cost barrier, is the largest obstacle preventing its widespread use" (p. 21).

Hallahan and Kauffman (1991) acknowledge the problems with cost effectiveness and the state of the art of the technology as it is presently available. They add that we have recently begun to realize that the most sophisticated alternative communication system is not always the one that will be the most useful for a given individual, and that it is essential that decisions about such systems be made on a highly individual basis.

Intelligent Computer-Assisted Instruction (ICAI) or Intelligent Tutoring Systems (ITS)

This application is the least developed of any discussed so far. Lockard and associates (1990) describe the concept: "An ITS engages the learner in dialogue to identify misconceptions, then remediates to correct them. . . . In theory, an ITS knows what to teach, to whom, when, and how. It is not constrained by the responses programmed into it, but rather than just repeating the same presentation as typical tutorials do, an ITS would analyze the cause of the error and remediate accordingly" (p. 189). In other words, the goal of ITS is to produce a machine tutor as effective as or more effective than a human tutor.

As previously stated, applications of ITS are scarce, and those that have been completed are very crude. Lockard and co-workers (1990) discuss early systems such as SCHOLAR (Rambally, 1986; Kearsley, 1987), which teaches South American geography; SOPHIE, which teaches electronic troubleshooting; and BUGGY, which deals with misconceptions in arithmetic.

Hannafin and Peck (1988) agree that the state of the art in ICAI is in its infancy: "Unfortunately, there are no fully functional ICAI systems in existence today. . . . We are not talking about today's technology, we are talking about tomorrow's" (p. 375).

Gagne (Twitchell, 1991) comments, "I am a little skeptical about ICAI. . . . I think, of course, if you want to develop some good computer-aided instruction, and you want to get funding for it, you call it ICAI" (pp. 34–35). In the same interview, Merrill criticizes ICAI on the grounds that most such programs are excellent with the subject matter being taught, but are poor instructors. Roberts and Park (1991) agree and comment: "The rhetoric surrounding this work often leaves the reader with the impression that ICAI systems that can intelligently teach any subject on any terminal are 'just around the corner,' and *this is clearly not the case*" (p. 133).

They go on to identify ICAI problems that must be solved, including (a) the inability of students to interact with the program using natural language, (b) the lack of complete understanding of how students learn specific subject matter and how this learning differs from the learning of experts, (c) the labor-intensive nature of ICAI system development, (d) the tendency to develop ICAI only for highly structured content areas such as mathematics, and (e) the need for very expensive hardware to run ICAI programs.

Lockard and associates (1990) echo these concerns and add that although many ICAI programs are described in the literature, most are not fully functional. The reason for this is easy to understand in light of Liebowitz's (1989) rule of thumb that building intelligent tutoring systems consisting of 60 hours of instruction requires about five person-years of development. This problem is compounded by the fact that ICAI programs are subject matter specific, and most authorities do not believe that generic, domain-independent programs are possible (Lianjing & Taotao, 1991). Liebowitz (1989) adds that developers should provide for feedback on the part of the expert and users, and that the user interface is an important consideration that needs to be improved in most programs.

Epstein and Hillegeist (1990) are optimistic about the future of ICAI but caution that existing applications often neglect attention to the role of the human teacher in the success of an ICAI application. These authors emphasize that human teachers must (a) teach students the necessary prerequisite skills and knowledge before the computer program is begun, (b) observe students as they use the program and capitalize on teachable moments that arise, (c) provide individual help for weaker students, and (d) help students generalize skills learned. These authors also provide an excellent section in which they list qualities of an ideal ICAI.

In summary, ICAI or ITS technology, like all the other applications of AI, is in its infancy. It is time-consuming to produce, and the most sophisticated programs run on expensive hardware not readily available to schools. The future of ICAI is uncertain, but most experts are optimistic that some useful programs will become available in the next few years. Some developers caution that the role of the teacher should be examined carefully and is crucial to the success of ICAI. Perhaps the major benefit of this innovation will be in research, where it has proven useful in helping to understand how children learn.

EXPERT SYSTEMS

An expert system is "a computer based system capable of solving complex problems (in a specific subject area) at the competency level of a human expert" (Merrill et al., 1992). Grabinger, Wilson, and Jonassen (1990) describe how expert systems are used:

Like a human expert, an expert system (computer program) is approached by an individual (novice) with a problem, the system queries the individual about the current status of the problem, searches its own data base for pertinent rules and information, processes the information, arrives at a decision and reports the solution to the user. (p. 3)

In addition, expert systems are often able to explain their reasoning (Lockard et al., 1990). Expert systems typically are made up of several modules including a *knowledge base,* an *inference base,* and a *user interface* (Van Horn, 1991). These components are developed through a complicated collaborative process involving the developer and experts whose expertise will be simulated by the software.

As we stated at the beginning of this chapter, expert systems have become the most available AI application for use in schools. Educational journals are full of articles about expert systems, and educational computing conferences feature numerous sessions related to them. Although expert systems are more common in schools *than are other applications of AI,* the reader should not assume that they are *commonly* found here. Pilato and Malouf (1991) suggest that expert system technology is coming of age but add that school implementation remains very rare.

As with other AI applications, expert systems are more common in non-school settings, especially commercial settings. An indication of this phenomenon is that a recent volume entitled *Innovative Applications of Artificial Intelligence* (Schorr & Rappaport, 1989) includes chapters on expert systems in aerospace, banking and finance, biotechnology, emergency services, law, manufacturing assembly, manufacturing design, media and music, military, operations management, personnel management, and retail packaging. No chapter on educational uses is included. It should be obvious from this brief discussion that there is more excitement about the *potential* of expert systems in education than about the accomplishments of such systems, since implementation has been sparse indeed.

In our discussions of AI applications earlier in this chapter, I referred to the philosophical problems and controversies evoked by AI, but for space reasons, I have avoided addressing these controversies in depth. However, no discussion of expert systems would be complete without some consideration of the philosophical questions and controversies they provoke.

Although expert systems have great potential for accomplishing important tasks in schools, they also have great potential for abuse. In the past, misuse of computers in schools has contributed to a backlash of public and professional opinion against their use. Although there are many reasons for the backlash (see Maddux, 1989), I believe that one of the main causes is a myth and related behaviors I have called *the Everest syndrome.* This syndrome is based on the belief that computers should be implemented in schools merely "because they are there." This is a dangerous belief because it can cause us to neglect to think critically about how computers *should* and *should not* be used in education. I believe many educators have been guilty of this error, and it has caused us to focus myopically on what can be done with technology and to neglect making the value judgments about what should be done. We have frequently acted as if computers *should* be used for whatever they *could* be used for.

Expert systems are a case in point. Although it is by no means an established fact that human expertise *can* be instilled into a computer program, neither has there been sufficient debate concerning whether or not such expertise *should* be computerized. I believe there are a number of reasons why conversion of pedagogical and related expertise to machine delivery should give us pause:

1. *There is a tendency to believe that computerizing an activity automatically improves that activity.* This is not necessarily so. Sometimes computerizing only streamlines, or speeds up, the activity, or makes it more efficient in some other way. Although this may make the activity more convenient, it does not necessarily improve the underlying idea on which the activity is based. Weizenbaum (1976) addresses this problem: "For example, there are computer programs that carry out with great precision all the calculations required to cast the horoscope of an individual whose time and place of birth are known. Because the computer does all the tedious symbol manipulations, they can be done much more quickly and in much more detail than is normally possible for a human astrologer. But such an improvement in the technique of horoscope casting is irrelevant to the validity of astrological forecasting. If astrology is nonsense, then computerized astrology is just as surely nonsense" (pp. 34–35).

One danger inherent in expert systems is that educators will make the mistake of believing that once an expert system has been created and implemented, improvement has taken place and no effort is needed to refine the ideas underlying the computerized techniques. In other words, expert systems may delude us into a false sense of security about what we are doing in education.

2. *Computerizing an activity often leads to acceptance of the status quo.* This problem is related to the one above. Once an expert system is implemented, there may be great resistance to changing any of the tasks it was designed to facilitate. Any organization has a finite amount of energy and money to devote to innovation. In my experience, consultants to businesses or to schools who suggest that the organization might want to work on refining some technique that has already been turned over to computer implementation are frequently greeted with "Are you kidding? We just spent X dollars and X months revising and computerizing that technique last year." In this way, moving to computer implementation often leads to a very conservative approach to further innovation.

3. *Users often expect far too much of computer applications.* This may be especially true of expert systems. Virtually every educational article on expert systems emphasizes that they should be viewed only as sources of second opinions and not as primary decision makers. However, many people associate computers with power, precision, and accuracy, and there is a very real danger that expert systems will be used to supplant, rather than supplement, human expertise.

The seriousness of the practice of using expert systems as primary decision makers is partially dependent on the extent to which expert systems can actually emulate human expertise and solve human problems. Although there is disagreement with regard to the quality of expert systems, most authorities admit that existing programs do not completely emulate human expertise.

Dreyfus and Dreyfus (1988) go even further and suggest that AI in general, and expert systems in particular, are one of the great commercial disappointments of our time. These critics maintain that no expert system to date has even come close to emulating the best and most complete human expertise, and that many companies dedicated to the development of such systems have given up the effort or gone bankrupt, or both.

Dreyfus and Dreyfus (1988) suggest that expert systems have had some limited success, and that their potential can be understood only through a consideration of the type and complexity of human problems they are designed to address. According to these writers, human expertise is applied to (a) structured problems and (b) unstructured problems. They suggest that expert systems have been developed for use in solving only structured problems, which are the least common problems and which they define as those that call for step-by-step, sequential, *if–then* solutions. "Here the goal and what information is relevant are clear, the effects of decisions are known, and verifiable solutions can be reasoned out" (p. 20). Examples of structured problems that have been successfully addressed by expert systems include mathematical manipulations, puzzles, delivery truck routing, and petroleum blending. Dreyfus and Dreyfus (1988) describe such an expert system, called AALPS, that can be used to determine the placement of objects in cargo planes, and can do so in minutes as compared to hours when carried out by human experts.

According to Dreyfus and Dreyfus (1988), however, *unstructured* problems have not yielded to computer solutions. These problems are the most common human problems and contain "a potentially unlimited number of possibly relevant facts and features, and the ways those elements interrelate and determine other events is unclear" (p. 20). Unstructured problem areas include management, nursing, economic forecasting, teaching, and all social interactions. Examples of unstructured problems include everyday tasks such as recognition of a human face, identification of a faint odor, determining socially acceptable behavior, and walking or riding a bicycle. Problems such as these are unstructured because they cannot be solved by developing specific sets of *if–then* rules.

If these authorities are correct, the future of expert systems in education is not nearly as rosy as some advocates would lead us to expect. Nearly all of our problems are unstructured problems, and the danger is that implementation of expert systems in education may lead us to apply a flawed, simplistic, *if–then* logic to their solution, even though such logic is effective only for other, highly structured problems.

Many advocates of expert systems do not agree with Dreyfus and Dreyfus (1988) and their assessment of the abilities and limitations of expert systems. It is too early to know whether they are correct.

By now, the reader will have gathered that there are some very real reasons why it would be prudent for educators to take a cautious approach to expert systems. However, expert systems, although still scarce, are becoming more common in education. Therefore, we turn now to a consideration, not of whether or not we should use them, but to aids and cautions for those who decide to accept them as an educational tool.

There are many books and articles available on expert systems in education. One of the most valuable is a recent compilation of 31 articles reprinted from *Educational Technology* (Educational Technology, 1991). Also helpful is a volume by Grabinger and associates (1990), entitled *Building Expert Systems in Training and Education,* and another by Kearsley (1987), entitled *Artificial Intelligence and Instruction.*

Examining these and other sources will reveal that many expert systems have been developed for education, but that most have been used only in research settings. Nevertheless, the experiences of these and other users and researchers may prove helpful.

Special education has been an area in which several researchers have concentrated their work on expert systems. Hofmeister and Lubke (1986) have developed an expert system for diagnosing learning disabilities. They concluded:

1. Evaluations conducted with prototypes indicate that expert systems can perform as well as humans in specific areas.
2. Some of the problems faced by special educators are similar to those encountered in other disciplines where expert systems have proven successful.
3. The process of assembling and organizing knowledge bases for expert systems is a productive activity in its own right. The development of the "if–then rules of a knowledge base clarifies existing knowledge and identifies areas where knowledge is needed." (p. 71)

Hofmeister (1986) and Parry and Hofmeister (1986) also developed and tested an expert system called Mandate Consultant, designed to provide a second opinion on the appropriateness of the decision-making process used in the development of individualized education programs (IEPs) for disabled students. Although he found that conclusions reached by the expert system compared favorably with those reached by human experts, he made the following recommendations:

1. The expert system should be expanded to cover more of the areas addressed by special education regulations, and more qualitative issues such as the instructional content of IEP goals and objectives should be addressed.
2. The expert system requires further evaluation in a field setting, with attention being given to factors specific to user acceptance, such as accessibility, response time, and attitudes.

Steele and Raab (1991) developed an expert system called MONARCH, designed to provide a second opinion for special education multidisciplinary teams who make eligibility and placement decisions, and to train pre-service and in-service teachers. These researchers concluded that the MONARCH could be helpful in preventing misdiagnosis of learning-disabled children. A disadvantage of this expert system was that it was written in Prolog, a difficult computer language, in which changes are very difficult to make. Steele and Raab emphasized that this difficulty could prevent needed updates as knowledge becomes more sophisticated, but chose to use Prolog rather than an authoring shell, since multiple copies were then legal.

Haynes, Pilato, and Malouf (1987) reviewed several special education expert systems and suggested that one problem is that many expert systems have no provision for recognizing and questioning data that look faulty. Another problem in designing special education expert systems is determining whose expert knowledge to build into the system. In special education, there is little consensus among many contradictory theories and approaches.

Jones (1984) discussed several prototype special education expert systems and concluded that the development of simplified shells for designing expert systems will greatly increase their availability. Jones also recommended consulting several experts when designing special education expert systems, since a diversity of opinions exist concerning many aspects of dealing with disabled children.

Pilato and Malouf (1991) discussed implementation of an expert system called SNAP, intended to help teachers mainstream special education students into regular education classes. Pilato and Malouf observed that expert systems have only rarely been introduced into schools, and they offered a number of suggestions for those who wish to implement an expert system in a school:

1. A "champion" or advocate is needed in the school.
2. Designers of expert systems must be well acquainted with the needs of users and be sure that the system takes advantage of teachers' "need to know."
3. The technology must fit into the world of the user. The system must be readily available and training must be provided.
4. A multiphase infusion strategy should be used, incorporating awareness, initial training, acceptance, and integration.

In summary, this review of expert systems has not been exhaustive. Representative articles were chosen to illustrate the state of the art in educational expert systems and problems and cautions in their use in special education and rehabilitation. Many other excellent articles have been published but were not included due to space limitations.

Some conclusions about expert systems seem in order. Expert systems are potentially useful and potentially dangerous if abused. They remain highly experimental, and most applications run on hardware not yet widely available in education. Their utility appears to be best when applied to structured, rather than unstructured, problems.

There is a type of expert system that is so new that I have been unable to find an application in special education or rehabilitation. Such expert systems are called *neural networks*. These systems are based on the principles of human neurological systems and employ "artificial neurons." Although it seems counterproductive to engage in yet another round of anthropomorphizing the computer,

Dreyfus and Dreyfus (1988) and many others believe that neural nets may solve some of the problems rule-based expert systems have in dealing with unstructured problems. They might be better at dealing with such problems since they are modeled after the human nervous system and may be better at responding to the whole situation, the "gestalt" of a problem. Neural networks are promising but highly experimental approaches.

CONCLUSIONS

The jury is still out on the utility of artificial intelligence in special education and rehabilitation. Currently, the greatest benefit comes from application of speech synthesis for individuals with speech disabilities. If cost comes down, robotics seems a good bet to provide worthwhile service for individuals with physical disabilities. Natural language processing may come of age but seems a prospect for the far-distant future. Intelligent computer-assisted instruction, or intelligent tutoring systems, will continue to appear and will prove useful so long as we remember that they can never replace a human teacher. Expert systems are highly ambitious undertakings but will probably continue to see service as providers of second opinions. Neural networks seem highly promising, but their implementation may have to wait a decade or more.

What is the upshot of all this? The reader is, of course, encouraged to draw his or her own conclusions. For what it is worth, my conclusion is that we should approach the implementation of artificial intelligence in education with great caution and care. Regardless of how "expert" systems become, the problem is that expertise in dealing with human beings, particularly in special education and rehabilitation, requires more than knowledge. Affective qualities such as compassion, empathy, wisdom, and so forth are also required in large measure. The problem is that computers do not now, nor will they ever, possess these qualities. Such qualities are unavailable to computers since they require human experiences in their formation. Weizenbaum (1976) made reference to this problem as follows:

> I have argued that the individual human being, like any other organism, is defined by the problems he confronts. The human is unique by virtue of the fact that he must necessarily confront problems that arise from his unique biological and emotional needs. . . . No other organism, and certainly no computer, can be made to confront genuine human problems in human terms. And, since the domain of human intelligence is, except for a small set of formal problems, determined by man's humanity, every other intelligence, however great, must necessarily be alien to the human domain. (p. 223).

If we keep firmly in mind that computers must always be alien to the human domain, we will not be tempted to turn over to them decisions that require uniquely human attributes such as human emotions.

Because a tool is dangerous does not mean that it should be abandoned. Artificial intelligence has great potential. We should keep in mind the following caution by Dreyfus and Dreyfus (1988), and in our work with disabled individuals, proceed to use, rather than misuse, our artificially intelligent tools:

> If we fail to put logic machines in their proper place, as aids to human beings with expert intuition, then we shall end up servants supplying data to our competent machines. Should calculative rationality triumph, no one will notice that something is missing, but now, while we still know what expert judgment is, let us use that expert judgment to preserve it. (p. 206)

REFERENCES

Anderson-Inman, L., Adler, W., Cron, M., Hillinger, M., Olson, R., & Prohaska, B. (1990). Speech: The third dimension. *The Computing Teacher, 17*(7), 35–40.

Barr, A., & Feigenbaum, E.A. (1981). *The handbook of artificial intelligence* (Vol. 1). Los Altos, CA: William Kaufmann.

Born, R.P., & Born-Lechleitner, I. (1987). Introduction. In R.P. Born (Ed.), *Artificial intelligence: The case against* (pp. vii–xxxv). London: Routledge.

Brody, H. (1989). The great equalizer: PCs empower the disabled. *PC Computing, July*, 82–93.

Bullock, L.M. (1992). *Exceptionalities in children and youth*. Boston: Allyn & Bacon.

Dear, B.L. (1986). Artificial intelligence techniques: Applications for courseware development. *Educational Technology, July, 26*(7), 7–15.

Dreyfus, H.L., & Dreyfus, S.E. (1988). *Mind over machine*. New York: Free Press.

Educational Technology (1991). *The Educational Technology anthology series, Volume 2: Expert systems and intelligent computer-aided instruction*. Englewood Cliffs, NJ: Educational Technology Publications.

Epstein, K., & Hillegeist, E. (1990). Intelligent instructional systems: Teachers and computer-based intelligent tutoring systems. *Educational Technology, 30*(11), 13–19.

Ferrara, J.M., Parry, J.D., & Lubke, M.M. (1985). Expert systems authoring tools for the microcomputer: Two examples. *Educational Technology, 25*(4), 39–41.

Geisert, P., & Futrell, M. (1990). *Teachers, computers, and curriculum*. Needham Heights, MA: Allyn & Bacon.

Grabinger, R.S., Wilson, B.W., & Jonassen, D.H. (1990). *Building expert systems in training and education*. New York: Praeger.

Hallahan, D.P., & Kauffman, J.M. (1991). *Exceptional children* (5th ed.). Englewood Cliffs, NJ: Prentice-Hall.

Hannafin, M.J., & Peck, K.L. (1988). *The design, development, and evaluation of instructional software*. New York: Macmillan.

Haynes, J.A., Pilato, V.H., & Malouf, D.B. (1987). Expert systems for educational decision-making. *Educational Technology, 27*(5), 37–42.

Hofmeister, A.M. (1986). Assessing the accuracy of a knowledge-based system: Special education regulations and procedures. Final Report, Department of Education Grant No. G008530236, Project #023BH50056, Logan, UT: Utah State University.

Hofmeister, A.M., & Lubke, M.M. (1986). Expert systems: Implications for the diagnosis and treatment of learning disabilities. *Learning Disabilities Quarterly, 9*, 133–137.

Hoseit, K., Liu, N., & Cook, A. (1986). Development and use of a robotic arm system with very young developmentally delayed children. *Proceedings of the Ninth Annual Conference on Rehabilitation Technology*. Minneapolis: Rehabilitation Engineering Society of America.

Jones, M. (1984). Expert systems: Their potential roles within special education. *Peabody Journal of Education, 62*(1), 52–66.

Kearsley, G. (1987) (Ed.). *Artificial intelligence and instruction.* Reading, MA: Addison-Wesley.

Lianjing, H., & Taotao, H. (1991). A uniform student model for intelligent tutoring systems: Declarative and procedural aspects. *Educational Technology, 31*(11), 44–48.

Liebowitz, J. (1989). Expert systems technology for training applications. *Educational Technology, 29*(7), 43–45.

Lockard, J., Abrams, P.D., & Many, W.A. (1990). *Microcomputers for educators* (2nd ed.). Glenview, IL: Scott Foresman/Little, Brown Higher Education.

Maddux, C.D. (1989). Computers in assessment: Is it time? *Diagnostique, 14,* 262–273.

Marsolais, E.B., & Kobetic, R. (1986). *Walking of paraplegic subjects with computer-controlled electrical stimulation.* (Report No. MSL 3). Cleveland: Motion Study Laboratory.

McFarland, T.D., & Parker, R. (1990). *Expert systems in education and training.* Englewood Cliffs, NJ: Educational Technology Publications.

Merrill, P.F., Hammons, K., Tolman, M.N., Christensen, L., Vincent, B.R., & Reynolds, P.L. (1992). *Computers in education* (2nd ed.). Boston: Allyn & Bacon.

Moore, G.B., Yin, R.K., & Lahm, E.A. (1986). Robotics, artificial intelligence, computer simulation: Future applications in special education. *Technological Horizons in Education, 14*(1), 74–76.

Parry, J.D., & Hofmeister, A.M. (1986). Development and validation of an expert system for special educators. *Learning Disability Quarterly, 9*(2) 124–132.

Petrofsky, J.S., & Phillips, C.A. (1983). Electrical stimulation of paralyzed individuals under feedback computer control. *IEEE Transactions of Biomedical Engineering, BME-30*(8), 510.

Pilato, V.H., & Malouf, D.B. (1991). Expert systems in schools: Solving the implementation paradox. *Educational Technology, 31*(8), 49–53.

Post, P.E., Howell, R.D., & Rakocy, L. (1988). Robot technology: Implications for education. *Educational Technology, 28*(1), 39–45.

Rambally, G.K. (1986). The AI approach to CAI. *The Computing Teacher,* April, 39–42.

Reese, H.W., & Overton, W.F. (1970). Models of development and theories of development. In L.R. Gulet & P.B. Baltes (Eds.), *Life-span developmental psychology.* New York: Academic Press.

Roberts, F.C., & Park, O. (1991). Intelligent computer-assisted instruction: An explanation and overview. In *Expert systems and intelligent computer-aided instruction.* Englewood Cliffs, NJ: Educational Technology Publications.

Schorr, H. (1989). Preface. In H. Schorr & A. Rappaport. (1989) (Eds.), *Innovative applications of artificial intelligence* (pp. xiii–xvi). Menlo Park, CA: AAAI Press.

Schorr, H., & Rappaport, A. (1989) (Eds.) *Innovative applications of artificial intelligence.* Menlo Part, CA: AAAI Press.

Searle, J.R. (1989). Minds, brains and programs. In R.P. Born (Ed.), *Artificial intelligence: The case against* (pp. 18–40). London: Routledge.

Shanker, S.G. (1989). The decline and fall of the mechanist metaphor. In R.P. Born (Ed.), *Artificial intelligence: The case against* (pp. 72–131). London: Routledge.

Steele, J.W., & Raab, M.M. (1991). MONARCH: An expert system for classifying learning disabled students. *Tech Trends, 36*(2), 38–42.

Twitchell, D. (1991). Robert M. Gagne and M. David Merrill: In conversation. *Educational Technology, 31*(1), 34–40.

Van Horn, R. (1991). *Advanced technology in education.* Pacific Grove, CA: Brooks/Cole.

Weizenbaum, J. (1976). *Computer power and human reason.* New York: W.H. Freeman.

Wetzel, K. (1991). Speech technology II: Future software and hardware predictions. *The Computing Teacher, 19*(2), 19–21.

Wilson, B.G., & Welsh, J.R. (1986). Small knowledge-based systems in education and training: Something new under the sun. *Educational Technology, November, 26*(11), 7–13.

Winston, P.H. (1984). *Artificial intelligence.* Reading, MA: Addison-Wesley.

Yin, R.K., & Moore, G.B. (1987). The use of advanced technologies in special education: Prospects from robotics, artificial intelligence, and computer simulation. *Journal of Learning Disabilities, 20*(1), 60–63.

PART III

Educational Policy Making

9

Litigation, Legislation, and Politics of Special Education: Implications for the Practitioner

M.L. Anderegg
Glenn A. Vergason

"Historically, society has tended to isolate and segregate individuals with disabilities, and despite some improvements, such forms of discrimination against individuals with disabilities continue to be a serious and pervasive social problem; discrimination against individuals with disabilities persists. . . ." (Section 2, Americans with Disabilities Act of 1990, P.L. 101–336)

This statement in recent federal legislation indicates the problem facing 43 million people in the United States and focuses on expanding the protection of their rights. It succinctly summarizes the progression of the development of legislation driven by the litigation and politics of hundreds of years.

Most current educators, whether specialized or general, would now agree with this purpose, but that has not always been true. From the earliest days of special education in this country, special educators realized the need to overcome discrimination and lack of services. Prior to 1975, leaders in the field believed specialized pedagogies and a need for specialized services existed that were unavailable in regular classrooms. Most textbooks surveying the topic of exceptional children reflected that belief by defining students with disabilities as students who differed so far from the norm that they would be expected to fail in regular education. Within that context, one can understand Will's (1986) belated charge that children with disabilities are required to fail before help can be enlisted.

The abandonment of that view of special education was prompted by federal legislation for which the litigation and politics of previous eras served as incentives. Litigation, legislation, and politics are three areas that have prompted

167

change in special education, most recently and most notably reflected in the movement known originally as the regular education initiative (REI).

This chapter addresses the issues surrounding the education of students with disabilities and examines how political and economic issues have permeated the practices of special educators, at times without their realization of what was happening. We will examine the historical changes in special education from the standpoint of the interaction between litigation and legislation as they address the rights of the disabled. We will discuss the most recent political roots of the REI that may affect future litigation and legislation. Finally, we will comment on how we believe these interactive factors should affect current practice in the field of special education. Throughout the following discussion, the reader may benefit from a perusal of Table 9.1, which highlights the significant legislation affecting special education.

Table 9.1 Significant special education legislation

P.L. 89–313 1965	Grants to state institutions and state-operated schools, first federal grant to target individuals with disabilities
P.L. 89–750 1966	First federal grant for children with disabilities at local school level rather than special schools or institutions
P.L. 93–112 1973	Rehabilitation services for all regardless of severity of disability, civil right enforcement under Section 504
P.L. 93–380 1974	First federal law to mention "appropriate education," guaranteed students and families right to examine student's records
P.L. 94–142 1975	Mandated FAPE, due-process, individualization, least restrictive environment, zero reject
P.L. 98–199 1983	Reauthorized school-to-work transition, parent training and information, funding for research in early intervention
P.L. 98–524 1984	Supported vocational education programs, provided equal access
P.L. 99–372 1986	Recovery of reasonable attorney's fees for prevailing parents or guardians in disputes over FAPE-related services
P.L. 101–336 1990	Ensured full civil rights for disabled
P.L. 101–392 1990	Assigns greater responsibility for inclusion of disabled in vocational training
P.L. 101 476 1990	Mandated transition services, added two categories to eligible, removed Native American education from Bureau of Indian Affairs, changed terminology
P.L. 101–496 1990	Funded protection, advocacy, specialized services for those with developmental disabilities

HISTORICAL CHANGES
Litigation and Legislation

P.L. 94–142 (1975), The Education of All Handicapped Children Act, changed the semantics used in discussing the education of students with handicaps. The act described special education as including specialized instruction and related services to provide appropriate education for each child with a disability. Further, recent reauthorization (P.L. 101–476, 1990) has changed the terminology, from *handicapped* to *disabled*. The emphasis on regular education as the root of the problem has virtually disappeared from the literature. In fact, P.L. 94–142, and its subsequent renewal in P.L. 101–476, gave preference to educating children with disabilities with their nondisabled peers whenever that was possible without sacrificing the potential to benefit from instruction. In response to this, one mother said, "For years they told me regular education was my child's problem and now they tell me it is the solution."

Educators not only told parents regular education was the solution, some advocacy and parent organizations even instituted such a strong top-down mandate that parents were made to feel guilty if they did not insist on total, all-day mainstreaming for their child. Changing the label to "inclusive" education did not necessarily change the focus. For example, the Georgia Advocacy Office recently (1991) stated that "all children with developmental special needs should be educated with their nonhandicapped peers in regular classrooms" (p. 2). They urged "Georgians to learn about and work for inclusive education" (p. 3) and stated unabashedly that they "hope that this issue paper will further that end" (p. 3). Such strong language is not unusual.

Within the past few years, the organization for parents whose children have severe disabilities (TASH) experienced a traumatic confrontation over just this issue. The election of its chief officer revolved around the issue of pressuring parents to insist on 100% mainstreaming or inclusion for their children. The winning candidate's platform emphasized case-by-case placement decisions, and he urged parents to resist guilt applied by professionals and others promoting total inclusion (Simpson, 1991).

Least Restrictive Environment

P.L. 94–142 (1975) indicated the desire of Congress to promote the education of these children with normal children or as near to normal children as would be feasible and noninjurious to all the students. This latter principle, the least restrictive environment, has been debated and litigated in the courts (Turnbull, 1990) because some have viewed the least restrictive environment as equivalent to mainstreaming. The term *least restrictive* does not appear in the law but was originally coined in the literature to describe the setting (regular classroom) of the academic instruction. Later, the term was applied to placements in the regular classroom where the major skills focus was on social skills rather than on academic skills.

In negotiations following the disposition of the *Daniel R.R.* case (1989), however, Reed Martin (attorney for the child's family) used the term *mingling* to refer to placement in regular education settings, with social skills as the target behavior without concern for academic achievement. While it is similar to Orelove and Sobsey's (1984) partial integration, we believe Reed Martin's distinction to be valid and would recommend this distinction be adopted by the profession in the interest of clarifying communication.

Efficacy Studies

Prior to 1968, a number of descriptive studies addressing the efficacy of special education were published. None could withstand Campbell and Stanley's (1963) tests for validity, however. Essentially those publications compared students with multiple disabilities who were more likely to be placed in special classes and students with milder disabilities who were not only more likely to be in general education but would also do better academically. In short, the efficacy "studies" described what would be obvious to any thinking person. The more involved the disability, the less likely the child was to be placed or be successful in the regular classroom. Lloyd Dunn, for years, taught his doctoral students to reject these studies because of their methodological deficiencies. Later, in his swan song, Dunn (1968) chose to use these same works to urge movement away from special classes as the sole delivery model. Those persons who know Dunn and his style of teaching recognize his intention to stimulate professionals to reexamine practices current at that time. Although the article was critical, there appears to have been little reason, at the time, to believe the discussion would be taken so out of context of his life's work and be used as the most frequent justification for future changes in special education. The difference arose from the climate of litigation that examined the whole idea of the rights of the disabled and whether discrimination had been practiced against them.

Landmark Litigation

The landmark cases of *Pennsylvania Association for Retarded Children (PARC) v. Commonwealth of Pennsylvania* (1971, 1972) and *Mills v. D.C. Board of Education* (1972, 1980) established the standard that all individuals with disabilities had the right to an education, regardless of the severity or nature of their disability. These cases not only articulated their right to an education but also asserted the potential for even the most severely disabled to make progress.

Perhaps the most notable contribution of the PARC case was contained in the provisions of the out-of-court settlement. That agreement made the state of Pennsylvania responsible for providing a free, appropriate public education (FAPE) to all school-aged children within its boundaries and providing due-process protections. These provisions, in sharp contrast to practices in the rest of the nation, provided a model for later federal legislation, which spread its protections both unilaterally and geographically. Although appropriate education was one of the provisions of P.L. 93–380 (1974), both FAPE and due-process provisions from the PARC case are easily recognizable in P.L. 94–142 (1975). The due-process provision was especially important because it linked educational rights to the Fifth Amendment.

Chronologically and ideologically linked to these cases were the landmark decisions in *Diana v. State Board of Education* (1970, 1973) and *Larry P. v. Riles* (originated in 1970; 1984 was the date of the last decision rendered), which set the stage for a major shift in educational programming. In both cases, minority children were overrepresented in special classes. The situation gave the appearance of a racially segregated program following a decade of strong civil rights protests, litigation, and legislation.

Together these cases set a precedent for reserving special classes for the more disabled and for employing a regular education model, with mildly disabled students being pulled out only when limited specialized instruction was needed. These cases also focused attention on the potential for cultural bias in testing.

It was only a matter of time before these four cases reshaped special education dramatically. We moved from special classes with specialized curricula and a heavy emphasis on pre-vocational and vocational preparation in the 1950s to a model where the regular classroom was both the model and the curriculum. The Carl D. Perkins Vocational Acts (P.L. 98–524 in 1984 and P.L. 101–392 in 1990) specifically supported vocational training for individuals with disabilities, but the regular classrooms remained the primary placement and vocational education has not made a great contribution (Halpern, 1973, 1974). Thus, during the 1980s, special education rendered its services primarily in a supportive role.

Resource-Room Model

The pullout, or resource, model became the educational vehicle for the vast majority of the more mildly disabled learners. It reigned supreme for about 15 years, with students being served in both regular education and special education. However, in the 1980s certain professionals, most notably Madeline Will (1984, 1986), then the Assistant Secretary of Education, took the position that all students with disabilities would be served better if they were in regular classrooms 100% of the time. She declared special education a failure despite the fact that only about one-third of the students' course work was provided through special education services (Capitol Publications, 1990). She ignored the fact that most of the services (67%) were being provided in the regular classroom. Consequently, there was a massive removal of children from special education services and vocational preparation settings. Amazingly, Will began a campaign to return all the students to the regular classroom completely.

Under this scheme, special education rendered its services through regular education or in a collaborative model. What Will advocated, and others have echoed or elaborated, has become known as the regular education initiative or, more recently, inclusive education (O'Brien et al., 1989; Stainback & Stainback,

1990). Plainly put, it recommends that education of all students occur in the mainstream.

By the beginning of the 1980s, the effect of major litigation on national policy was beginning to dwindle, in large part because of the effects of what Michenberg (1980) called the "glacial pace of the judicial process" (p. 60). Since general education services cost less than special education services, many agree the political climate of a nation in recession provided the primary impetus for REI, and the effect of politics on special education rose to new prominence.

Political Roots of the Regular Education Initiative

The foundation for the politics that spawned the REI was quite possibly laid in the 1960s. The Camelot era, with its Great Society movement and student activism, set a tone of reformation whose expectations exceeded all probability of fulfillment. The successes were, at best, only partial victories; at the same time, the fact that a family as prominent and accomplished as that of John F. Kennedy acknowledged a sibling's disability, and shared with the country how their family had dealt with it, had an impact. Later, when the family supported the development of the Special Olympics, more attention was focused on attending to the potential of individuals with disabilities (Kauffman & Hallahan, 1990).

Effect of the Media

The military conflict in Southeast Asia seems, in retrospect, to reflect accurately a reasonable pendulum swing from the euphoric optimism of the preceding decade. A combination of the technology and affordability of television provided the American public with daily immersion, via televised news, into the violence of the Vietnam war. As veterans disabled in that war returned home, picked up their lives, and began to take their place in society, the nation's attention was once again focused on the potential of people with handicaps.

While the impact of the immediacy of televised coverage provided ample involvement in the war, it also demonstrated the potential of "that little box in the living room." Of all the policy makers who used television to further their ends, William Bennett (Secretary of Education in the 1980s) was perhaps most effective in gaining public support with his wall-chart test results and oversimplified "solutions" to complex issues (Baker, 1991). For example, he was quite successful in selling the idea that further increases in educational funding were futile. This latter proposal was especially insidious because he purported to speak from research findings, which, in actuality, said the opposite, but the public was not aware of that.

Convinced that spending more money on education was useless, it is little wonder that the decline in Congressional funding for education from 1981 to 1988 totaled nearly $15 billion. Vergstegen and Clark (1988) said that if the Administration's budget requests had been granted, the total decline would have been $46.5 billion in 8 years. Kauffman (1990) warned us of how prevalent that "made-for-television" mentality still is and urged professionals to hold politicians accountable.

The politics of the 1980s clearly reflected the use and abuse of electronic media in policy development and implementation. The hedonism of the era may well have been a backlash against the disillusionment of the 1970s and the disappointments of the 1960s (Clark & Amiot, 1981; Kauffman & Hallahan, 1990). National political concerns spilled over and were reflected in policy decisions concerning education. The 1960s' pursuit of civil rights on the basis of race, creed, and religion set the stage for the 1970s' pursuit of civil rights on other bases, like gender, age, and handicapping condition. But the cure for social ills is expensive, and the results are slow in becoming great enough to measure.

Sociological Changes

Not until the 1980s did the civil rights leaders realize the difference between integration and desegregation. By then, so many ill-conceived court-mandated implementations existed that leaders like Jesse Jackson despaired of that error. It is noteworthy, given that climate, that the 1980s' educational legislation contained few additional supports for the civil rights of persons with disabilities.

The cost of the previous three decades of reform and the lessons learned from it set the stage for the educational reforms of the mid-1980s. The national budget was a disaster. The economy was experiencing a series of recessions (some called it one ongoing recession). The level of the national debt had reached the point that Congress passed a law requiring federal budgets to be balanced. The Keynesian economics that had pervaded federal spending since the New Deal era were falling into disrepute as theory continued to collide with reality. President Reagan called for a resurgence in private enterprise to compensate for what government not only could not do, but could no longer afford to try to do. Diminuation, deregulation, decentralization, disestablishmentism, and deemphasis of federal focus on education and educational funding were hallmarks of the Reagan years (Clark & Amiot, 1981). The dominant theme focused on returning both control and responsibility (especially fiscal responsibility) to the state and local level.

Reaganomics

The Reagan administration proposed the use of block grants to give state and local governments control of how federal funds were spent. The idea was to reduce the total allotment, lump all social service funds into one pot, and leave it to state and local agencies to decide how the money would be spent. Advocates for persons with disabilities opposed the policy so fiercely that special education wound up being left out of the block grant program. As a result, not only did special education get increased funding, the experience also demonstrated the political strength that advocates could muster and suggested an avenue for future endeavors.

We believe, with Kauffman, Hallahan, Clark, Amiot, and others, that, in similar manner, the regular REI was born from a political imperative to reduce educational spending. Extra funding for the education of poor and low achievers could not be tolerated in the political and sociological climate of the Reagan/Bush administration. Where the previous decades had emphasized the need for additional funding for intervention for unsuccessful learners, policymakers of the 1980s tried to reduce costs, substituting competition and promises for funding.

The REI, in fact, was seen by some as a "trickle-down theory of educational benefit" demanded by Reagan's economic strategy where educational excellence was defined as doing more with less (Kauffman, 1989). As Kauffman and others pointed out, the initiative was promoted by Reagan's political appointees and those who benefited from the appointments (Baker, 1991; Clark & Amiot, 1981; Kauffman, 1990). Kauffman concluded that the image of reform was far more important than the essence of results. As another example of that emphasis, Kauffman noted that the changes in education following publication of *A Nation At Risk* (National Commission on Excellence in Education, 1983) consisted almost entirely of higher academic standards, emphasis on competition, calls for stricter discipline, and exhortations for teachers to do better. These increased demands without improved supports could only ensure failure for students who were already struggling.

These demands, however, were no different from the demands of reformers since the days of Plato. Contemporary reformers differ from their earlier counterparts in that earlier governments had no legislated commitment to educate all learners. Another difference is the recent priority for public relations and image building over substantive change (Clark & Astuto, 1988; Kauffman, 1989), requiring attention to a few carefully selected specific "issues with high emotional appeal" and solutions offering "simplistic answers to complex problems" (Kauffman, 1989). Ginsberg and Wimpelberg (1987) noted that the national commissions on which Reagan depended had, as a primary function, "political agenda-setting" (p. 345).

In fact, the nature of the change following the Commission's work was reminiscent of a popular cartoon where the industrious wife persists from year-to-year in confusing her lazy ne'er-do-well spouse's motion with movement. Like Flo, we sought results where change was the primary agenda. Were not the consequences so serious for those most dependent on others for their defense, the politics of educational reform and the litigative and legislative products would make a humorous satire.

EFFECTS ON CURRENT PRACTICE

Weintraub and Abeson (1976) pointed out years ago that "public policy determines the degree to which minorities, in this case, the handicapped, will be treated inequitably by the controlling majority" (p. 7). Note that they addressed equity rather than equality. They considered it axiomatic that minorities can expect to receive only the amount of power or resources that the majority are willing to relinquish. In this chapter, we have traced the degree of surrender that has been experienced and we have described how, during recessionary times, even that which is given can be taken back. We have described how the latter was accomplished. Whether the reclamation of power occurs in hostile confrontation or subtle seduction does not lessen the impact.

If parents and educators do not consider the effect of litigation, legislation, and politics on public policy, they will fail to raise their voices, and students with disabilities and their parents can forget the dream of equitable treatment. Instead, they will receive equal treatment that will result, as it always has, in diminished preparation for adult life. Students who leave school equipped with maximum expectations and minimal skills cannot expect to lead independent adult lives in the kind of competitive society we now live in, and much less in that of the twenty-first century.

Realistically, we need to look carefully, too, at the basis of the current demands for "inclusion." It is now, and will be for several decades of economic recovery, politically correct to develop policies that decentralize control in order to control demands for funding. It is doubtful that even the political changes in Soviet-block countries will substantially permit redirection of Congressional budgetary priorities in favor of special education. Thus far, none of the 1992 Presidential hopefuls has given the state of special education any public consideration.

Certainly if desegregation or its newest form, inclusion, is examined, there can be no basis for saying a student should not be educated or does not have the right to be educated in the mainstream. But the key word in all this is *educated.* Although the plaintiffs in *Brown v. Board of Education* (1954) demanded integration, they and the nation settled for desegregation. Only later would leaders such as Jesse Jackson recognize that desegregation focused on geographic proximity, whereas integration addressed civic equity. We, in special education, do not need to waste two decades rediscovering that difference. Rather, we should seek meaningful integration just as *Brown* tried to do and settle for no less, whether that means mingling or mainstreaming as determined by the severity of the child's disability.

According to a recent study (*Education of the Handicapped,* 1989), 74% of the parents of children with disabilities surveyed ($n = 1,000$) were satisfied with the level of their children's mainstreaming, whereas 7% would prefer less mainstreaming. Among the students themselves, 78% said their schoolwork was interesting and 88% said their teachers were helpful. Based on this and similar subsequent reports such as the Robert Woods Johnson study, as much as the children want the opportunity to compete, few would want to give up modifications in instruction or environment. After years of working toward workplace accommodations, why would we give up educational accommodation?

Although equality for all is an admirable goal, we wonder if professionals, parents, and advocates who have endorsed these concepts have faced the reality of what they are saying. If they got what they say they want, we would return to "a golden age of schooling" that, as Cuban (1990) reminded us, never did exist. We might do well to remember, as Greenberg (1990) did, that the total mainstreaming of the one-room schoolhouse was a matter of necessity, not of virtue. One has only to look at the dropout rate under the equity of individualized placement decisions to be mortified of the possibilities under programmatic placements. Greenberg (1990) warned that a voluntary return to such a notion "would make Pollyanna look like a hard-bitten cynic" (p. 3C).

There is something distinctly American about a phrase like "fuller integration," but the fact is, it has already been provided in earlier legislation, including a process for developing an individual educational program (IEP). Provision has also already been made for individualizing the placement decision based on the child's IEP. No programmatic decisions are to be made, and each case must be separately determined, with students being served in placements that best serve their needs. Robert Davilla (Assistant Secretary of Education) has consistently affirmed the department's commitment to case-by-case determinations (R.R. Davilla, personal communication, February 2, 1990; February 28, 1990; July 17, 1990). We advocate a return to that concept of least restrictive environment, free of politically driven mandates that discount individual needs to be competitively prepared for adulthood. Stephens (1988) reminded us of the following:

> The present system of special education and its relationship to general education did not occur through fiat. Rather, it evolved from societal forces, including economic and welfare mechanisms. These were a part of the same drive for equality that contributed to expanded civil rights for women, racial and ethnic minorities, and for the economically disenfranchised. (p. 61)

No amount of romanticizing can dissolve the realities of how we got where we are today. Like it or not, REI, or inclusions, is deeply rooted in litigation, legislation, and politics.

REFERENCES

Baker, K. (1991). Yes, throw money at schools. *KAPPAN, 72,* 628–632.

Campbell, D.T., & Stanley, V.C. (1963). *Experimental and quasi-experimental designs for research.* Boston: Houghton Mifflin.

Capitol Publications (1990). Regular educators have a stake in disabled students' success. *Education of the Handicapped, 16*(7), 1.

Clark, D.L., & Amiot, M.A. (1981). The impact of the Reagan administration on federal education policy. *KAPPAN, 62,* 258–262.

Clark, D.L., & Astuto, T.A. (1988). *Educational policy after Reagan: What next?* Occasional paper No. 6. Charlottesville, VA: University of Virginia, Policy Analysis Center.

Cuban, L. (1990). Reforming again, again, and again. *Educational Researcher, 19*(1), 3–13.

Dunn, L.M. (1968). Special education for the mildly retarded: Is much of it justified? *Exceptional Children, 35,* 5–22.

Education of the Handicapped (1989). Parents, educators applaud special ed but see weak spots, poll shows. *Education of the Handicapped 15*(16), 1–3.

Georgia Advocacy Office (1991). *Promoting inclusion.* Atlanta: Georgia Advocacy Office.

Ginsberg, R., & Wimpelberg, R.K. (1987). Educational change by commission: Attempting "trickle down" reform. *Educational Evaluation and Policy Analysis, 9,* 344–360.

Greenberg, P. (1990). Latest "educationist" fad on the wrong track. *The Register-Guard* (Eugene, OR), *April 22,* p. 3C.

Halpern, A. (1973). General unemployment and vocational opportunities for EMR individuals. *American Journal of Mental Deficiency, 80,* 81–89.

Halpern, A. (1974). Work-study programs for the mentally retarded: An overview. In P. Browning (Ed.), *Mental Retardation: Rehabilitation and counseling* (pp. 120–127). Springfield, IL: Charles C Thomas.

Kauffman, J.M. (1989). The regular education initiative as Reagan-Bush education policy: A trickle-down theory of education of the hard-to-teach. *Journal of Special Education, 23,* 256–278.

Kauffman, J.M. (1990). President's message addressing reform. *CCBD Newsletter, November,* 2.

Kauffman, J.M., & Hallahan, D.P. (1990). The politics of special-education 'backlash.' *Education Week, October 24,* 25,27.

Michenberg, N.H. (1980). A decade of deinstitutionalization: Emerging legal theories and strategies. *AMICUS, 5*(3,4), 54–63.

National Commission on Excellence in Education (1983). *A nation at risk: The imperative for educational reform.* Washington, D.C.: U.S. Government Printing Office.

O'Brien, J., Snow, I., Forest, M., & Hasbury, D. (1989). *Action for inclusion.* Toronto: Frontier Press.

Orelove, F.P., & Sobsey, R.J. (1987). *Educating children with multiple disabilities: A transdisciplinary approach.* Baltimore: Paul H. Brookes.

Simpson, R. (1991). Focus on autistic behavior: Editor's note. *Journal for the Association of Severely Handicapped, 6*(2), 1.

Stainback, W., & Stainback, S. (1990). *Support networks for inclusive schooling.* Baltimore: Paul H. Brookes.

Stephens, T.M. (1988). Eliminating special education: Is this the solution? *Journal of Teacher Education, 39*(3), 60–64.

Verstegen, D.A., & Clark, D.L. (1988). The diminution in federal expenditures for education during the Reagan administration. *Phi Delta Kappan, 70* (2), 134–138.

Weintraub, F.J., & Abeson, A. (1976). New education policies for the handicapped: The quiet revolution. In F.J. Weintraub, A. Abeson, J. Ballard, & M.L. LaVor (Eds.), *Public policy and the education of exceptional children.* (pp. 7–14). Reston, VA: Council for Exceptional Children.

Will, M. (1984). Let us pause and reflect – but not too long. *Exceptional Children, 49,* 246–252.

Will, M. (1986). Educating children with learning problems: Shared responsibility. *Exceptional Children, 52,* 411–415.

LEGAL DECISIONS

Brown v. Board of Education, 347 U.S. 483 (1954).

Daniel R.R. v. El Paso, 874 F.2d 1036 (5th Cir. 1989).

Diana v. State Board of Education, Civ. Act. No. C-70–37 (N.D. Cal. 1970, further order, 1973).

Larry P. v. Riles, 343 F.Supp. 1306, aff'd, 502 F.2d 963, further proceedings, 495 F.Supp. 926, aff'd, 502 F.2d 693 (9th Cir. 1984).

Mills v. D.C. Board of Education, 348 F.Supp. 866 D. D.C. (1972): contempt proceeding EHLR 551:643 C.D. D.C. (1980).

Pennsylvania Association for Retarded Children (PARC) v. Commonwealth of Pennsylvania, 334 F.Supp. 1257, 343 F.Supp. 279 (E.D. Pa. 1971, 1972).

10

Transition from School to Adulthood for Young People with Disabilities: Critical Issues and Policies

Paul Wehman

Within the past decade transition from school to adulthood for youths with disabilities has been a consistent goal for persons and families in special education, rehabilitation, vocational education, and other related disciplines. Rarely has one topic dominated the field the way transition has for such a sustained duration. This continues to be an exciting area that has cut across the Reagan administration and into the Bush administration and in which there continues to be strong bipartisan support in Congress. Transition reflects the interests of so many people in so many different professional disciplines. There are, in fact, tens of thousands of young people with disabilities who are leaving the public schools and who are looking for post-secondary opportunities in the community colleges and in the work force, and for their rightful place in the community.

Anyone who reviewed the transition literature as little as 10 years ago would have been hard pressed to find any mention of transition in the federal legislation. Identification of specific sources of money within the federal budgets would have been difficult as would have been finding a distinct professional body of research literature in transition. However, in the past 8 to 10 years there has been a dramatic spawning of post-21 follow-up studies, increased authorizations and appropriations of state and federal dollars, and, perhaps most importantly, a heightened interest on the part of parents, families, and individuals with disabilities about the importance of planning for transition.

The unemployment rate for people with disabilities continues to hover in the 50% to 75% area depending on which survey you choose to review (U.S. Commission on Civil Rights, 1983). Such levels of unemployment are clearly unconscionable and unacceptable as we move into the twenty-first century. It has become abundantly clear to those professionals in the field, as well as to concerned family members, that truly the only way to alter this disturbing unemployment rate is to significantly emphasize work opportunities and experiences in the schools and for the public schools themselves to go through critical self-examination of the curriculum offerings that are provided.

Recently, Secretary of Labor Lynn Martin released a report from the Secretary's Commission on Achieving Necessary Skills (*Richmond Times Dispatch,* Wednesday, July 3, 1991). The Commission was charged with studying the vocational needs of the approximately 50% of high school students who do not go to college, including those with disabilities. In this report, the Commission analyzed 15 jobs, such as chief electrician, bank teller, nurse, and truck driver, and found *little* connection between what the schools were actually teaching and the specific work requirements in industry. The one-year study drew on educators, public officials, business people, and so forth, and identified five major competencies. These were:

- *Resources* (i.e., allocating time, money, and material)
- *Interpersonal skills* (i.e., working on teams, teaching others, serving customers)
- *Information* (i.e., how to acquire and process data)
- *Systems* (i.e., understanding social, organizational, and technological systems)
- *Technology* (i.e., selecting equipment and tools)

This particular study, which was reported in most of the local and national newspapers (*Richmond Times Dispatch,* Wednesday, July 3, 1991), will be a cornerstone of the Bush administration's educational plan, which is titled *America 2000: The President's Education Strategy.*

THE U.S. PLAN FOR EDUCATION REFORM

What is important to identify in both Secretary Martin's report and in the Bush administration's educational plan strategy, discussed below, is that young people with disabilities can and will need to participate in the long-term planning and development of the U.S. strategy for helping young people, disabled or nondisabled, improve work opportunity. According to a report from the Office of the White House Press Secretary (April 18, 1991) the *America 2000: The President's Education Strategy* document builds on four related themes:

1. Creating better and more accountable schools for today's students
2. Creating a new generation of American schools for tomorrow's students
3. Transforming America into a nation of students
4. Making our communities places where learning will happen

These four themes are essential for special educators, rehabilitation personnel, and vocational educators to take into account as they plan curriculum, develop new service-delivery models, and identify objectives for young people with disabilities.

For too long, young adults with disabilities have been treated as a separate group, segregated from "normal" kids. They have not been integrated into the curriculum, service-delivery, and post-secondary opportunities in which nondisabled youth have had the opportunity to participate. Parents and professionals must take a closer look at what is happening to *all* youth in this country in terms of work opportunities and likelihoods for successful integration into the community if they are to discern the *optimal* ways to smooth the transitions into adulthood.

It should be noted that the integration of nondisabled and disabled youth is not simply a philosophical notion, but one that is born of pragmatic reasons. Without question there will be increasing demands for a *diversified* labor force as we come into the twenty-first century. Work opportunities will abound in selected areas such as entry-level service occupations in the hotel and restaurant industries, the child-care industries, the technologies, inventory management, and clerical support. These are all areas where people with disabilities, if sufficiently trained and exposed to the work environment, will make a contribution to society and to business and industry and will at the same time better their own lives.

What this chapter is about is how to help young people with disabilities experience meaningful transitions from school to adulthood, particularly in the workplace. I will look closely at what these "transitions" are. This chapter focuses on the functional and practical applications of programs, models, and examples of how successful integration into the workplace can occur. For example, why do some students, regardless of level and/or type of disability, do so well at work? Why do others perform so poorly? In this chapter, the focus is not only on people with mental disabilities or physical disabilities, but also on those with cognitive disabilities, hearing disabilities, visual disabilities, and emotional disabilities. Transition is for *all* young adults.

I have drawn extensively on literature, demographic trends, and movements that affect nondisabled young adults because it is only from studying this group of people and the direction in which the society is going that we will be able to effectively plan and implement effective transition programs. We cannot exclusively identify vocational education programs for people with disabilities as if they exist in isolation from business, industry, and the work force in general. Therefore, not only do I draw heavily on what the 1980s have taught us about interagency planning, service-delivery models, systematic instruction, and other useful strategies, but I will also place these technologies in the context of what America 2000 — the labor force in the twenty-first century — will look like.

INDIVIDUALS WITH DISABILITIES ACT: WHAT THIS MEANS FOR TRANSITION

The reauthorization of the Education for the Handicapped Act (EHA) became law on September 30, 1990 under a new name, the Individuals With Disabilities Education Act (IDEA). The act replaces the term *handicapped* in the legal language with the term *children with disabilities*. It also now allows private citizens to sue states or state departments of education if they violate the law.

The IDEA's new definition of "transition services" requires that these services be included in students' individual education programs (IEPs) and makes changes in transition programs authorized under Part C of the law. The definition states,

Transition services means a coordinated set of activities for a student, designed within an outcome oriented process, which promotes movement from school to postschool activities, including postsecondary education, vocational training, integrated employment, including supported employment, continuing adult education, adult services, independent living or community participation. The coordinated set of activities shall be based upon the individual student's needs taking into account the student's preferences and interest and shall include instruction, community experiences, development employment, and other postschool adult living objectives, and when appropriate acquisition of daily living skills and functional vocational evaluation.

IEPs, under the new law, must now include a statement of the needed transition services for the student, beginning not later than age 16 years and annually thereafter. When determined appropriate for the student, a statement of needed transitional services is required at age 14 years or younger. These statements should include, when appropriate, a description of the interagency responsibilities or linkages or of both before the student leaves the school setting. The IDEA also encourages federally funded transition programs to develop and disseminate exemplary programs and practices that meet the unique needs of students who use assistive technology and services.

Although the new law stops just short of mandating individual transition plans with the specificity of IEPs, it nevertheless provides an incredibly positive requirement and challenge to the more than 16,000 local education agencies to include transition planning and implementation into IEPs for all children with disabilities. Previous legislation spoke only in passing about transition and did not provide a definition; it also did not provide the comprehensive nature of transition services and did not discuss the role of interagency responsibilities. Transition planning is at best difficult given the fact that multiple local agencies have to be involved. From the beginning we have always known that effective transition cannot be managed by only a local rehabilitation agency, a local Association for Retarded Citizens program, or the local school system. All must work together. In our earlier writing (Wehman et al., 1988) this challenge was acknowledged. IDEA, however, has now raised this challenge as an issue to all school systems to reach out to other agencies in establishing interagency linkages.

Therefore, for the purpose of this chapter, the federal definition of transition services noted above will be used. All discussion, information, and references about transition services are drawn from the IDEA's new definition.

A final word is in order about the IDEA and its impact on transition. Clearly, no law can "make" service providers, school districts, and state agencies enact policies and procedures that they do not want to enact. In this way, the transition services definition is nothing more than a piece of paper with words on it. However, for the first time we have in a federal law a requirement for providing transition services for youth as they prepare for movement into adulthood. This is a very positive development that should not be minimized, and well-meaning professionals, certainly families and advocates, and above all young people with disabilities should take full advantage of this law and what it means.

TRANSITION: WHAT PROGRESS HAS BEEN MADE OVER THE PAST DECADE?

With the extensive amount of activity that has occurred in recent years in the area of transition nationally, as well as dozens of local and state conferences that have been held, it is not unreasonable to ask: How are we doing? What progress are we making? Are we making an impact or a difference? While this chapter addresses at length ways to improve transition outcomes, I would be remiss not to discuss some of the very definite gains that have been made to date. Therefore, what follows is a brief list of some of the different positive developments that have accrued.

Increased Awareness of Post-21 Outcomes for Youth with Disabilities

A decade ago, there were virtually no post P.L. 94–142 follow-up studies. Now there are probably a good 15 to 20 published studies documenting the poor employment outcomes of young adults who leave school. These studies go to great lengths to document the shortcomings of the service-delivery system and the public schools, vocational rehabilitation deficiencies, and other breakdowns in the service-delivery system. These data have given rise to papers such as that by Edgar (1987), who have even queried about the justifiability of secondary special education and its value in general. We do not view these doubts, skepticism, and questions in an altogether negative way. Instead we view them as a positive step for documenting the need for the critical self-examination of service providers and what they are doing with and without business and industry in providing work opportunities for people with disabilities. Furthermore, the high dropout rate, which has been increasingly documented (i.e., 25% to 30%; Table 10.1), provides further fuel for the challenges that lie ahead in this area. Nevertheless, the substantial amount of data that have now been accrued are an important foundation for future changes.

Positive Legislative Advances

The Individuals with Disabilities Education Act and the impact that it is having on children with disabilities cannot be viewed in a vacuum from other legislation. The Rehabilitation Act Amendments from 1986, which focused extensively on improving independent living opportunities, client rights, and supported employment opportunities, for the first time offer a major avenue of transition opportunity for young adults. Also, there was some limited language related to transition and the importance of transition services in the Rehabilitation Act.

Furthermore, on July 26, 1990, President Bush signed into law the Americans with Disabilities Act, which many are hailing as a civil rights law for all people with disabilities. Briefly, this law provides for accessibility, nondiscrimination, and greater entrance into work and community sites and use of public transportation and telecommunications. If, in fact, this law achieves a reasonable degree of successful implementation, the "spill-over" effect for young adults coming into a world that is less discriminatory against people with disabilities can be only extremely positive. Neither of these laws was in place a decade ago. There is every reason to believe that more rigorous legislation that reflects advances in medical rehabilitation, vocational rehabilitation, and behavior intervention will continue to develop as we move toward the twenty-first century, and young adults should benefit from this.

Advances in Behavioral and Rehabilitation Technology

Slowly but surely, progress is being made in the most effective ways to provide vocational and behavioral intervention for individuals with all levels of disabilities. While this progress is painfully slow at times, the reality is that more people than ever with severe disabilities can and should be employed in the workplace. Robotics, electronics, computer technology, advances in telecommunication, and increasingly more skilled providers of behavioral intervention techniques are helping individuals with disabilities become more independent and vocationally more marketable. The technologies are available and have been tested to be effective. However, they are not being used anywhere to the extent that is necessary to make transition work in communities. These advances are the fuel that can provide credibility to people working in jobs that less than a decade ago no one thought would ever be possible for positive development.

Family and Student Attitudes

There was a time less than two decades ago that young adults with severe disabilities could not even get into school. These students were fortunate if they could get to the Association for Retarded Citizens for a partial day program. The 1976 P.L. 94–142 changed that. Then, as we entered the 1980s, students and their families were happy to be bussed to schools, to have services from 9:00 a.m. to 3:00 p.m., and to exercise their due process, when appropriate, for receiving occupational, physical, speech, or other related therapies as needed. However, as the decade drew to a close, and as we moved into the 1990s, it became increasingly clear to those families and individuals that more functional, real-life community work experiences and, yes, even job placement before exiting school are necessary and essential means for transition. Finally, the focus is turning to what it is that the student wants and what it is that the family wants instead of what the teacher wants or what the school system wants. We are beginning to see a

Table 10.1 Why Disabled Students Left School, 1987–88

State	Graduated with Diploma	Graduated with Certification	Reached Maximum Age[1]	Dropped Out	Other[2]
Alabama	29.45%	26.91%	1.36%	26.78%	15.50%
Alaska	43.77	5.67	0.28	39.94	10.34
Arizona	56.96	4.85	1.59	31.07	5.52
Arkansas	55.20	15.60	2.14	23.95	3.10
California	20.34	10.00	3.62	11.26	54.783
Colorado	63.73	4.11	1.49	29.67	0.99
Connecticut	88.82	4.44	4.22	2.15	0.37
Deleware	38.11	13.40	2.45	39.39	6.64
District of Columbia	33.88	39.18	6.53	8.57	11.84
Florida	42.34	8.86	4.93	29.50	14.37
Georgia	33.75	23.53	1.40	32.85	8.47
Hawaii	61.94	24.91	2.08	5.19	5.88
Idaho	56.00	10.37	2.22	23.11	8.30
Illinois	59.89	2.46	4.09	33.56	0.00
Indiana	50.10	9.85	4.21	26.42	9.41
Iowa	57.81	4.89	0.81	23.72	12.76
Kansas	57.20	0.00	0.99	22.82	18.99
Kentucky	53.21	4.97	1.24	29.51	11.07
Louisiana	16.39	27.70	1.24	31.38	23.28
Maine	53.81	7.48	2.20	30.21	6.30
Maryland	41.55	3.46	25.83	29.16	0.00
Massachusetts	64.79	0.00	3.66	31.55	0.00
Michigan	20.95	1.70	1.90	16.28	59.16
Minnesota	68.09	0.00	0.00	31.91	0.00
Mississippi	15.45	56.40	1.50	22.39	4.27
Missouri	35.16	14.08	1.03	32.86	16.88
Montana	55.74	12.67	0.51	18.75	12.33

Nebraska	39.06	5.29	3.82	15.86	35.98
Nevada	49.49	29.98	3.49	14.37	2.67
New Hampshire	28.76	8.50	2.18	45.83	14.73
New Jersey	67.01	0.00	0.93	29.29	2.78
New Mexico	49.66	4.31	2.35	27.32	16.36
New York	31.33	18.87	3.42	46.38	0.00
North Carolina	39.24	19.71	1.50	30.45	9.10
North Dakota	54.44	6.78	2.80	23.83	12.15
Ohio	72.85	2.60	1.72	17.65	5.17
Oklahoma	60.79	5.29	1.54	25.06	7.32
Oregon	38.44	9.81	0.56	26.46	24.74
Pennsylvania	41.63	1.86	1.45	17.37	37.68
Puerto Rico	6.66	6.07	13.37	73.89	0.00
Rhode Island	42.75	0.00	3.85	38.53	14.87
South Carolina	33.65	26.06	5.53	26.20	8.56
South Dakota	29.97	37.23	0.94	17.59	14.26
Tennessee	14.88	22.11	1.16	40.61	21.24
Texas	33.62	40.93	0.00	25.45	0.00
Utah	53.13	2.38	1.14	29.95	13.40
Vermont	52.20	4.55	1.79	37.72	3.74
Virginia	40.02	16.88	1.52	29.55	12.03
Washington	39.82	6.09	0.47	33.82	19.80
West Virginia	53.44	5.47	2.01	27.12	11.97
Wisconsin	68.26	4.87	2.42	17.38	7.07
Wyoming	61.26	2.25	3.60	30.03	2.25
Average	41.99%	11.26%	2.50%	27.40%	16.85%

[1]The age limit for receiving special education services varies from state to state.

[2]Many of the "other" category may have droped out, died or moved without contacting school officials.

Reprinted with permission from Education Department, Office of Special Education Programs, Data Analysis System.

(From Wehman P, Moon W, Everson J, Wood W, & Barcus JM: Transition from school to work: new challenges for youth with severe disabilities. Baltimore: Paul H. Brookes Publishing Company, 1988, with permission of the publisher.)

gradually increasing emphasis on real work experiences. As these attitudes permeate the school system and more and more parents of younger children come to expect these services, there will be a compelling pressure on all school systems and school boards to alter their curricula to reflect what in effect the private sector is saying that they want right now, that is, functional skill training that is consistent with the skills required for success in business and industry.

School systems must train students to be able to work in hotels, retail stores, fast-food restaurants, factories, warehouses, offices, libraries, and hospitals. Students must be able to take orders, know how to work within the team, be able to be cross-trained into other jobs fairly quickly, and be able to take initiative. If the schools are not prepared to train students to do this, the United States as a whole will suffer because the labor force will not be able to meet the demands that will be presented as we move into the twenty-first century.

Impact of Federally Funded Model Demonstrations

A final positive advance that needs to be discerned is the impact of discretionary grant programs that the federal government has funded over the past eight years. Through the excellent work of Dr. Frank Rusch and his colleagues at the University of Illinois, outcome data from the dozens and dozens of model programs have been reported. For example, in their compendium of product profiles, 1988, they indicate the following:

1. Forty-two of the fifty states have developed and implemented at least one service-delivery model focusing on transition.
2. Product services have been provided in metropolitan areas, several small towns, and rural areas, and about 20% have provided state-wide services.
3. Of those youths being served, over half have a learning disability, whereas about 20% have been diagnosed as having mental retardation or a developmental disability. Students with diagnoses in at least 19 other categories have also been reported.
4. As of January, 1988, it was estimated that over 127,000 young people with handicapping conditions were helped by model programs alone.
5. Nearly all model demonstration projects provide training to professionals, business communities, and parents. Well over 20,000 persons have benefited from this training.
6. The majority (65%) of reporting projects indicated collaborative interagency agreement between state agencies.

WHAT ARE TRANSITIONS?

A great deal has been written about transition in recent years. However, a very small amount of the literature specifically is directed at what transitions are and at the challenges they entail for 16- to 25-year-olds. In this section we briefly touch on several major transitions that young people with disabilities, as well as their nondisabled counterparts, encounter as they come to the end of their schooling. It is important to understand what these transitions are because they form the basis for planning curriculum and service-delivery strategies to help provide independence and coping skills before the student leaves school.

Anxiety Over Finding Employment and Financial Independence

Most young people, whether or not they are labeled as having a disability, have concerns about what they will do when they are finished with school. As Secretary of Labor Martin's report indicated, approximately 50% of high school students in the United States do not go on to college of any type and, of course, most people with disabilities are in this group. The inability to know how to find a job and the inability to have specific vocational skills to be employed in the workplace are major sources of anxiety, as they well should be for people with all types of disabilities. Without some form of employment, the departing students are immediately dependent and will continue their dependence on their parents or on society in the form of Social Security allowances.

The ability to be employed upon leaving school, therefore, is important for at least two major reasons: (a) the need to have productive activity everyday in a meaningful vocation is important to one's self-esteem in American society, and (b) working in competitive employment provides an opportunity for receiving wages and benefits that, therefore, lead to greater independence and mobility within the community at large. Hence, the *first transition* that teachers, service providers, rehabilitation personnel, family members, and others should be focusing on is reducing anxiety over unemployment and economic insufficiency. This can be done by aggressively training a wide range of occupational skills well before the student leaves and, furthermore, allowing the student to practice those skills in real work environments, ideally through a real job while the student is still in school.

Community and Home Living Arrangements

The next transition that most individuals with disabilities and others feel in their adolescent years is: Where do I live when I leave school? Must I always live with Mom and Dad? Will I have to live in a room by myself? These are very important questions and significantly influence the way people look at themselves and the types of friends they have.

Burchard, Hasazi, Gordon, and Roe (1991) looked at lifestyle normalization, community integration adjustment, and personal satisfaction for 133 adults with mild and moderate mental retardation who were living in small group homes. The study indicated that persons who lived in supervised apartments achieved the most normative lifestyles with greater personal independence and community integration while reporting levels of lifestyle satisfaction and personal well-being similar to those of persons living with their own families. Studies such as this one and the work of Bruininks and associates (1987) point out time and time again the critical aspect of this transition. In fact, in the 1985 model that

Halpern promulgated, he made community living one of the major components of his model. Clearly, one cannot look at movement from school to adulthood without close examination of what type of living arrangement the person can look forward to upon leaving school.

Independent Mobility

All too often, we take for granted our ability to move around within the community as well as in and out of the community. Most people drive automobiles, and those who do not have access to public transportation or friends who can help them get around the community. Independent movement around the community is critical for the purposes of going to movie theaters, convenience stores, grocery stores, the park, church, and work, and, in general, for being able to feel independent in the way one can use one's time. One of the great difficulties that people with disabilities face is a lack of independent mobility.

Lack of mobility can be caused by an individual's ambulation problems or lack of accessibility to public places. However, more often than not, it is caused by the person's inability to have access to an automobile or a driver's license or because only a limited number of friends are willing to drive the person. Lack of mobility may also reflect living in an area where there is no public transportation. As children, we are generally chauffeured from place to place, but as we move into our teen years, this becomes more and more of an independent need. Such a transition is a critical one.

In reviewing the transition literature, it is amazing that so little reference has been made to the complexity of this transition in smoothing out the opportunity for independence.

Changing Peer Relationships

One of the more popular topics that has begun to appear in the literature over the past several years has been the importance and need for friendships in the lives of people with disabilities. Not only is there a need for friendships, there must also be a sensitivity to the changing nature of peer relationship as one moves from a middle school to a high school and then out of the high school into an adult environment. Once a person moves into an adult environment, he or she is expected to be increasingly independent in identifying friends, networking socially with other people, and initiating social activities. Obviously, some people are better at this and do better than others at developing such relationships. However, this is clearly a cause of stress and anxiety for many people with disabilities who have not been sufficiently empowered to have the network available for meeting different people.

One can also see that a lack of a job, poor living quarters, and restricted mobility are all factors in inhibiting peer relationships. Developing new friends, maintaining old friendships, and meeting the challenge of changing peer relationships is a critical transition for all people with disabilities.

Sexuality and Self-Esteem

As most teenagers grow into adulthood, they begin to establish their own sets of values, levels of confidence, and choices in how they choose to interact with members of the opposite sex. These aspects are very important in the way a person sees himself and particularly in establishing good self-esteem. Socialization, the way one dresses, hair styles, and recreational activities are but some of the ways to express sexuality, both in a dating format and in groups. Too little attention has been paid to this important transition, and we believe that with increased focus in this area, some of the other transitions will fall into place more smoothly as the individual becomes a young adult.

WHAT ARE THE CRITICAL TRANSITION ISSUES AS WE HEAD INTO THE TWENTY-FIRST CENTURY?

It is appropriate to give some thought and time to reviewing what are the cutting-edge issues that we must focus on as we move into the next decade and as we try to help people with disabilities overcome the transition challenges and make integration into the workplace and community a reality. Several issues are discussed briefly in the following:

Student Choice

The transition models advanced in the early to mid 1980s by Wehman and associates (1988) and Halpern and colleagues (1983) did not focus nearly enough on student choice, family choice, and self-determination. Choices of school, type of job, type of work arrangement, and nature of instruction were all assumed to be controlled unilaterally by the special education teacher and school system. Fortunately, more progressive thinking has been moving in the direction of much greater focus on choice, self-determination, self-advancement, and, generally, freedom. A number of professionals, parents, and advocates have begun to write in this regard (e.g., Turnbull et al., in press; Turnbull, Turnbull, Summers, Rhoader, and Gordon, 1989, as well as many of the pioneers who promoted the passage of the Americans With Disabilities Act). This philosophy is a very important aspect of planning for transition because the focus of control shifts from service providers to the person who is receiving the service and who should be making decisions. We believe that this is more than an initiative, priority, or theme, but instead will shortly become the only way to provide services. We believe that if service providers do not honor the need for a student- or client-focused way of planning services, services will be out of business.

What are the implications for a student- and family-oriented approach to transition planning? These implications are significant indeed and involve students being directly involved in writing IEPs and individual transition plans, going out to workplaces and identifying the jobs they want, and vetoing unfair vocational evaluation practices. They further involve students directly picking the type of skills that they believe will be useful.

Secondary Curriculum Reform

Transition should be perceived as movement for all youth with disabilities who are leaving public school programs and entering adulthood. It should be viewed as a "right." The goals of special education programs should be to prepare students with disabilities to live and work in their communities. This major change in focus will expand the role of education from preparing individuals for transition to include making the initial placement in appropriate community settings, with sufficient time for follow-along before exiting school. As Edgar (1987) has noted, a very critical and hard look at the quality of the secondary special education curriculum is in order. Although all blame cannot be placed on the public school system and specifically on the secondary/special education teacher, there is little question that there needs to be a far greater relationship between what is happening in the schools and what is required in business and the workplace.

Better Dissemination of Information About Transition

The general public needs to be much more aware of the contributions that young adults with disabilities can make. More general print and audiovisual means, such as public and network TV, newspapers, radio, and popular magazines, must be accessed. Presentations of local providers and regular publications, such as newsletters, that reach direct service providers should be commonplace. It is essential that local Chambers of Commerce, Lions Clubs, Kiwanis Clubs, and other civic groups be aware of the capabilities of young adults with disabilities and be there to give them a "helping hand" similar to other young adults within the community. This can happen only if there is a much broader publicity within the general public.

More Direct Assistance to State and Local Education Agencies

While we have good models for transition services developed over the past 5 years, it is now time for more local agencies *to test* the effectiveness of these models. State agencies must concentrate on transition *outcomes,* not on the process. In other words, how many students with learning disabilities get into community colleges and graduate, or how many students with severe and profound handicaps are placed into supported employment "real jobs" before graduation? How many more students with severe physical disabilities are receiving rehabilitation engineering services and culminating those services with real jobs? We now know what best practices should be, but we don't know the extent to which they are being implemented. Significantly, more dollars need to be flowing into local education agencies and communities at large specifically for this purpose. Transition is not exclusively a school issue. It is a community issue.

Anticipated Service Needs: Waiting List for Adult Services

The vast majority of students with more severe disabilities are leaving school and, unfortunately, joining an ever-expanding waiting list with little hope of timely placements into useful programs. Families, educators, adult service providers, and advocates must develop strategies that work together to improve this situation, which has been created by tight budgets and misplaced fiscal priorities. It is a cruel hoax, indeed, to maintain a student for 10 to 15 years in public schools and then put him or her on a waiting list for services, in some cases for 3 to 10 years. The emphasis is on in-service training. Many teachers have been in this field for as long as 5 years and never have had any of the transition training that current personnel preparation programs are beginning to provide. It is crucial that discretionary programs meet these needs by funding competent in-service providers to reach teachers through innovative techniques (i.e., video courses, computer networking, technical assistance, and other strategies are but some of the ways to begin refurbishing the special education teachers). For the most part these teachers need direct help in their school or agency by professionals who have been directly involved in transition planning and implementation in the past.

SUMMARY

This chapter is intended for special education professionals, vocational educators, rehabilitation counselors and evaluators, parents, families, advocates, and, last but not least, university students in training. Major points that must be considered in reviewing critical transition issues in the 1990s are:

1. *The student and family* (i.e, the customer is usually right). Listen to the student and family and to what they are saying. What hints are they giving in terms of what they need and what are they showing. These are the critical features that will make for a student-oriented program.
2. *A close look at what business and industry require.* The new generation of teachers will look carefully at how they spend every day with students in classes and critically evaluate whether the skills, objectives, and activities that they are focusing on have direct relationship to what the local employer needs and what is needed to maintain a dependable work force. Is the teacher using ditto sheets, work books, or blackboard work that has no bearing whatsoever on what the labor force needs? Is the curriculum being influenced by what business says is required and needed or are curriculum objectives generated by bureaucrats who have no real-life experience? These outmoded policies can and must change.
3. *Integration of all young people with disability into the workplace and school.* It is our belief and hope that when the year 1997 arrives, or 1998 or 1999 or even hopefully 1995, that special schools, segregated

work activity centers, and programs that are designed only for handicapped people will become a thing of the past. We know from our own consistent experience with people with disability that they perform better in normal work environments and natural and community environments. Perpetual segregation does not help overcome the transitions that were discussed earlier. Integration must be an outcome, not a process. Integration must be a goal toward which educators, parents, and professionals work together.

REFERENCES

Bruininks, R., Rotegard, L., Lakin, K.C., & Hill, B. (1987). Epidemiology of mental retardation and trends in residential services in the United States. In S. Landesman & Vietze (Eds.), *Mental retardation* (pp. 252–272). Washington, D.C.: American Association on Mental Retardation.

Burchard, S.N., Hasazi, J.S., Gordon, L.R., & Roe, J. (1991). An examination of lifestyle and adjustment in three community residential alternatives. *Research in Developmental Disabilities, 12,* 127–142.

Edgar, E. (1987). Secondary programs in special education: Are many of them justifiable? *Exceptional Children, 53,* 555–561.

Halpern, A. (1985). Transition: A look at the foundations. *Exceptional Children, 57*(6), 479–486.

Halpern, A. (1985). Transition: A look at the foundations. *Exceptional Children, 57*(6), 479–486; Turnbull, H.R., III, Bateman, D.F., & Turnbull, A.P. (in press) Family empowerment. In P. Wehman, (Ed.), *The ADA mandate for social change,* Baltimore: Paul H. Brookes Publishing Co.; Turnbull, H.R., III, Turnbull, A.P., Bronicki, G.J., Summers, J.A., & Roeder-Gordon, C. (1989). *Disability and the family: A guide to decisions for adulthood.* Baltimore: Paul H. Brookes Publishing Co.

Office of the White House Press Secretary. (1991). *America 2000: The President's Education Strategy* (Fact Sheet). Washington, DC.

Rusch, F.R. (1990). *Supported employment: Models, methods, and issues.* Sycamore, IL: Sycamore Press.

Rusch, F.R. (1988). *Transition program evaluation,* Urbana, Illinois, Transition Institute, University of Illinois.

Turnbull, A., Bateman, D., & Turnbull, R. (in press). Americans with Disabilities Act and family involvement. In P. Wehman (Ed.), *Americans with Disabilities Towards Self-Determination.*

Turnbull, H.R., III, Bateman, D.F. & Turnbull, A.P. (in press). Family empowerment. In P. Wehman (Ed.), *The ADA mandate for social change.* Baltimore: Paul H. Brookes Publishing Co.

U.S. Commission on Civil Rights. (1983). *Accomodating the spectrum of individual abilities.* Washington, DC: U.S. Commission on Civil Rights.

U.S. Department of Education. (1991). *America 2000: An Education Strategy.* Washington, DC: U.S. Department of Education.

U.S. flunks high schools on student job skills. (1991). *Richmond Times-Dispatch.* July 3, p. 1.

Vocational Training News. (1991). 22(45), November 14.

Wehman, P., Moon, M.S., Everson, J., Wood, W., & Barcus, J.M. (1988). *Transition from school to work: New challenges for youth with severe handicaps.* Baltimore: Paul H. Brookes.

Washington Post, Editorial, October 13, 1991.

11

School to Community Transition for Youth with Disabilities

Philip Browning
Caroline Dunn
Clarence Brown

In 1990, President Bush held an educational summit with the National Governors' Association Task Force on Education. The purpose of this meeting was to take the first step in a long-term commitment to support needed educational reforms. The outcomes of this event and its resulting document, *America 2000: An Educational Strategy* (Bush, 1991), set forth six goals for this nation's public schools. Most appropriate to this discussion is the second of these goals: "By the year 2000, the high school graduation rate will increase to at least 90 percent" (p. 19). In order to achieve this goal for the general student population, our schools will have to increase their current graduation rate by 19% within the next 8 years. This goal will be an even greater challenge for students with disabilities, since their current graduation rate is only 55% (SRI International, 1988).

While the *America 2000* graduation goal may be unrealistic for students with disabilities, the fact remains that we are faced with a dismal record regarding the adult adjustment outcomes of former special education students. Furthermore, we must confront this dilemma by acknowledging that our performance over the past 30 years has not been commensurate with the resources expended to ameliorate the problem (Brolin, 1992).

The purpose of this chapter is to address some of the essential considerations that must be attended to by our nation's secondary special education schools and other transition-related services and programs, if we expect to have any success in improving on the current plight of youth with disabilities. First, however, the reader is given a short history of the past initiatives that have been directed toward the goal of preparing these students for a successsful adult life. Second, functional assessment and curricula are addressed as two major school-related considerations. Finally, a brief discussion of several other issues acknowledges the fact that the problem and issues of transition certainly extend beyond the teacher in the classroom.

A BRIEF HISTORY

There have been three national movements within the past 30 years directed toward the improvement of secondary high school programs for students with disabilities. The reader is referred elsewhere for a more extensive historical perspective of these movements (Browning et al., 1992; Halpern, 1992). The first of the three movements began in the early 1960s and was embodied by cooperative work/study programs. The general goal of these programs, which were agreements between the public schools and the local offices of vocational rehabilitation, was ". . . to create an integrated academic, social, and vocational curriculum, accompanied by appropriate work experience, that was designed to prepare students with mild disabilities for eventual community adjustment" (Halpern, 1992, p. 203). Cooperative agreements between vocational rehabilitation and schools sprang up throughout the country and, according to one national survey, served over 96,000 students (Browning & Brummer, 1974).

With the establishment of the Office of Career Education, U.S. Office of Education, career education became a major priority of the second movement during the 1970s. As one major outcome of this career-focused movement, the Council for Exceptional Children approved the Division of Career Development as its twelfth division in 1976 and shortly thereafter established the nationally refereed periodical *Career Development for Exceptional Individuals.*

The third movement, referred to as *transition,* emerged in the early 1980s when Madeleine Will, former Commissioner for the Office of Special Education and Rehabilitative Services (OSERS), U.S. Department of Education, authored a paper about the concepts and policies that were to guide OSERS in its effort to improve the transition from school to work for all individuals with disabilities. This paper presented the school-to-work "bridges" model and a definition that described transition as ". . . an outcome oriented process encompassing a broad array of services and experiences that lead to employment" (Will, 1984, p. 2). Subsequently, other definitions have emerged in the literature (for example Halpern, 1985; Brolin, 1992), including OSERS' more recent one:

> The term "transition services" means a coordinated set of activities
> for a student, designed within an outcome-oriented process, which
> promotes movement from school to post-school activities, includ-
> ing post-secondary education, vocational training, integrated
> employment (including supported employment), continuing and
> adult education, adult services, independent living, or community
> participation. The coordinated set of activities shall be based
> upon the individual student's needs, taking into account the stu-
> dent's preferences and interests, and shall include instruction,
> community experiences, the development of employment and
> other post-school adult living objectives, and, when appropriate,

acquisition of daily living skills and functional vocational evaluation. (The Individuals with Disabilities Education Act P.L. 101–476, 602 [a] [19])

Also, this past decade saw the enactment of federal legislation that served as the major initiative to address the transition problem. Section 626 of the 1983 Amendments to the Education of the Handicapped Act (P.L. 98–199), "Secondary Education and Transition Services for Handicapped Youth," provided funds for the development of training programs and related services in order to improve secondary special education programs. In 1986, Congress authorized additional legislation (P.L. 99–497) to both improve and expand the secondary programs and their accompanying transitional services.

The latest of the legislative initiatives is the 1990 Amendment to P.L. 94–142, now known as The Individuals with Disabilities Education Act (IDEA). The two important aspects of this amendment that are transition-related focus on (a) improvements in transition planning for individual students through modification of the individual education program (IEP) process and (b) improvements in planning for program capacity to support the service needs identified for individual plans.

Another federal initiative is the new program that enables the Secretary of Education to make one-time, 5-year competitive grants to state rehabilitation and education agencies. One of the objectives that must be accomplished by those awarded this grant is that they ". . . increase the availability, access, and quality of transition assistance through the development and improvement of policies, procedures, systems, and other mechanisms for youth with disabilities and their families as those youth prepare for and enter adulthood (Federal Register, 1991, p. 66290).

In summary, our past commitments to transition have prepared us better than any time before to confront the transition problems because we now possess (a) a conceptual and definitional framework for direction; (b) an awareness of and, in some instances, good understanding of issues and problems that must be resolved; (c) exemplary service models that should be implemented on a broader scale; (d) knowledge of good instructional and service-delivery methods to be applied; (e) an inventory of functional assessment and curricular materials for practice; and (f) a legislative grounding for change. We now have a substantive foundation for drafting the nature and direction of this decade's transition policies, programs, and practices.

SCHOOL-RELATED ISSUES

This nation's schools must incorporate more effective programs and practices if they expect to prepare students with disabilities for a more successful transition into work and community life. This section focuses on functional assessment and curricula as two areas that are critical to school-based efforts for improving transition.

Assessment: A Functional Approach

Assessment is an important educational and service-delivery ingredient for the planning, programming, and placing of youth with disabilities from school to work and into the community. The need for and importance of a functional assessment approach for secondary students in transition have been well documented (Agran et al., 1987; Browning & Brechin, 1992; Elrod, 1987; Elrod & Sorgenfrei, 1988; Halpern et al., 1982).

The authors contend that the problem in conducting functional assessments is not a lack of tools with which to practice. DeStefano, Linn, and Markward (1987), for example, in their assessment of the current status of instrumentation for student assessment in transition programs, reported 144 assessment instruments derived from the transition projects funded by OSERS during the 1985–1987 period. Rather, a more pressing need is for practitioners to incorporate a definition of functional assessment into their work and to be sufficiently knowledgeable about the major assessment approaches and their respective applications.

A definition of functional assessment should serve as the basis for the assessment process, guiding practitioners to use measurement information in a more utilitarian way. When considering the following definition, it is important to keep in mind the fact that transition (a) is longitudinal in nature, beginning with the students no later than in the ninth grade and most often continuing through post-secondary education; (b) requires a systematic plan that is cooperatively designed and collaboratively implemented by interagency personnel and significant others; and (c) is outcome oriented in terms of the youth's personal, vocational, residential, and community success. It is within this context that Browning and Brechin (1992) have tailored the following definition of functional assessment in transition:

> The on-going process of obtaining and properly utilizing both person and environment-based assessment information intended for the purpose of aiding its users in decision-making regarding individualized program planning and implementation of needed educational, vocational, and community-based services for youth with disabilities in transition.

Functional assessment requires, among other things, that the user have a good knowledge base regarding the two general approaches to measurement. One major approach is known as norm-referenced testing, which compares an individual's performance (intelligence, ability, aptitude, trait) to the performance of his or her peers. A major assumption underlying this *traditional approach* is that standardized measures of existing aptitudes, interests, and traits can be used to predict subsequent learning, performance, and adjustment. This assumption continues to be empirically challenged, however, especially in terms of standardized or norm-referenced test results applied to the more severely, developmentally disabled (Halpern et al., 1982).

The second major approach to assessment is known as criterion-referenced testing. This more *contemporary approach* assesses a person's development of particular skills in terms of absolute levels of mastery. Thus, rather than comparing the individual's performance to the performance of the norm of a group, his or her performance is compared to an objective standard and linked directly to specific instructional and training objectives.

Many leaders in the field believe the contemporary approach is required if the results of evaluation are to have direct implications for program planning and implementation. In other words, rather than using the traditional approach of measuring traits to predict performance, the more functional position is that one should assess directly the competencies that will be taught and base subsequent decisions on the results of that assessment.

Moreover, assessments need to be conducted throughout the entire transition period rather than serving as a data-based resource for only a single point in time. The kinds of assessment information needed will vary at different stages of the transition process. In addition, transition team members may need information that is uniquely related to their particular service area. Rather than each team member being responsible for obtaining information only for his or her own decision-making use, it is suggested that team members cooperatively and systematically develop an assessment plan that indicates the types of assessment information needed by each throughout the process. This element would help minimize duplication of information-gathering efforts, as well as lessen the resources needed for obtaining such information.

In summary, successful transition for most youth with disabilities requires an array of educational, vocational, and community-based services that are provided by different interagency personnel and delivered at different stages in the transition process. Also essential to its success are the collaboratively developed plans that are designed for each individual in the transition program. Central to this premise is that the soundness of these transition plans is based, in part, on the proper use of assessment information. It is here that assessment should play a critical role in that, by definition, it is "functional" only in so far as the results of one's measured performance are properly applied to decision making.

Curricula: A Functional Approach

One of the most critical elements in the transition process is the curriculum implemented during the school years. Unfortunately, much of the emphasis on improving transition has neglected this foundation, focusing instead on formal transition planning and the identification and availability of various post-secondary services (Cronin et al., 1992). While these are critical elements of successful transition, the importance of the curriculum and experiences students are exposed to during their school years cannot be neglected.

A variety of curricular approaches are used with secondary students with disabilities. The various orientations or models differ with regard to the amount of time students spend with special versus regular education teachers, and the extent to which the curriculum is special or different from the regular curriculum (Polloway et al., 1989b). The time students spend with the special education teacher may range from little or no time to the majority of the school day, and the curriculum followed may range from the regular education curriculum to a novel curriculum.

A Functional Emphasis. Professionals have criticized the curricular emphasis of many secondary programs. In a discussion of the current needs and concerns regarding transition efforts, for example, Halpern (1992) has said that there is a deficiency in what is taught at the secondary level and suggested that too much emphasis is placed on remedial academics and not enough is placed on functional skills. Brolin (1992) concurred, explaining that most schools continue to emphasize academic skills development at the expense of training in the affective, social, vocational, and daily living domains. Because of such practice, secondary curriculum has been proposed by OSERS' Coordinator for Secondary and Transition Program as one of five needed reform areas for the 1990s (Halloran, 1992).

Several studies have examined curricular content at the secondary level. Halpern and Benz (1987) and Benz and Halpern (1986, 1987), for example, studied secondary special education practices for students with mild disabilities, focusing on curricular implications. One of the findings they reported is that 65% of the teachers included in the survey indicated that a more appropriate curriculum was needed. This study was replicated (Brown et al., 1992) in order to identify major, unmet needs in terms of secondary special education practice and program components. Approximately 70% of the 302 special education teachers who responded to the survey indicated a need for more appropriate curricula, which supports the findings of the Halpern and Benz studies. Also, the special education coordinators rate "more appropriate curricula" as one of the top four options for improving secondary special education programs.

A number of curriculum guides, materials, and kits are now available for the secondary special classroom teacher. We have elected to highlight several of them, particularly because of their functional nature in terms of the content domains they emphasize. One popular curriculum that has been adopted by many teachers is known as *Life Centered Career Education: A Competency Based Approach* (Brolin, 1989). This curriculum includes (a) daily living skills, personal-social skills, and occupational guidance preparation competency units; (b) sources of instructional materials and other resources; and (c) student competency assessment and planning for individualized education program. Also accompanying this life-centered approach to learning is a curriculum-based, criterion-related assessment instrument (Bucher & Brolin, 1987). This knowledge-based test battery, which is designed to assess the competency level of the secondary students in the curriculum areas, consists of 89 subcompetency tests. The battery was developed with the assistance of expert special education item writers and was field tested extensively throughout the United States.

Wilcox and Bellamy (1987a) developed *The Activities Catalog,* which is considered to be an alternative curriculum for youth and adults with severe disabilities. This catalog is a field-tested curriculum that helps prepare young adults with disabilities for integrated home, leisure, and work settings. It is based on a functional approach to achieving performance goals through the mastery of activities. Step-by-step instructions are provided for each activity. Over 100 specific activities are subsumed under the three content areas of leisure, personal management, and work. *The Activities Catalog* is supplemented by a book (Wilcox & Bellamy, 1987b) that serves as an introduction and guide to the curriculum system. Furthermore, it outlines the alternative approach and describes the procedures for using *The Activities Catalog* in high school, work, or residential settings.

Irvin, Halpern, and Beckland (ND) developed a *Skills for Independent Living Kit,* which emphasizes nine areas of practical life activity, such as job search skills, budgeting, and health. This curriculum includes more than 250 instructional objectives and is accompanied by the Social Prevocational Information Battery (Halpern & Irvin, 1986), which consists of nine tests designed to assess knowledge of skills and competencies regarded as important for the community adjustment of students with mild mental retardation. The nine subtests are job search skills, job-related behavior, banking, budgeting, purchasing habits, home management, and physical health. The battery is intended primarily for junior and senior high school levels. The nine areas measured reflect five long-range educational goals: (a) employability, (b) economic self-sufficiency, (c) family living, (d) personal habits, and (e) communication.

An example of an excellent curriculum that is focused on specific content domain is *Working II — Interpersonal Skills Assessment and Training for Employment* (Foss & Vilhauer, 1986). This curriculum incorporates field-tested methods for teaching handicapped persons the social content required for successful employment. It provides a nine-step teaching procedure designed to develop knowledge based on behavioral mastery of key social competencies. Included with the teacher's guide are three videotapes entitled, (a) "Interaction with Supervisors," (b) "Interaction with Co-Workers," and (c) "An Introduction to the Teaching Procedures used in the Working II Program." Accompanying this curriculum is The Test of Interpersonal Competence for Employment (Foss et al., 1986), which has 61 items designed to assess skills that have been empirically identified as important for job tenure.

These are but a few of the many curricular materials with a functional emphasis for secondary students with disabilities. Other efforts have been directed toward the need for functional curricula. For example, functional curriculum is increasingly emphasized in special education teacher-preparation programs and textbooks (see Falvey, 1989).

A Vocational Emphasis. The employment of persons with disabilities is a major dilemma facing this nation. A 1983 study conducted by the U.S. Commission on Civil Rights, for example, found an unemployment rate approaching

50% to 78% for individuals with disabilities. Also, it was estimated from the results of a Harris telephone poll (Chadsey-Rusch, ND) that 67% of all Americans with disability, between the ages of 16 and 64, are not working and that 75% of those who are working are likely to be employed only part-time.

In addition to the unemployment problem for the general population of people with disabilities, Rusch, Chadsey-Rusch, and Szymanski (1992) note that special education students have only a 35% chance of obtaining full-time employment after leaving school. Clearly, our performance record demonstrates that the status of employment opportunities and successes for our youth with disabilities continues to be a major economic dilemma (Rusch & Phelps, 1987).

A career and vocational focus is a critical component needed for transitional programs. Its importance has been well documented, both with vocational functional assessment (Berkell, 1987; Dick, 1987; Leconte & Neubert; 1987; Stodden & Ianacone, 1981; Stodden et al., 1987) and vocational functional curriculum programs (Foss & Vilhauer, 1986).

In a statewide survey of secondary special education programs (Brown et al., 1992), only 22% and 20% of a random sample of 302 of Alabama's secondary special education teachers reported that their students were instructed in "community work sites" and "in-school work sites," respectively. Such practices must be corrected if we expect to have any impact on the students' employment success. Again, the problem is not a lack of tools with which to assess or teach/train, but rather the awareness, knowledge, and actual practice of the teachers/service providers.

In addition to assessment, the teaching of career and vocational domains, and the provision of work experience, there is also a need to use job placement resources in the community that are designed to facilitate training and paid employment (Brechin, 1992; Wehman et al., 1988). The Vocational Rehabilitation On-the-Job Training (OJT) is an important wage subsidy program, for example, reimbursing employers for additional costs incurred in training students with disabilities. The Job Training Partnership Act (JTPA), which subsidizes up to 50% of wages for up to 6 months during an on-the-job training program, provides programs for preparing youth and unskilled adults for entry into the labor force. Another economic incentive for employers to hire persons with disabilities is the Targeted Jobs Tax Credit Program (TJTC). The economic incentive of this program is the sizable reduction in a company's federal income tax liability based on the amount of wages paid to each worker who qualifies the employer for the credit. Also, the Association for Retarded Citizens On-the Job Training Project, which is funded through Title IV of the Jobs Training Partnership Act, reimburses an average of $500 to employers who participate in job training of people with disabilities.

Parents of students with disabilities historically have been concerned about losing financial and medical benefits if the student goes to work. Fortunately, such concerns are being addressed by the Social Security Administration, under Social Security Work Incentives, which provide incentives for recipients to enter the work force. In fact, since 1980, many barriers to employment have been alleviated for Social Security recipients, and work incentives have been added and liberalized under the Social Security Disability Amendments of 1980. Finally, employment provisions of the Americans with Disabilities Act offer promise in enhancing job opportunities for students with disabilities. The Act, which will eventually affect all private employers with fifteen or more workers and all places of public accommodations and services, includes a number of prohibitions that apply to job application procedures, hiring, advancement, employee compensation, training, discharge of employees, and other terms and privileges of employment.

Finally, special education must become involved in the rapidly growing "partnership" movement between education and business (Tindall, 1992). Our society's private business/industry sector is becoming increasingly involved in our nation's educational welfare. In addition to viewing such participation as simply a moral obligation, the private sector considers this new commitment as a solution to many problems that now face the U.S. workforce. Also, their linkage with education is considered by many to be a good long-term investment in that the eventual outcome will be more and better prepared workers for tomorrow's labor force.

Interestingly, this movement is just beginning to be recognized with respect to special education. Freedman and Aschheim (1988), for example, examined several business–education partnerships in Massachusetts that serve at-risk students and students with disabilities. Alliance for Business brings together under one umbrella organization several school–business collaborations while adding new programming in response to regional needs. Mini-grants are provided to teachers for such things as curriculum development and a partnership newsletter. The involvement of special education students in such education–business partnerships must be expanded and strengthened. Furthermore, according to Tindall (1992), "It is the responsibility of Local Education Agencies to see that education–business partnerships include special education students" (p. 337).

A Self-Directed Emphasis.   Although specific, behaviorally based daily living skills are indeed essential for the successful school-to-community transition for many students with mental disabilities, the importance of other complementary skills is beginning to be discussed in the field. These are generic, cognitive-behavioral skills that help students to better self-manage, self-regulate, and self-direct their own lives (Browning, 1992). Unfortunately, such self-directed skills are said to be conspicuously absent from most educational programs for students with disabilities (Mithaug et al., 1988).

Cognitive-behavior skills are different from the typical behavioral daily living skills in that they (a) involve covert cognitive processes that mediate behavior; (b) are generally applicable across situations, settings, and people; and (c) require a cognitive-behavioral, multiple instructional approach to training (Browning & White, 1986). Social problem solving, goal setting, and requesting assistance are skills that enable students with disabilities to augment their levels of self-determination.

Social problem solving is a cognitive-behavioral strategy that can enable one to manage and regulate one's own life more effectively and independently. According to Mithaug and associates (1987), ". . . the core of a transition program should focus upon instructing students to solve problems independently . . ." (p. 501). This skill is required for successful adjustments to social and life situations during postschool years (Alley & Deshler, 1979). Goal setting is another important cognitive-behavioral life-enhancement strategy to teach handicapped learners of adolescent and young adult age. The reasons are many, including (a) the attributes or properties of goal setting are well known; (b) the effects of goal setting with respect to task performance are well known; and (c) it is a strategy for self-direction, self-management, and self-achievement, all of which are enabling features of independent living. Requesting assistance is also an important cognitive-behavioral strategy for personal management. The ability to solicit, obtain, and use help is an important life skill that is relevant across a life span. Also, this skill requires a level of cognitive sophistication in that for one to initiate help seeking, one ". . . must become aware of obstacles to goal attainment, must learn to view other people as resources valuable for goal achievement, and must learn means of enlisting others to help attain these goals" (Nelson-LeGall, 1985, pp. 70–71).

Related to the issue of what cognitive-behavioral skills are to be taught is the matter of using appropriate methods for teaching them. Such intervention involves a number of procedures to instate, modify, or extinguish cognitions, feelings, and/or behaviors (Harris, 1982). *Cognitive-behavior modification* (CBM) is the popular term used for this instructional consideration and refers to a series of procedures designed to teach learners to take an active role in modifying their own behavior (Marshall, 1985). In other words, rather than relying on an external agent to manipulate behavior, there is a concentration on activating the learner to act as his or her own behavior change agent (Rooney & Hallahan, 1985).

Self-management strategies have implications for preparing students with disabilities to assume greater responsibility for their own lives (Kurtz & Neisworth, 1976). The two major types of self-management strategies are self-instruction and self-monitoring techniques. Self-instruction training has been identified as the procedure of verbally directing oneself, either overtly or covertly, to prompt, direct, or maintain behavior (Rusch et al., 1985). Simply, the assumption is that what one says to oneself will have a subsequent impact on one's behavior. According to Whitman (1987), this cognitive-behavioral training strategy has special implications for people with mental disabilities because of ". . . its emphasis on teaching production of relevant verbal cues and the use of those cues as an attention-focusing device, a vehicle for processing information, and a means of regulating motor behavior" (p. 220). The special need for this approach with these individuals is that they have difficulty generating their own verbal cues to guide their performance (Gow & Ward, 1985). Thus, there is need for the use of verbal self-instruction training. The second type of self-management approach to training is self-monitoring techniques (i.e., self-observation, self-reinforcement, self-evaluation, and cue regulation) that require the person to assess his or her behavior and make decisions regarding appropriateness (Mickler, 1984). Like self-instruction, these techniques shift the locus of control for prompting, directing, and maintaining behavioral performance from external agents to the individual.

It is not only the abilities and skills that are important for self-direction, however, but also the "opportunities" for one to make choices and decisions about one's own preferences and destiny. Thus, while in-school experience may be devoted to the learning of self-directed skills, out-of-school experiences are essential for meaningfully applying those skills. If we are serious about increasing our emphasis on preparing secondary students for a more self-directed way of life, we also need to give consideration to how they can meaningfully apply these learned skills outside the classroom.

Self-help/self-advocacy groups serve as one opportunity for accomplishing this goal (Rhoades et al., 1986). Unfortunately, however, these self-directed activities have been limited primarily to those of post-secondary age. In addressing this shortcoming, Browning and Rhoades (1986) developed a resource guide to assist secondary teachers and other service providers with materials for establishing self-help/self-advocacy groups for individuals with developmental disabilities. This material, which is based on the People First self-advocacy organization, consists of a five-part video series and accompanying training manual. The user witnesses self-advocates running their own organization and speaking as experts on their own behalf.

OTHER CONSIDERATIONS

While the primary focus of this chapter has been on the school setting, it is essential to acknowledge the fact that the concept, definition, and practice of transition extend far beyond the classroom walls in terms of issues, policies, and program practices. For the purpose of this chapter, we have elected to highlight only a few of the many other important considerations.

Interdisciplinary Collaboration

Transition is truly an interdisciplinary process that requires an interface between different service-delivery systems (Szymanski et al., 1992). Interagency cooperation and planning are areas that must be addressed with regard to transition planning (Bates et al., 1992; DeStefano & Snauwaert, 1989; Heal et al., 1990; Johnson et al., 1987; Johnson et al., 1982). In fact, federal and state statutes mandate interagency collaboration that will enable service agencies to determine the effectiveness of transition-related programs and services.

Obstacles to efficient interagency cooperation and planning include (a) inconsistent organizational patterns across agencies, (b) discontinuity in the geographic areas covered by programs, (c) differing application procedures for service eligibility, and (d) varying planning cycles and fiscal years (Edgar et al., 1984).

Therefore, a consistent policy framework is required at all levels. Such a framework includes ". . . policy goals, understanding of service eligibility and entitlement requirements, commonly shared language and information among service delivery systems, and consensus on the type and scope of services provided within each level of the services delivery system" (Johnson et al., 1987, pp. 522–523).

System's Change at the Local Level

While one of the initiatives in the new 1990 amendments to P.L. 94–142 is a focus on planning in terms of the individual, another indicates how there must be improvements in planning for program capacity in order to support the service needs identified for individual plans. One approach for improving a state's capacity to deliver effective programs and services in order to produce successful outcomes is through local transition teams (Everson & McNulty, 1992).

Oregon is the first state to have fully developed and incorporated this approach into its state plan. Halpern, Benz, and Lindstrom's (1992) model, referred to as the *Community Transition Team Model* (CTTM), includes procedures and materials for implementation in local communities by groups known as the "community transition team." The model includes as members of the local transition teams the full array of people who are concerned about secondary special education and transition programs in their community (i.e., persons with disabilities and their parents, school personnel, adult agency personnel, and members of the general public such as employers). The viability of this system's approach at the local level is evidenced, in part, by the fact that currently five other states are replicating the system on a statewide basis.

Follow-Along Strategies

Follow-along strategies are being increasingly endorsed by leaders in the field on the premise that effective transition services must be based on both an outgoing and systematic evaluation of the postschool outcomes of individuals leaving education (Halpern, 1990; Johnson et al., 1987). A number of follow-up studies have been funded (a) to examine the impact of basic skills or minimum competency testing on students with disabilities, (b) to determine the relationship between secondary programming with post-secondary outcomes, and (c) to document the experiences of special education students as they exit from school. Halpern (1990), in his review of follow-up studies for tracking school leavers in special education, noted that a total of 27 such studies have been concluded. The problem, however, is that in the 27 studies reviewed, only 7 indicated longitudinal (follow-along) intent in the design and not one of the studies reflected a strong "follow-along" strategy being implemented. Investigators need to demonstrate the utility and impact of a follow-along system developed specifically for tracking school leavers with disabilities. Important methodological considerations for increasing our contributions in this area are provided by Blackorby and Edgar (1992).

Consumer Directed

An expected outgrowth of the consumerism movement that began in the 1970s is that many people with disabilities have come to discover the right to speak out and be heard. Furthermore, the people we serve and their significant others have been major builders of our contemporary professional philosophy and practice. As secondary advocates, for example, the parents of exceptional children planted the seed of special education as we now know it. As for primary advocates, adults with disabilities laid the foundation for today's rehabilitation. As we plan ahead, we must acknowledge the significant role primary consumers and their advocates have had, and will continue to have, in drafting tomorrow's agenda.

Also, there is evidence that the area of self-determination will become a priority of the 1990s. In 1989, for example, OSERS sponsored a national conference on the topic, and the first of 29 recommendations resulting from this event reads: "The enabling of people with disabilities to determine their own futures [should] be seen as the top priority in all government policy making functions" (*Self-Determination*, 1989, p. 6). Also, Dr. William Halloran, OSERS's Secondary and Transition Program Coordinator, envisions self-determination as one of five major transition issues that may characterize the 1990s (Halloran, in press). As discussed in the functional curriculum section, we must seriously direct our attention to enhancing the abilities and opportunities of youth in transition so that they can better direct their own lives (Browning, 1992).

SUMMARY

The purpose of this chapter was to discuss some of the crucial components of transition. School-related issues included the areas of functional assessment and functional curriculum. Furthermore, the authors elected to give emphasis to the curriculum question of what to teach, with special attention devoted to the need to incorporate "vocational" preparation, experiences, and opportunities and "self-directed" learning into the secondary curriculum. Many of the important secondary classroom issues were not addressed in this chapter, such as individualized program planning, community-based instruction, and so forth. Finally, the problems of transition certainly extend beyond the classroom walls. For this chapter, four such considerations were briefly discussed, including interagency collaboration, local transition teams, follow-along systems, and consumer participation in determining the nature, focus, and direction of transition programs and services.

REFERENCES

Agran, M., Martin, J., & Mithaug, D. (1987). Transitional assessment for students with mental retardation. *Diagnostique, 12,* 173–184.

Alley, G., & Deshler, D. (1979). *Teaching the learning disabled adolescent: Strategies and methods.* Denver: Love Publishing Company.

Bates, P., Bronkema, J., Ames, T., & Hess, C. (1992). State-level interagency planning models. In F. Rusch, L. DeStefano, J. Chadsey-Rusch, L. Phelps, & E. Szymanski (Eds.), *Transition from school to adult life* (pp. 115–129). Sycamore, IL: Sycamore Publishing Company.

Benz, M., & Halpern, A. (1986). Vocational preparation for high school students with mild disabilities: A statewide study of administrator, teacher, and parent perceptions. *Career Development for Exceptional Individuals, 9,* 3–15.

Benz, M., & Halpern, A. (1987). Transition services for secondary students with mild disabilities: A statewide perspective. *Exceptional Children, 53,* 507–514.

Berkell, D. (1987). Vocational assessment of students with severe handicaps: A review of the literature. *Career Development for Exceptional Individuals, 10,* 61–75.

Blackorby, J., & Edgar, E. (1992). Longitudinal studies in the postschool adjustment of students with disabilities. In F. Rusch, L. DeStefano, J. Chadsey-Rusch, L. Phelps, & E. Szymanski (Eds.), *Transition from school to adult life* (pp. 371–386). Sycamore, IL: Sycamore Publishing Company.

Brechin, C. (1992). Resources in Alabama for job placement. In P. Browning (Ed.), *Transition in Alabama: A profile of commitment* (pp. 77–82). Auburn, AL: The Program for Training and Development, Department of Rehabilitation and Special Education, College of Education, Auburn University.

Brolin, D. (1989). *Life centered career education: A competency based approach* (3rd rev. ed.). Reston, VA: Council for Exceptional Children.

Brolin, D. (1992). The transition movement: Here we go again. In P. Browning (Ed.), *Transition in Alabama: A profile of commitment* (pp. 21–29). Auburn, AL: A Program for Training and Development, Department of Rehabilitation and Special Education, College of Education, Auburn University.

Brown, C., Browning, P., & Dunn, C. (1992). *Secondary special education programs in Alabama: A statewide study.* Auburn, AL: A Program for the Study on Disability, Department of Rehabilitation and Special Education, Auburn University.

Browning, P. (1992). *A self-directed model for students in transition.* Manuscript submitted for publication.

Browning, P., & Brechin, C. (1992). *Assessment in transition: A frame of reference for practice.* Manuscript submitted for publication.

Browning, P., & Brummer, E. (1974). Rehabilitating the mentally retarded: An overview of Federal-State impact. In P. Browning (Ed.), *Mental retardation: Rehabilitation and Counseling* (pp. 71–79). Springfield, IL: Charles C Thomas.

Browning, P., & Rhoades, C. (1986). *Self-advocacy for people with developmental disabilities: Teachers resource book and five-part video series.* Santa Monica, CA: James Stanfield Publishing Company.

Browning, P., & White, W. (1986). The teaching of life enhancement skills using interactive video-based curricula. *Education and Training of the Mentally Retarded, 21,* 236–244.

Bucher, D., & Brolin, D. (1987). The life-centered career education (LCCE) inventory: A curriculum-based, criterion-related assessment instrument. *Diagnostique, 12,* 131–141.

Bush, G. (1991). *America 2000: An educational strategy: A sourcebook.* U.S. Department of Education, Washington, DC: Author.

Chadsey-Rusch, J. (ND). Roles and responsibilities in the transition process: Concluding thoughts. In J. Chadsey-Rusch & C. Hnaley-Maxwell (Eds.), *Enhancing transition from school to the work place for handicapped youth: Personnel preparation implications* (pp. 221–237). — University of Illinois at Urbana–Champaign, Office of Career Development for Special Populations, College of Education, A Publication of the National Network for Professional Development in Vocational Special Education.

Cronin, M., Patton, J., & Polloway, E. (1992). *Preparing for adult outcomes: A model for developing a life skills curriculum.* Manuscript submitted for publication.

DeStefano, L., Linn, R., & Markward, M. (1987). *Review of student assessment instruments and practices in use in secondary/transition projects.* University of Illinois at Urbana–Champaign: Secondary Transition Intervention Effectiveness Institute.

DeStefano, L., & Snauwaert, D. (1989). *A value-critical approach to transition policy analysis.* University of Illinois at Urbana–Champaign: Secondary Transition Intervention Effectiveness Institute.

Dick, M. (1987). Translating vocational assessment into transition objectives and instruction. *Career Development for Exceptional Individuals, 10,* 76–84.

Edgar, E., Horton, B, & Maddox, M. (1984). Postschool placements: Planning for public school students with developmental disabilities. *Journal for Vocational Special Needs Students, 6,* 15–18, 26.

Elrod, G. (Ed.). (1987). Transition-related assessment. *Diagnostique, 12* [Special Issue].

Elrod, G., & Sorgenfrei, T. (1988). Toward an appropriate assessment model for adolescents who are mildly handicapped: Let's not forget transition! *Career Development for Exceptional Individuals, 11,* 92–98.

Everson, J., McNulty K. (1992). Interagency teams: Building local transition programs through parental and professional partnerships. In F. Rusch, L. DeStefano, J. Chadsey-Rusch, L. Phelps, & E. Szymanski (Eds.), *Transition from school to adult life* (pp. 341–352). Sycamore, IL: Sycamore Publishing Company.

Falvey, M. (Ed.). (1989). *Community-based curriculum: Instructional strategies for students with severe handicaps.* Baltimore: Paul H. Brookes Publishers.

Federal Register (1991), p. 66290.

Foss, G., Cheney, D., & Bullis, M. (1986). *TICE: Test of Interpersonal Competence for Employment.* Santa Monica: CA: James Stanfield & Company.

Foss, G., & Vilhauer, D. (1986). *Working II — Interpersonal skills assessment and training for employment: Teacher's guide* [24 video lessons with assessment scale]. Santa Monica, CA: James Stanfield & Company.

Freedman, S., & Aschheim, B. (1988). *Innovation with impact: Industry-education partnerships in Massachusetts.* No. 153 11. Quincey; Massachusetts State Department of Education.

Gow, L., & Ward, J. (1985). The use of verbal self-instruction training for enhancing generalization outcomes with persons with an intellectual disability. *Australia and New Zealand Journal of Developmental Disabilities, 11,* 157–168.

Halloran, B. (1992). Transition services requirement: Issues, implications, challenge. In P. Browning (Ed.), *Transition II in Alabama: Another profile of commitment.* Auburn, AL: A Program for Training and Development, Department of Rehabilitation and Special Education, College of Education, Auburn University (this is the keynote paper delivered at the May, 1992, statewide conference on transition and to be published in the proceedings).

Halpern, A. (1985). Transition: A look at the foundations. *Exceptional Children, 51,* 479–486.

Halpern, A. (1990). A methodological review of follow-up and follow-along studies tracking school leavers in special education. *Career Development for Exceptional Individuals. 13,* 13–28.

Halpern, A. (1992). Transition: Old wine in new bottles. *Exceptional Children, 58,* 202–211.

Halpern, A., & Benz, M. (1987). A statewide examination of secondary special education for students with mild disabilities: Implications for the high school curriculum. *Exceptional Children, 54,* 122–129.

Halpern, A., Benz, M., & Lindstrom, L. (1992). A systems change approach to improving secondary special education and transition programs at the local community level. *Career Development for Exceptional Individuals, 15,* 109–120.

Halpern, A., & Irvin, L. (1986). *Social and prevocational information battery–revised.* Monterey, CA: CTB/McGraw-Hill.

Halpern, A., Lehmann, J., Irvin, L., & Heiry, T. (1982). *Contemporary assessment: For mentally retarded adolescents and adults.* Baltimore: University Park Press.

Harris, K. (1982). Cognitive-behavior modification: Application with exceptional students. *Focus on Exceptional Children, October,* 1–17.

Heal, L., Copher, J., & Rusch, F. (1990). Inter-agency agreements (IAA's) among agencies responsible for the transition education of students with handicaps for secondary schools to post-secondary settings. *Career Development for Exceptional Individuals, 13,* 121–127.

The Individuals with Disabilities Education Act, P.L. 101–476, 602 (a) (19) (1990).

Irvin, L., Halpern, A., & Beckland, J. (ND). *Skills for independent living kit.* Monterey, CA: CTB/McGraw-Hill.

Johnson, D., Bruininks, R., & Thurlow, M. (1987). Meeting the challenge of transition service planning through improved interagency cooperation. *Exceptional Children, 53,* 522–530.

Johnson, H., McLaughlin, J., & Christensen, M. (1982). Interagency collaboration: Driving and restraining forces. *Exceptional Children, 48,* 395–399.

Kurtz, P., & Neisworth, J. (1976). Self control possibilities for exceptional children. *Exceptional Children, 42,* 212–217.

Leconte, P., & Neubert, D. (1987). Vocational education for special needs students: Linking vocational assessment and support. *Diagnostique, 12,* 156–167.

Marshall, K. (1985). Cognitive behavior modification in the classroom: Theoretical and practical perspective. In C.S. Simon (Ed.), *Communication skills and classroom success.* San Diego, CA: College-Hill Press.

Matson, J. (1988). Teaching and training relevant community skills to mentally retarded persons. *Child & Youth Services, 10,* 107–201 [Special Issue].

Mickler, M. (1984). Self-management skill training for educable mentally retarded persons. *Journal of Special Education, 18,* 143–149.

Mithaug, D., Martin, J., & Agran, M. (1987). Adaptability instruction: The goal of transition programming. *Exceptional Children, 53,* 500–506.

Mithaug, D., Martin, J., Agran, M., & Rusch, F. (1988). *Why special education graduates fail: How to teach them to succeed.* Colorado Springs, CO: Ascent Publications.

Nelson-LeGall, S. (1985). Help-seeking behavior in learning. In E.W. Gordon (Ed.), *Review of research in education* (Vol. 12). Washington, DC: American Educational Research Association.

Polloway, E., Patton, J., Epstein, M., & Smith, T. (1989a). Comprehensive curriculum for students with mild handicaps. *Focus on Exceptional Children, 21,* 1–12.

Polloway, E., Patton, J., Payne, J., and Payne, R. (1989b). *Strategies for teaching learners with special needs.* (4th ed.). New York: Merrill.

Rhoades, C., Browning, P., & Thorin, L. (1986). A self-help advocacy movement: A promising peer support system for mentally handicapped people. *Rehabilitation Literature, 47,* 2–6.

Rooney, K., & Hallahan, D. (1985). Future directions for cognitive behavior modification research: The quest for cognitive change. *Remedial and Special Education, 6,* 46–51.

Rusch, F., Chadsey, J., & Szymanski, E. (1992). The emerging field of transition services. In F. Rusch, L. DeStefano, J. Chadsey-Rusch, L. Phelps, & E. Szymanski

(Eds.), *Transition from school to adult life: Models, linkages, and policy* (pp. 5–15). Sycamore, IL: Sycamore Publishing Company.

Rusch, F., Morgan, T., Martin, J., Riva, M., & Agran, M. (1985). Competitive employment: Teaching mentally retarded employees self-instructional strategies. *Applied Research in Mental Retardation, 6,* 389–407.

Rusch, F., & Phelps, L. (1987). Secondary special education transition from school to work: A natural priority. *Exceptional Children, 53,* 487–493.

Self-Determination (1989). The proceedings from a national conference sponsored by the Office of Special Education and Rehabilitative Services (OSERS), held in Arlington, VA, January 9–10.

SRI International. (1988). *OSEP national longitudinal study.* Washington, DC: U.S. Department of Education, Office of Special Education.

Stodden, R., & Ianacone, R. (1981). Career/vocational assessment of the special needs individual: A conceptual model. *Exceptional Children, 47,* 600–608.

Stodden, R., Ianacone, R., Boone, R., & Bisconer, S. (1987). *Curriculum-based vocational assessment: A guide for addressing youth with special needs.* Honolulu: Center Publications, International Education Corp.

Szymanski, E., Hanley-Maxwell, C., & Asselin, S. (1992). Systems interface: Vocational rehabilitation, special education, and vocational evaluation. In F. Rusch, L. DeStefano, J. Chadsey-Rusch, L. Phelps, & E. Szymanski (Eds.), *Transition from school to adult life* (pp. 153–171). Sycamore, IL: Sycamore Publishing Company.

Tindall, L. (1992). Business linkages. In F. Rusch, L. DeStefano, J. Chadsey-Rusch, L. Phelps, & E. Szymanski (Eds.), *Transition from school to adult life: Models, linkages, and policy* (pp. 321–340). Sycamore, IL: Sycamore Publishing Company.

Wehman, P., Moon, W., Everson, J., Wood, W., & Barcus, J. (1988). *Transition from School to Work: New challenges for youth with severe disabilities.* Baltimore, MD: Paul H. Brookes Publishing Company.

Whitman, T. (1987). Self-instruction, individual differences, and mental retardation. *American Journal of Mental Deficiency, 92,* 213–223.

Wilcox, B., & Bellamy, G. (1987a). *The activities catalog: An alternative curriculum for youth and adults with severe disabilities.* Baltimore, MD: Paul H. Brookes Publishing Company.

Wilcox, B., & Bellamy, G. T. (1987b). *A comprehensive guide to the activities catalog: An alternative curriculum for youth and adult with severe disabilities.* Baltimore: Paul H. Brookes Publishing Co.

Will, M. (1984). *OSERS programming for the transition of youth with disabilities: Bridges from school to working life.* Washington, DC: Office of Special Education and Rehabilitative Services, U.S. Office of Education.

Transition Services Requirement: Issues, Implications, Challenge

William D. Halloran

The 1970s marked a decade of special education issues characterized by concerns with equal access for all students with disabilities, appropriate education conducted in the least restrictive environment, individualized educational planning, and due process assurances under the law for students and their families. Ten years later, as the special education community took stock of its accomplishments since the passage of P.L. 94–142, it could point to progress in these areas and mark the achievements.

But follow-up studies conducted in the early 1980s (Edgar et al., 1986; Hasazi et al., 1985; Mithaug & Horiuchi, 1983) revealed that despite this emphasis on equality, integration, and independence (seen in P.L. 94–142 and other legislation), large numbers of special education students leaving public education were entering segregated, dependent, nonproductive lives. Two-thirds of adults with disabilities were not employed, and others were served in segregated programs or were not provided with a program at all. Consumers became concerned that school experiences, despite their exemplary quality, would lead to an "aging out" into meager adult services. These findings, along with concern on the part of parents, professionals, and policymakers, gave rise to the issues of the remainder of the 1980s: early intervention, transition from school to work, maximum participation in regular education, family networking, and follow-up/follow-along responsibilities. These issues expanded the role and responsibility of public education to younger and older age groups. They also emphasized the importance of developing relationships between the school and elements of the community, such as families, employers, adult service agencies, and social services. While in the 1970s, accountability through increased documentation and legal resources was stressed, emphasis shifted toward assessing real-life outcomes associated with special education in the 1980s. Education agencies began to identify adult adjustment goals for their students in the areas of post-secondary education, employment, and independent living; to plan educational programs and work experiences to achieve those goals; and to follow up on graduates and school leavers in an effort to gauge the effectiveness of school programming.

TRANSITION: THE FEDERAL INITIATE

Transition was first introduced in federal legislation in the 1984 Amendments to the Education of the Handicapped Act, P.L. 98–199. The Amendments drew specific attention to the need to improve the scope and quality of transition services. The U.S. Department of Education's Office of Special Education and Rehabilitative Services defined the critical components of transition planning and put new demonstration programs into place throughout the country. These components of transition include:

1. Effective high school programs that prepare students to work and live in the community
2. A broad range of adult service programs that can meet the various support needs of individuals with disabilities in employment and community settings
3. Comprehensive and cooperative transition planning between education and community service agencies for the purpose of developing needed services for completers, leavers, and graduates

Many successful programs adapted these critical components in their conceptualization and development. However, the overriding principle in successful programs was that services are shaped by the needs of the youth being served.

The research and demonstration efforts supported by the federal discretionary program have stimulated the development of new and unique approaches throughout the country. These programs demonstrated that public education can assist youths with a variety of disabilities and levels of impairments in making the adjustment to adult life in their communities. They set in place interagency cooperation between school and adult programs. They also provided instructional support systems to ensure that an individual with disabilities could succeed in real work settings.

Studies of program effectiveness have shown that three essential components are necessary for all levels of disability. First is the need for families of youths with disabilities to be included as partners in the development and implementation of purposeful activities that maximize independence. The family is a major facilitator of transition. Second, transition programs must be community-based, and opportunities to experience and succeed in employment and other aspects of community life must be provided. The third component is the need for working partnerships with employers to ensure that efforts of the schools are consistent with employers' needs. Programs that prepare youths with disabilities for employment should include measurement of employers' and employees' satisfaction. Additional strengths lie in effective and systematic coordination of agencies, organizations, and individuals from a broad array of disciplines and professional fields.

The interest in transition and the success of early demonstrations led to the expansion of the federal discretionary program through the *Education of the Handicapped Amendments of 1986*, P.L. 99–457. P.L. 99–457 included more specific language to shape state-level transition policy as states were encouraged to develop state-level interagency agreements for the provision of transition services and required to report information on the status of students with disabilities exiting secondary education.

Although transition-related language and the accompanying discretionary dollars prompted a flurry of research and demonstration activity across the country, federal legislative actions prior to 1990 provided no definition of transition, no mandate for providing transition services, and no mechanism for funding other than through model demonstration projects. Therefore, states and localities were allowed to provide and fund transition services in programs serving secondary-level youth with disabilities at their own discretion. These circumstances resulted in considerable heterogeneity in the extent and manner in which states responded to the federal transition initiative. The heterogeneity existed along a number of dimensions: the type of state-level policy; the nature of interagency agreements; the designations of a lead agency in transition planning; the age at which transition services begin; the type of services available; and the manner in which transition planning was conducted (Repetto et al., 1990; Snauwaert & DeStefano, 1990).

For some states, lack of federal prescription created opportunities for individualization as they went about constructing state-level policy and local service-delivery systems that were based on the education, adult service, and employment context of their states. The high level of local control increased ownership and commitment to these systems. Transition service delivery was optimized because of such factors as specific local or state-level knowledge of anticipated service needs of students exiting school, available resources, personalities, politics, and reducing barriers to service delivery. As a result, a number of states are currently operating efficient, effective systems of transition service delivery that differ greatly from each other, yet achieve desirable results within their jurisdiction (DeStefano & Wermuth, 1991). In other states, in the absence of a federal mandate, little has been done to create a system of transition service delivery. Both efforts have resulted in a national pattern of transition services in which there exist pockets of excellence and pockets of great need.

The 1990 reauthorization of the Education of the Handicapped Act created the Individuals with Disabilities Education Act (IDEA). The IDEA now requires that transition services be made available to all students age 16 and older, or age 14 or younger if appropriate, with the services being updated on an annual basis. Section 1401 of IDEA defines transition services as:

> . . . a coordinated set of activities for a student, designed within an outcome-oriented process, which promotes movement from school to post-school activities, including post-secondary education, vocational training, integrated employment (including supported employment), continuing and adult education, adult services, independent living, or community participation. The coordinated set of activities shall be based upon the individual student's needs, taking into

account the student's preferences and interests, and shall include instruction, community experiences, the development of employment and other post-school adult living objectives, and, when appropriate, acquisition of daily living skills and functional vocational evaluation. [The Individuals with Disabilities Education Act, P.L. 101–476, 20 U.S.C. Chapter 33, Section 1401 (a) (19)]

This new requirement represents a major policy shift regarding transition from permissive "when appropriate" services to prescriptive, required services. The required services include transition curriculum, community experiences, and the development of employment and other independent living objectives. In addition to the mandate, the legislation details the process of service provision in four ways:

1. By providing a definition of transition services
2. By listing the set of activities that make up transition services and detailing the basis for determining which activities are appropriate for an individual student
3. By specifying the process by which a statement of needed transition services is to be included in a student's individualized education plan (IEP)
4. By describing the responsibilities of the educational agency to monitor the provision of services

Clearly, transition planning will soon become an essential component of the educational process. Prior to the passage of P.L. 101–476, some states used P.L. 98–199 and P.L. 99–457 as springboards to foster the development of transition-related activities at both the state and local levels, whereas other states did not. However, with the passage of the IDEA, states and local educational agencies are now mandated to provide transition services. Many state and local educational agencies have developed policies that mandate the provision of services similar to those outlined in P.L. 101–476 and have been providing those services for a number of years (Repetto et al., 1990; Snauwaert & DeStefano, 1990). For other states and localities, the definition contained in P.L. 101–476 may dramatically change the scope and settings in which secondary-level education is provided to youth with disabilities.

REFORMS NECESSARY TO EXPAND AND IMPROVE SERVICES

As we begin the 1990s we witness the legislative changes that have moved transition services from a privilege to an entitlement. Just as the issues of the 1980s reflect an extension or elaboration of those of the previous decade, the issues of the 1990s build upon the central themes of independence, interagency linkages, and curriculum and policy reform based on maximizing real-life outcomes for youth with disabilities. Five issues are identified that may characterize the transition issues for the 1990s: self-determination, secondary curriculum reform, graduation/high school completion, anticipated service needs, and public policy alignment. A review of recent research is presented for each issue along with implications for policy makers and professionals charged with the implementation of the transition requirements of IDEA. These issues should be considered as parents, educators, and other professionals interact with their colleagues in developing educational reforms in response to *America 2000* (U.S. Department of Education, 1991) and other initiatives for reforming our educational enterprise.

Self-Determination: The Ultimate Goal of Education

Issues of independence, self-sufficiency, and the capacity to make informed decisions are beginning to emerge in the rehabilitation and education literature as essential attributes for successful community integration of persons with disabilities (Mithaug, Martin, Agran, & Rusch, 1988). Thomas (1982) postulates that cultural attitudes toward persons with disabilities progressed through three stages: the first phase, in which a person with a disability was considered helpless; a second phase, in which skilled professionals became involved in helping those with disabilities; and a third stage, in which persons with disabilities exhibited self-determination and began to question their roles as passive recipients of help. Despite Thomas' claim that cultural attitudes have progressed through these three stages, there is a lack of evidence supporting the claim that parents, professionals, and other helpers have actualized the third phase and developed strategies to ensure that persons with disabilities learn and are provided the opportunity to practice self-determination in their education and other facets of their personal lives.

For persons with disabilities, *self-determination* means "running risks, challenging rules, and acquiring resources" (Varela, 1986). It also involves "knowing your basic human rights; taking responsibility for your life; and asking for help because you want or need it" (McGill, 1978). Acquiring these personal characteristics and the information base that enables self-determination may be thought of as a developmental process that begins in early childhood and continues throughout adult life (Ward, 1988). The acquisition of these traits should not be assumed to be a natural occurrence but rather the result of purposeful strategies, properly implemented, to achieve the desired outcome of independence. This notion has some very important implications for special education. In a paper addressing the achievement of educational excellence, Wang (1987) stated, "of particular interest is the reexamination of the student's functioning in classroom learning and learner outcomes." Similar sentiments were expressed by Mithaug and associates (1988) when they indicated that the primary goal of special education and, in fact, of all education is to increase student responsibility for managing their own affairs. Actualizing this emphasis would require a major change in the current approach to educating, parenting, or planning for children and youth with disabilities. At present, the student is rarely seen as a participating team member and, in fact, is rarely even present during the IEP process.

Implications

The implied outcome of the transition services requirement of IDEA is to assist youth with disabilities to become well-adjusted, suitably employed members of their communities. Transition services are based on the student's needs, taking into account the student's preferences and interests. The public agency responsible for the development of the transition services component of the IEP must include the student to ensure that his or her needs, preferences, and interests are addressed. Students must be active participants throughout the decision-making process afforded through the IEP meeting. It is unrealistic to expect students to become well-adjusted, active members of the community if they are not afforded opportunities to become active members in decisions that affect that future. There is an increasing realization within the field that it is unrealistic to expect satisfactory career development and transition outcomes when intervention is delayed until students reach high school (Clark et al., 1991). The ultimate question of what schools want students to know or be able to do when they leave school is critical. It is equally critical that schools ask what they want their students to know or be able to do when they reach middle school, or junior high school, or high school. Preparing a student for independence or transitioning can never start too early. Reform aimed at a goal of self-determination must consider control for learning and performance as a shared responsibility among teachers, parents, and the student him/herself, with primary control residing with the student.

Secondary Curriculum Reform: Completing Initial Transitions

Will (1984) defined transition as a bridge between the security and structure offered by the school and the many choices and responsibilities of adult life. She went on to suggest that transition can be conceptualized as an outcome-oriented process encompassing a broad array of services and experiences leading to employment. Halpern (1985) expanded the notion to include outcomes other than employment, such as level of integration and the quality of a person's social and interpersonal network. By all accounts it would seem that a successful transition from school to work and adult life is an important outcome associated with effective schooling and service provision (Wilcox & Bellamy, 1982).

Edgar's work (Edgar, 1987) and that of others (Hasazi et al., 1985; Mithaug & Horiuchi, 1983) indicate that students exiting special education programs often experience significant difficulty making the transition to adult and working life. Research by Mithaug and Horiuchi (1983); Hasazi, Gordon, and Roe (1985); Hasazi, Gordon, Roe, Hull, Finch, and Salembier (1985); Fardig, Algozzine, Schwartz, Hensel, and Westling (1985); Wehman, Kregel, and Seyfarth (1985); Gill (1984); and Edgar, Levine, and Maddox (1986) provide a discouraging picture of the post-school adjustment of individuals who have left special education.

> The truth is that secondary curriculum for special education students appears to have very little, if any, impact on their eventual adjustment to community life. A logical conclusion is that major change in secondary programs for special education is urgently required. . . . The only solution is a radical shift in focus of secondary curriculum away from academic to functional vocational, independent living tasks. (Edgar et al., 1986)

Shill (1988) analyzed 315 individual education plans (IEPs) from high schools in suburban and urban districts in the state of Washington and found that functional objectives occurred in just 31% of the IEPs, and only 2% of the objectives specified generalized outcomes. It appears that while we are looking for more positive living and employment outcomes for youth with disabilities, less emphasis is being placed on the "functionality" of our current educational efforts.

Special education students need knowledge and skill in the academic subject areas. At the same time they need to be able to apply that knowledge and skill to solve problems once they leave school. In their book, entitled *Why Special Education Graduates Fail,* Mithaug and co-workers (1988) indicated that, in addition to teaching basic academic skills and appropriate classroom behaviors, special education teaches passive responding and dependency — the major post-school problems of special education graduates. As stated in the previous section, students must be encouraged to think critically, solve problems independently, make choices, set their own goals, decide what to do, initiate action, evaluate their work, and adjust accordingly. In addition, special education students must be given the opportunity to apply skills learned in real settings, in mainstream classes, in the community, and on the job. A logical conclusion is that significant reform is necessary in secondary special education curricula and practice, making it community referenced, community based, and geared to real-life outcomes expected for all students.

Implications

The role of education must be expanded to *include* making initial employment and independent living placements in appropriate community settings and providing sufficient time to "follow-along" before students exit public school programs to determine whether additional support is necessary and to evaluate program effectiveness. The transition services provisions of IDEA appear to support this expansion. Transition services are to be outcome-oriented and must include curriculum, community experiences, and the development of employment and other post-school adult living objectives.

Graduation/High School Completion: Functional vs. Academic

The increase in regular education graduation requirements is drastically affecting the flexibility of special education programming for students with mild disabilities. More and more states are setting minimum standards that must be met for any student to graduate from high school. These standards usually include earning a specified number of Carnegie units, passage of a minimum competency test, and certain course and credit requirements. Although there is a well-recognized need for a high school education that results in the development of basic competencies, this concept is in actuality being interpreted as academic competencies rather than life-skill competencies.

In some states and localities, students, parents, and teachers are forced into a planning dilemma related to graduation requirements. In some cases, if students wish to receive a regular diploma, they must focus on academic requirements, leaving no time for course work in vocational education, career education, and experiences that relate to the development of social skills and independent living — all areas of well-documented need for students with disabilities. It appears that not only is curricular reform necessary as stated in the previous section, but accompanying policy change must occur for students to be maximally prepared for adult life.

Exiting data indicate that almost all youth with disabilities who are in regular education programs leave school before age 19. The majority of these individuals do not graduate with a "regular" diploma. Estimates indicate that over 30% might drop out of school prior to the age of graduation (Halloran & Ward, 1988). Recent studies and reports indicate that it cannot be assumed that the earning of a diploma can be equated with being prepared to live and work in our communities. The National Council on Disability (1989) reported that students with disabilities are lagging behind their peers without disabilities. The *Twelfth Annual Report to Congress on the Implementation of the Education of the Handicapped Act* (U.S. Department of Education, 1990) indicated that 47% of all students with disabilities do not graduate from high school with either a diploma or certificate of completion. This figure is corroborated by data from a National Longitudinal Study (Wagner & Shaver, 1989). This study indicated that 44% of students with disabilities failed to graduate from high school, and 36% of the students with disabilities dropped out of school. Employment data for people with disabilities are similarly discouraging. While the national unemployment rate is about 6%, almost two-thirds of all Americans with disabilities between the ages of 16 and 24 are not working (Harris & Associates, 1986). These studies suggest that many factors contribute to this situation, including attitudinal, physical, and communication barriers; lack of appropriate training opportunities; and scarcity of effective transition planning and service programs. None of the studies recommended a stronger academic approach for youth with disabilities; however, questions have been raised regarding the academic emphasis at the expense of more functional, community-referenced instruction.

Implications

The transition services requirements of IDEA appear to be calling for an increase in functional programming directed toward improving employment and independent living outcomes. This presents a dilemma for 50% to 70% of the secondary-aged youth with disabilities whose educational placements are predominantly in regular classes. This group includes the students reported to be served in regular-class and resource-room environments. The question is: *Can it be expected that regular classes or resource rooms have the capacity to meet the new functional requirements in IDEA?* Research and information obtained from needs statements for model demonstration grants would indicate that the answer is no. The problem of regular education classes being responsive to the new transition requirements (i.e., functional programming) is further complicated by the viewpoint of many professionals that any form of "separate education" is inherently unequal. However, it is regular education (regular-class and resource-room) placement that appears to be the education environment from which students are rejected.

Programs are needed that are aimed at continuing to engage or to re-engage such students. Reform is needed to provide for intensive instruction to prepare youth to live and work in their communities and to foster the availability of services in normalized, age-appropriate settings such as adult education, post-secondary vocational education, and community colleges, which will help to eliminate the stigma of returning to the same high school. Many state and local education agencies have established policies that consider the acquisition of a high school diploma as a point of termination of eligibility for special education regardless of whether the student is under the state's maximum age for services or has had the opportunity to experience functional programming. The provisions in IDEA would allow educational agencies to issue diplomas and continue enrollment of students, if they have not had the opportunity to complete the transition services component of their IEP, as long as they are under the state's maximum age for services. Reform efforts at the state and local level should review policy related to this issue to ensure that policies will not penalize students from receiving these opportunities.

Anticipated Service Needs: Waiting Lists for Adult Services

Today, educational programming for students with severe disabilities has as its goal to prepare students to live an adult life in integrated community residential and work settings. This goal remains reasonable as long as the necessary support services are available to maintain or enhance the person's maximum level of independence, productivity, and community participation once the responsibility of the educational system has ended (Wilcox & Bellamy, 1982). Unfortunately, needed services are frequently in short supply. The growing discrepancy between the service needs of youth with severe disabilities who leave school, along with the capacity of existing adult services to provide for these needs, has a grave impact on families and other caregivers who are often shocked to learn that the full service mandate terminates after school years (McDonnell et al., 1985). Deinstitutionalization and the P.L. 94–142 mandate for a free appropriate public education have led to an implied promise of responsive community-based adult services. This promise has been unfulfilled for many school leavers as they remain on waiting lists for months or years or enter segregated employment and residential settings.

Some might argue that the problem of waiting lists and the paucity of responsive adult programs and services are not legitimate concerns of the special education community. The fact is that the momentum to integrate students with severe disabilities into the mainstream of society has been increasing rapidly, brought on largely through the efforts of the school. Innovative instructional practices have been developed to prepare youth to work and live in society. Increasing numbers of today's youth with severe disabilities have had the benefit of community-referenced curricula focused on the acquisition of age-appropriate functional skills required for success in integrated domestic, community, recreational, leisure, vocational, and educational environments (Brown et al., 1976; Ward & Halloran, 1989). In addition to providing new technology and a focus to prepare students to be maximally independent, integrated, and productive in society, many school programs are now successful in preparing students with severe disabilities for gainful employment through work experience and supported employment programs (Rusch et al., 1987; Vogelsberg, 1986). Unfortunately, as in the case of most community-based adult services such as recreation and residential programs, there also is a shortage of supported employment programs for students who are exiting secondary school programs prepared to work (DeStefano et al., 1988).

Community-referenced, functional education implies that the concepts and skills learned by students will be applied in community settings. If the end result in public education for persons with severe disabilities is placement into a segregated setting or the experience of a long delay for service where regression or loss of skills is likely to occur, then the entire educational process becomes futile and without meaning.

Implications

The problems of waiting lists and lack of appropriate adult services are complex and difficult to solve, and go beyond what education alone can solve. If the 1990s are to be credited with the solution to these problems, much needs to be accomplished. A logical first step might be to assess individual service needs during transition planning and to discuss those needs with agencies providing adult services. This will help to identify what is possible as well as the gaps in needed services locally, regionally, and at the state level.

IDEA states that transition services means a "coordinated set of activities" that promote movement from school to post-school activities. Expansion of IEP requirements calls for the public agency responsible for IEP development to include representatives of other public agencies involved in the planning and provision of services. Despite the merits of inclusion of outside agencies in transition planning, assurance of participation of agencies other than education has been difficult to achieve. The gaps in service and responsibility that exist in the articulation between mandated educational services and eligibility-determined systems such as rehabilitation, mental health, and public-assistance programs mitigate against effective provision of services. In the absence of a federal mandate for adult services, reform efforts at the state and local level will have to be targeted to the development of needed services as well as revision of interagency agreements to define financial and service responsibilities among agencies. Increased articulation and planning between education agencies and adult service providers have resulted in better coordination of services and a more efficient use of scarce resources leading to improved outcomes for transitioning students. These efforts should continue, be encouraged, and be expanded.

Public Policy Alignment: Supporting Education Efforts

The commitment to integration and the provision of transition services necessitates a reform in our secondary special education programs to ensure that all youth with disabilities have the opportunity to become well-adjusted, suitably employed members of their communities. As we become more focused on programming for future environments, the need for reform in current educational policy and procedures will become apparent. The coordinated services provisions of IDEA will also necessitate the alignment of policy and procedures to enable the development of working relationships between education agencies and adult service providers.

In addition to the reforms in practice mentioned earlier, there is also a need for policy alignment in federal programs. This would include the Supplemental Security Income (SSI) Program and aspects of the Fair Labor Standards Act (FLSA) administered by the U.S. Department of Labor. The SSI Program has often been considered a disincentive to employment and other aspects of independence. Consequently, some well-meaning educators and rehabilitation professionals were reluctant to assist people with severe disabilities to enroll in the SSI program. The notion of promoting a payment program that might act as a disincentive to participation in training and employment programs would be contrary to the commitment to assist individuals in maximizing their potential for self-sufficiency (Halloran, 1991). Several incentives to participate in training and employment have been introduced to the SSI program since 1980. These changes sought to remove some of the economic barriers associated with working and allow for the continuation of benefits until a recipient's earnings and employment benefits would ensure coverage. Two major work incentives included in the current SSI program are the Plan to Achieve Self Support Program (PASS) and the Impairment-Related Work Expenses (IRWE) provisions. These incentives and the Medicaid health insurance program are assets that eligible youth with disabilities should be linked with.

The issue relating to the FLSA has become a barrier to the implementation of community-based training programs. Both the FLSA and community-based training efforts are for the benefit of the student with disabilities, rather than for the benefit of employers. The intent of the FLSA is to ensure that individuals are not exploited in our nation's workplaces. The intent of community-based training for students with disabilities is to provide structured educational activities that will lead to employment in their communities. Community-based training has been demonstrated to be an extremely effective strategy for improving employment outcomes. However, a number of programs have been forced to reduce their services after being cited for failure to pay commensurate wages to students in a variety of community situations.

Implications

Educators must become familiar with the benefits and incentives associated with the SSI program. The State Systems for Transition Services for Youth with Disabilities Program created in the IDEA requires participating states to develop procedures to be used to ensure that youth and their families who are eligible for the disability programs of the Social Security Administration are provided information, training, and referral services (U.S. Department of Education, 1991). The benefits and incentives of the SSI program have been used effectively to enable students to continue in paid employment positions after they have completed school. The SSI incentives have been used to continue support services that have been developed by school programs to enable students to secure and maintain employment. Examples of these supports include subsidized transportation under the IRWE provisions and the payment of job coaches and trainers under the PASS provisions.

Community-based instruction has become recognized as a primary method for preparing and assisting individuals with disabilities to make the transition from school to community life. Community-based instruction refers to systematic teaching of life skills in the actual environments in which the students apply them. These environments include the world of work where curricular content is based on ecological inventories to determine the skills needed to be employed. The need to develop systematic instructional strategies to prepare individuals for employment and independent living requires the development of well-articulated programs that clearly delineate the student as a trainee rather than as an employee. The public education agency must also ensure that at any point in time at which the education program becomes secondary to the performance of productive work, an employment relationship will begin along with commensurate compensation in accordance with the provisions of the FLSA. Public education agencies will have to acquire a working knowledge of the FLSA to ensure that their programs prohibit exploitation and violations of labor laws. The U.S. Department of Education and the U.S. Department of Labor are currently involved in discussions to provide guidance to education agencies in program development to ensure that the trainee vs. employee distinction can be made to satisfy the FLSA requirements. Reforms at the federal level are expected to be reflected in revision of practice and definition of programs at the state and local level. These reforms should result in well-articulated, community-based vocational education programs that will demonstrate compliance with both the IDEA provisions and those of the FLSA.

SUMMARY

Prior to the passage of P.L. 101–476, the Individuals with Disabilities Education Act, transition services were treated as a discretionary program in federal legislation. The discretionary program authorized by P.L. 98–199 and strengthened by P.L. 99–457 was intended to stimulate research and the development of demonstration programs to address concerns of Congress regarding the rather poor outcomes of many students exiting special education programs. Halpern (1992) links the transition movement to two similar movements: the career education movement in the 1970s and the work/study movement of the 1960s. Both of these areas of program emphasis were similar to the transition movement prior to IDEA. However, the IDEA provisions represent a major policy shift from permissive to prescriptive, required services. This policy shift differentiates transition services from the movements of the 1960s, 1970s, and 1980s, which encouraged improved services to achieve educational outcomes without a clear statement of entitlement for all youth with disabilities.

This chapter identified five issues that may greatly influence the implementation of the transition services entitlement: promoting self-determination among students in special education, curriculum reform resulting in real-life outcomes for students, reducing competition between increased graduation requirements and functional education, anticipating and accommodating service needs of students exiting public education, and the need for realignment of public policies to support transition efforts in education and to maximize the cooperation needed to achieve successful outcomes. These issues and implications should be considered as students, parents, educators, and other professionals interact with their fellow citizens and colleagues to ensure that all discussions involving educational reform include measures of excellence relating to positive outcomes achieved by students with disabilities exiting public school programs.

The inclusion of the requirement for transition services is a positive social and legislative move. For the past several years, beginning with the 1983 report *A Nation at Risk,* there has been a nationwide focus on restructuring and improving our nation's schools. *America 2000* has stimulated broad-based reform efforts to measure the progress of individuals, schools, districts, states, and the nation to ensure that our education enterprise will meet or exceed world-class standards. A major issue in our reform efforts will be to ensure that all students are included in performance standards and that performance standards are realistic for all students. The requirement that transition services be a coordinated set of activities, designed within an outcome-oriented process to promote movement from school to post-school environments, establishes the framework for special education reform. Our challenge is to address those issues necessary to ensure effective transition services for students with disabilities while ensuring that reform in our educational system addresses diversity and accommodates the unique needs of all students.

REFERENCES

America 2000: An education strategy sourcebook. (1991). Washington, DC: U.S. Department of Education.

Brown, L., Nietupski, J., & Hamre-Nietupski, S. (1976). The criterion of ultimate functioning and public school services for severely handicapped children. In M.A. Thomas (Ed.), *Hey don't forget about me! Education's investment in the severely and profoundly handicapped.* Reston, VA: The Council for Exceptional Children.

Clark, G., Carlson, B.C., Fisher, S., Cook, I.D., D'Alonzo, B. (1991). Career development for students with disabilities in elementary schools: A position statement of the Division of Career Development. *Career Development for Exceptional Individuals, 14*(2).

DeStefano, L., Wermuth, T. (1991). IDEA (P.L. 101–476): Defining a second generation of transition services. In F. Rusch, L. DeStefano, J. Chadsey-Rusch, L. Phelps, & Szymanski (Eds.), *Transition from school to adult life* (pp. 537–549). Sycamore, IL: Sycamore Publishing Company.

DeStefano, L., Winking, D.L., & Rusch, F.R. (1988). *Supported employment in Illinois: Job coach issues.* Champaign: University of Illinois, The Transition Institute.

Edgar, E. (1987). Secondary programs is special education: Are many of them justifiable? *Exceptional Children, 53,* 555–561.

Edgar, E., Levine, P., & Maddox, M. (1986). *Statewide follow-up studies of secondary special education students in transition.* Working Paper of the Networking and Evaluation Team. Seattle: CDMRC, University of Washington.

Fardig, D.B., Algozzine, R.F., Schwartz, S.E., Hensel, J.W., & Westling, D.L. (1985). Postsecondary vocational adjustment of rural, mildly handicapped students. *Exceptional Children, 52,* 115–121.

Gill, D. (1984). *An employment related follow-up of former special education students in Pierce County, Washington.* Tacoma, WA: Vocational/Special Education Cooperative (ERIC Document Reproduction Service no. Ed 250 854).

Halloran, W. (1991). Supplemental security income. Benefits and incentive provision to assist people with severe disabilities toward economic self-sufficiency. *American Rehabilitation, 17,* 21–27.

Halloran, W., & Ward, M. (1988). Improving transition programming. Changing special education's focus. *The Pointer, 32*(3), 43–46.

Halpern, A.S. (1985). Transition: A look at the foundations. *Exceptional Children, 51,* 479–486.

Halpern, A.S. (1992). Transition: Old wine in new bottles. *Exceptional Children, 58,* 202–211.

Harris, L., & Associates. (1986). *Disabled Americans' self perceptions: Bringing disabled into the mainstream. (Study no. 854009).* New York: Lou Harris and Associates.

Hasazi, S.B., Gordon, L.R., & Roe, C.A. (1985). Factors associated with employment status of handicapped youth exiting high school from 1979–1983. *Exceptional Children, 51,* 455–469.

Hasazi, S.B., Gordon, L.R., Roe, C.A., Hull, M., Finch, K., & Salembier, G. (1985). A statewide follow-up on post high school employment and residential status of students labeled, "Mentally Retarded." *Education and Training of the Mentally Retarded, 20,* 222–235.

McDonnell, J., Wilcox, B., Boles, S., & Bellamy, G.T. (1985). *Do we know enough to plan for transition? A national survey of state agencies responsible for services to persons with severe handicaps* (Grant No. G00–83–02159). Washington, DC: U.S. Department of Education, Office of Special Education Programs.

McGill, J. (1978). *We are people first — A book on self-advocacy.* Lincoln, NE: Nebraska Advocacy Services.

Mithaug, D.E., & Horiuchi, C.N. (1983). *Colorado statewide follow-up survey of special education students.* Denver, CO: Colorado Department of Education.

Mithaug, D.E., Martin, J.E., Agran, M. & Rusch, F.R. (1988). *Why special education graduates fail: How to teach them to succeed.* Colorado Springs, CO: Ascent Publications.

National Commission on Excellence in Education (1983): *A nation at risk: The imperative for educational reform.* Washington, DC: U.S. Department of Education.

National Council on Disability (1989). *The education of students with disabilities: Where do we stand?* Washington, DC: National Council on Disability.

Repetto, J.B., White, W.J., & Snauwaert, D.T. (1990). Individualized transition plans (ITP): A national perspective. *Career Development for Exceptional Individuals, 13*(2), 109–119.

Rusch, F.R., Trach, J.T., Winking, D.L., Tines, J., & Heal, L. (1987). Introduction to supported employment in Illinois: Status of the initiative. In J.S. Trach & F.R. Rusch, *Supported employment in Illinois: Program implementation and evaluation.* Champaign: University of Illinois, The Transition Institute.

Schill, W.J. (1988). Do IEP's support transition? *Individualized Educational Programs and Transition.* Project TROPHY. Seattle: University of Washington.

Snauwaert, D.T., & DeStefano, L. (1990). A comparative analysis of state transition planning. In F.R. Rusch (Ed.), *Supported employment: Models, methods, and issues.* Sycamore, IL: Sycamore Publishing Company.

Thomas, D. (1982). *The experience of handicap.* New York: Methuen & Co. Ltd

U.S. Department of Education (1990). *Twelfth annual report to Congress on the implementation of the Education of the Handicapped Act.* Washington, DC: U.S. Government Printing Office: 0–272–000:QL3.

U.S. Department of Education (1991). State systems for transition services for youth with disabilities: Final rule. *Federal Register, 56*(245), 66290–66295.

Varela, R. (1986). Risks, rules, and resources: Self-advocacy and the parameters of decision making. In J. Summers (Ed.), *The right to grow up: An introduction to adults with developmental disabilities,* Baltimore, Paul H. Brookes.

Vogelsberg, R.T. (1986). Competitive employment in Vermont. In F.R. Rusch (Ed.), *Competitive employment issues and strategies* (pp. 35–49). Baltimore: Paul H. Brookes.

Wagner, M., & Shaver, D. (1989). *Educational programs and achievements of secondary education students: Findings from the National Longitudinal Transition Study.* Menlo Park, CA: Stanford Research Institute.

Wang, M.C. (1987). To want achieving educational excellence for all students: Program design and student outcomes. *Remedial and Special Education, 8,* 25–34.

Ward, M.J. (1988). *The many facets of self-determination.* Washington, DC: National Information Center for Handicapped Children and Youth (NICHCY Transition Summary 7).

Ward, M.J., & Halloran, W. (1989). Transition to uncertainty: Status of many school leavers with disabilities. *Career Development for Exceptional Individuals, 13*(2), 71–81.

Wehman, P., Kregel, J., & Seyfarth, J. (1985). Employment outlook for young adults with mental retardation. *Retardation Counseling Bulletin,* 90–99.

Wilcox, B., & Bellamy, G.T. (Eds.) (1982). *Design of high school programs for severely handicapped students,* Baltimore, Paul H. Brookes.

Will, M. (1984). *OSERS programming for the transition of youth with disabilities: Bridges from school to working life.* Washington, DC: U.S. Department of Education, Office of Special Education and Rehabilitative Services.

Index